IT'S A WOMAN'S WORLD
A MEMOIR

*Stories of Women Who Made
a Difference in My Life*

By Marie Fenton Griffing
Edited by
Lila Lizabeth Weisberger

To order additional copies of this book, contact:
Xlibris Corporation
1-888-795-4274
www.Xlibris.com
Orders@Xlibris.com
131480

MARIE FENTON GRIFFING
Resume

FROM: 1981 to 2004: Freelance beauty/health/fitness writer. Articles published in Cosmopolitan, Good Housekeeping, Teen News, Fort Lauderdale Magazine, Globe Communications. Also did public relations work for Windjammer Barefoot Cruises; Soloman & Soloman Organization; North American Pageant; Calendar Girl Pageant. Presently writing my plebe autobiography "REAL WOMEN," and a series of children's stories; also a poetry book titled "Sunflowers Do Die & Other Poems" and "To Be A Child Again and Other Poems."

FROM 1970 TO 1981: Employed by Hearst Corp., NYC. Editor-in-Chief of Good Housekeeping Beauty Book, Cosmopolitan Beauty Guide, Cosmopolitan Super Diets & Exercise Guide. Wrote books published on beauty & health (see below).

FROM 1968 TO 1970: Women's Editor of The Rockland Journal News, Nyack, NY (a Gannett Newspaper). Did layouts; managed three reporters.

FROM 1965 TO 1968: Freelance writer in beauty/health. Books published.

FROM 1960 TO 1965: Beauty Editor of Teen Magazine.

FROM 1955 TO 1960: Freelance writer for LA Times Home Magazine

FROM 1946 TO 1954: Assistant Society Editor, Associate Editor of The Los Angeles Times Home Magazine; First Women's Correspondent in Europe for the Los Angeles Times. Co-publisher of European Traveler in Paris.

BOOKS PUBLISHED FROM 1965 TO 2004: From Teen to Twenty (McFadden-Bartell); The Leslie Uggams Beauty Book with Marie Fenton (Prentice Hall); Palmer's School Journalism Home Study Course; Pamper Your Feet; Baths for Beauty & Relaxation; Cheater's Diet (all by Dell Publishing); Fitness for the Working Woman (Contemporary Books);

Aerobics (Dell Publishing); How To be A Beauty Pageant Winner (Simon & Schuster); Flatten Your Tummy (Globe Communications).

REFERENCES: Helen Gurley Brown, Cosmopolitan Magazine; John Mack Carter, Director of Hearst Enterprises.

BACKGROUND
A FINISHED LIFE—AN UNFINISHED BOOK:
FROM THE EDITOR

Marie born April 11,1925
Died Sept 20, 2012
Ashes into the ocean under the moonlight Oct 20, 2012

Bill moves into the Independent Living apartment that they planned to move into together on January 13, 2013

Marie wrote her memoirs for 30 years or more with the goal of having it published. Her life ended before she was able to meet this goal. Thus this book is being published posthumously. The choices made were at the discretion of Lila Lizabeth Weisberger, Book Designer and Editor of "It's A Woman's World," after consultation with Marie's family and friends.

Marie was a member of my poetry peer group. We discussed and wrote original poetry, explored well-known poetry, worked in online groups and shared our writing. We became fast and special friends. I wanted to learn from Marie what enabled her to maintain her optimism and contentment in the face of the illnesses that she and her husband endured year after year. Each year I would seek an answer from her and each year she would respond "I explained that to you last year."

Now when I read her book, I finally understand Marie's way of facing the world was to never lose sight of the sunshine and love. She had the ability to welcome all that came into her life much as described in "The Guest House," a poem by Rumi.

I was very much like the traveler who had in his possession an item of great financial worth and was ready to give it up to learn how Marie lived and loved fully despite harsh and debilitating illnesses and major losses.

After her death it became apparent that I was the one she expected to see to it that her book was published. This was a final gift I could give Marie, knowing that it was a gift she was giving to her readers. Working on her book and reading intimate details of her life, I finally learned the answer to my perennial question.

Lila Lizabeth Weisberger celebrates Marie

"A wise woman who was traveling in the mountains found a precious stone in the stream. The next day she met another traveler who was hungry, and the wise woman opened her bag to share her food. The hungry traveler saw the precious stone in the wise woman's bag, admired it, and asked the wise woman to give it to him. The wise woman did so without hesitation.

The traveler left, rejoicing in his good fortune. He knew the jewel was worth enough to give him security for the rest of his life.

But a few days later he came back, searching for the wise woman. When he found her, he returned the stone and said, 'I have been thinking. I know how valuable the stone is, but I give it back to you in the hope that you can give me something much more precious. If you can, give me what you have within you that enabled you to give me the stone.'" from: "The Wise Woman's Stone"

from "Chicken Soup for the Woman's Soul"

DEDICATION

Bill to Marie:

"The minister from hospice came to our home carrying a small roundish stone like you'd find on the beach. He placed it on top of Marie's book "Sunflowers Do Die." Gaining strength after a wave of weakness and pain, Marie was able to put her small hand on the stone and to meet my hand already holding half of the stone. Her small fingers and mine touched and held. The minister said words of praise and prayer over our hands holding on together. An essence of Marie and our love was transported into the stone.

Marie, I keep the stone on top of the book and touch it each morning when I get up and then bid you goodnight with a gentle touch on the stone. During the day I touch it, stroke it and feel you are still with me. I miss you so. I will love you forever."

Contents

CHAPTER FOUR: MY NEW CAREER YEARS
(1960 TO 1967)

CHAPTER FIVE: MY STRUGGLING YEARS
(1968-1972)

CHAPTER SIX: MY AWAKENING YEARS . . . .
(1972 TO 1974)

CHAPTER SEVEN: MY REBIRTH YEARS
(1974 TO 1976)

CHAPTER EIGHT: MY TRANSITION YEARS . . . .
(1976 to 1986)

CHAPTER NINE: MY LIFE COMES TOGETHER AGAIN . . . .
(1985 to 1987)

CHAPTER TEN: ADAPTING TO MY NEW LIFE
(1990-1997)

CHAPTER ELEVEN: MY SECOND REBIRTH
(1997 - 2004)

*Marie died before Chapter eleven,
and Chapter twelve were written.*

CHAPTER TWELVE: MY HAPPY ENDING
(2004 - ON & ON)

INTRODUCTION

WHEN I FIRST decided to write my autobiography some years back, I was confused as to how I should approach it—use recorded "dead" facts about my family, then interject my own "dead" facts about my life like most autobiographies have been written over the years—or look back on my life in a different way? After all, I am not a famous celebrity, politician, artist or rock singer—just an average woman, a retired journalist, magazine editor, writer of ten how-to books and three poetry books, wife (twice), and mother who for over 60 years used her craft to make a living, survive financial disaster raise, educate her three children, attain a certain degree of recognition through her publications, pull herself up by the "bootstraps" when everything seemed like it was "going down the drain" build a new life and now happily living out her "platinum years" in Florida where for 26 years she keeps working on her memoirs. Wow! Did I really do all those things?

Then I read in some literary magazine that the "plebian autobiography" is getting attention from certain publishers these days. That idea struck an idea in my mind—focus in on a specific area of my childhood, adult and aging years that made the most difference in the eight decades I've lived.

Suddenly, one night, it all became so simple for me—even a unique theme for the book: "Women Who Made a Difference in My Life!" I would center my work on that theme. Even though I had been raised in a two-parent family with a father, brother and uncles, it was the female members of the large family that influenced me as a child and an adult. Plus, as I started to write my outline going onto later decades, I discovered there were wonderful experiences I had with many women of all ages who gave me tremendous support, urged me on to bigger and better things. I first worked on getting the facts correct—like birthdays, deaths, marriage dates, places, travels, career moves, family upheavals, and illnesses. Plus, I began looking at old photos I had.

But when it came to looking back at my past, I had to rely on my own perception of the particular happening and like most people who write about themselves, we are vulnerable in that we try to recall the exact words, the feelings which are the essence of an experience. Sometimes those aspects were very clear to me; they somehow stuck in my mind over all the years—other times, I had to rely on the female interpretation as I know myself today and how I must have felt and reacted those decades ago. Oftentimes, all of the above were shadowy, but the best version of each experience as I could remember it. The writing style I chose for my book is simple—short sentences, short dialogue, as if I were writing in my diary. This style was comfortable for me and unlike the commercial work I used to do or the how-to and poetry books I've written.

Even though I sought to make each chapter different, to show the wonderful individuality of the women who made a difference in my life, to bring out the revolving changes and growth that I experienced, I sensed that it was possible that other women who read my book would find something in themselves—something that they could relate to and say, "Yeah, I felt that way, too."

My "plebian" biography is a new form—a true-to-life recording of a woman's development . . . me. No person's life is too dull to write about—and the longer a person lives, the more stories there are to tell. I have found that as the circle turns, I now am passing on some of my knowledge, my "wisdom" to young women—as it was passed on to me. And the most wonderful thing is that the longer I live, the more I learn from other women of all ages and the smarter I get.

CHAPTER ONE

MY FORMATIVE YEARS
(1930s to Middle 1940s)

1. AUNT FANNY—ONE OF MY SADDEST DAYS

A S I SKIPPED home one sunny spring day from St. John's Elementary school in Los Angeles, I did not have a worry in the world. My house was just down the block and as always, I called out the address number of each house I passed until I got to 1628 . . . mine. The late afternoon sun shone brightly, illuminating the broken pavement on the sidewalk. When a breeze blew, I concentrated on the moving shadows reflecting on the cement from the tree branches above.

"Step on a crack, break your father's back," I sang as I hopped over the irregular cement lines. My plaid canvas bookcase swung from side to side on my shoulder. I heard the screech of blackbirds and knew what they were after. I grabbed my case and held it atop my head.

"Pests, go away!" I cried out, waving my free arm around. I was used to the birds descending on me during early spring and accepted it as a normal nature happening. They liked to pluck out my hair to stuff in their nests.

I felt unusually carefree this day. It was almost time to celebrate my 10th birthday—April 11, 1935.

I stopped for a second at Mrs. Brady's hibiscus bush, abloom with glorious red flowers. The bright yellow stamens always intrigued me—so perfectly fashioned. I picked a bright crimson flower and tucked it over my ear. I knew by evening it would fold up its petals and die. Unlike most other flowers, the hibiscus barely survives a whole day, which I thought was sad.

By now my thoughts were on meeting my best friend, Chuppie, who lived across the street from me. We always met after changing into our play clothes. I rubbed my fingers around the 10 pennies in my school uniform pocket just to make sure they were still there. I could almost taste the sweetness of the different candies that Chuppie and I would buy at the store around the corner. We loved to watch old Mr. Gordon, the owner, carefully pour the gumballs and jelly beans into the tiny brown paper bag.

Onward I skipped. It felt good to feel my hair blowing in the soft wind. My small two-bedroom frame house with one large palm tree in the front yard seemed to shake as I approached—a cool breeze blew around my neck.

I quickly walked down the dirt driveway toward the back yard. My first duty when arriving home from school was to feed 'Whitey' my rabbit. I raised him from a tiny bunny that Aunt Fanny gave me two years before for an Easter present.

Whitey was big and beautiful now. I loved to cuddle him for hours on my lap while doing homework or listening to a favorite program on the radio. I always put him back in his cage in the yard with a goodnight kiss. His fur was soft and pure white. It was fun to see his pink nose quiver when I'd brush my cheek against his head. I loved him dearly.

"Hi Fanny, I'm home," I called out as I reached the spacious yard filled with fig, quince, peach and all sorts of fruit trees. I opened the gate to a fenced flower garden abloom with row upon row of gladiolas, irises, calla lilies and geraniums. It felt nice to trickle my fingers over their colorful petals. My Aunt Fanny scented our house every Friday with magnificent bouquets from the garden.

I never questioned why Fanny lived with my parents, my brother and me, but I did wonder about it. She was different but no one ever talked about it. One day she would be jolly, the next, quiet and moody. Sometimes she frightened me with outbursts about people trying to hurt her. As a child, I was confused, and it wasn't until many years later that my mother told me Aunt Fanny was mentally ill. Despite this, she was a bright, creative and intuitive person.

I laid my bookcase on the ground in the garden and darted toward Whitey's cage. He wasn't there. "Oh, shoot!" I said, "He's escaped again." I looked around. Then a shadow on the ground caught my eye. I looked above to the branches of the fig tree that shaded his cage and saw Whitey hanging by his neck. His big, beautiful white-furry body was lifeless!

I stood stiff, in shock. Then I started shaking my arms up in the air, screaming, "Fanny, Fanny, come quick!"

The screen door creaked open. Fanny slowly descended the back porch steps. A long white dress wafted around her heavy-set body. Her grey-peppery hair pulled back into a knot set off a calm, tranquil face almost free of wrinkles. As she walked toward me, she put both hands over her mouth to stifle the weeping sounds that nevertheless escaped for me to hear.

MARIE FENTON GRIFFING

I pointed toward Whitey, swinging back and forth in the afternoon breezes. "What happened? Who?" I whispered under my sobs.

After clearing her throat, Fanny's eyes focused on the ground, she quietly said, "Little Marie, Whitey was getting too fat, too big and old. I put him out of his misery. He didn't want to be caged anymore. I set him free."

I stared at her in disbelief. Then I reached up to the branches and with much difficulty finally untied the rope. I laid Whitey's stiffened body on the ground and just looked at him—he looked like he was sleeping. Then I grabbed him up in my arms and hugged him to my chest, kissed his head but his little pink nose didn't quiver. Rocking back and forth, I rubbed his legs and stroked his body, murmuring all the time, "Whitey, I love you, I love you." He didn't move.

My Aunt Fanny stood quiet. I looked up at her. "Why did you do this Fanny?" Her face was solemn. She didn't answer.

"I'm going to tell Mother and Daddy when they come home. You just wait. You're a wicked, mean woman. I hate you!"

Then out of exhaustion, I plopped myself on the ground and rocked Whitey again. Fanny approached me, softly patted my head, then reached down and stroked Whitey. "I'm sorry, so sorry," she said, "I won't do it again."

I looked up at her face and saw tears streaming down her cheeks, her eyes filled with pain. I had never seen her cry before. I grabbed a hold of her legs and hugged them tightly. Then I got up and hugged her wide waist, my tears wetting her soft cotton dress. Whitey dropped to the ground.

"It's okay, it's okay," I repeated hugging her more tightly.

Fanny and I buried Whitey in a shallow grave under the fig tree. We made a small cross from branches then both said a silent prayer. When my mother got home later, she tried to comfort me. That night I cried myself to sleep.

When I went to confession the next Saturday, I told the priest about my angry feelings. He said something I've never forgotten. "It was normal for you to feel much anger and frustration about this but because you gave quick pardon to someone you love even though she hurt you so deeply, shows you have a wonderful capacity to forgive. You will find this virtue rewarding in many years to come. Go in peace!"

This experience has been imprinted in my memory for 70 years. I'll never forget it. Why? I don't know, but it did not destroy my warm feelings for Aunt Fanny.

2. AUNT FANNY—GETTING MY PERIOD

THE FALL OF 1936 seemed to come so quickly. My summer vacation was filled with much fun playtime and meeting new friends. The only way I could measure the quick passing of June, July and August was when I went with my mother to buy school clothes. My shoe size was larger. My uniforms didn't fit anymore around my chest. I was developing breasts. I was so pleased and proud—like the movie stars I idolized. I grew, as they say "like a weed." My mother was amazed and said it was due to the California sunshine. Little did I know what this quick growth meant.

There was a family with four young boys about my age who moved into a house up the block. My girlfriend Chuppie and I talked them into playing touch football, softball and other games. At first, they didn't like playing with "girls," but for lack of playmates I guess, they joined in our after-school on-the-street activities. We'd play "kick the can," "cops and robbers" and "G man." They were rough boys but Chuppie and I kept up with them—in fact, we won most of the games.

We decided to form a club—we called ourselves "The Great Six." In my backyard we built a clubhouse out of orange crates. Chuppie and I were so physically active during that fall that we really felt we were "one of the boys." We even cut our hair short; our mothers were horrified.

Then the days grew shorter and the starting of school cut down on our time together. I looked forward to weekends when we'd all play our favorite games.

One morning in late winter, I woke up early and saw blood on my pajama pants. I was frightened. I thought—did I hurt myself climbing the fence into Mrs. Mooney's yard to steal some cumquats off her tree yesterday afternoon? Or was it because I practiced 20 leg splits last night? I threw the pj's into the wash bin.

All day in class my underpants felt wet and in the girl's bathroom I discovered more blood on them. I was scared and petrified and slowly walked home holding my legs together. I went straight to my bedroom and found a strip of white linen material folded on my bed. "What's that?" I thought. I walked out of the bathroom where I had washed up and saw Aunt Fanny sitting on my bed. "Marie, you are having your sick time," she said in a matter-of-fact tone. "Your mother will tell you all about it when she comes home from work. She'll bring you some special pads. For now, let's tie this cloth between your legs, then you put on a clean pair of underpants."

I thought to myself—"sick time?" I didn't feel sick. I didn't understand what was happening to my body, that's all. Aunt Fanny was calm as she tied a string around my waist and then attached the linen fold between my thighs. I guess I was relieved that it wasn't my 20 splits that caused the bleeding.

The cloth felt weird between my legs. My mother didn't come home from work until I was almost asleep. She turned on the light and sat on the edge of my bed. I vaguely heard her tell me how I was becoming a young woman and that I must be careful about jumping around and playing all those silly games with the boys. That was it. Only later, talking it over with Chuppie who was three years older than I, did I find out what this was all about.

The next morning while eating my cold cereal and feeling the thick Kotex between my thighs, I wondered about my "sick time." Did it really mean I couldn't play touch football with boys? I sighed, "I can't live without that!"

I rushed into the kitchen. "Fanny, I have to play a basketball game today. I'm the forward on the team . . . they need me. Mother says not to jump around. I've got my 'sick time'—what shall I do?"

She smiled at me, giggled a bit and patted her hands on her heavy apron. "You are all right. In four days the bleeding will stop but it will come back again next month. Go ahead and do what you want. You'll be fine—go win your game."

And our team did win that day. Since taking the wise advice of my Aunt Fanny (and not my Mother's), I accepted my menstrual period with "a grain of salt." After another discussion with Chuppie, she and I decided it was just a nuisance, but one we had to live with. We didn't like it, especially because it made us feel different from the boys. They never had a "sick time."

It's interesting to look back and reflect on the changing of words from "sick time," to "the curse", popular in my teens, then finally to "my period" when I was twenty. Today girls know about this and sex before parents decide to discuss it with them. I thank my stars that Aunt Fanny showed me how to take this eventful body change in my stride instead of surrendering to "old world" myths.

3. AUNT FANNY—KNITTING LESSONS

IN MY EARLY teens, I noticed that my mother would give five dollars every Friday to Aunt Fanny. It was like an allowance. Sometimes, Fanny would give me a dime or a quarter to go to the movies. I liked that and always gave her a big hug. Most of her "weekly allowance" was spent at Kresses dime store, a few blocks from our house. She would come home with bags filled with fabrics and yarns. She always made her own clothes and hats but knitting, crocheting and tatting were her favorite pastimes.

I was fascinated with the way she could twist the yarn around and off the needles so swiftly. Her fingers seemed to fly in all directions. A scarf was born or an afghan came to me for my bed. She even crocheted colorful flowers for her hats. Everything she made was so lovely and perfectly crafted.

My fascination with her work grew until one day while Fanny and I were listening to Myrt & Marge on the radio, I asked her to teach me how to knit. She seemed happy with this request and my first project was a hot pad, which I proudly gave to my mother. At first it was difficult but I persevered and graduated to the scarf which I gave to my Aunt Tony in Milwaukee because it got cold there in the winter, and then a sleeveless vest which I wore all the time even in 80 degree weather.

I remember her patience with me when I lost a stitch or knitted when I should have purled. I liked sitting close to her; she sometimes smelled like the lemon blossoms on the tree in our yard. We would giggle a lot too, especially when my fingers got tangled up in the yarn.

One thing that impressed me when she was working on a piece was how calm her face looked. It seemed as if she were in another world. Sometimes on rainy weekends when I was forced to stay indoors, I turned to my knitting project and found myself entering that same tranquil space that Fanny must have experienced.

*   *   *

To "fast forward" for a moment, I continued taking on a new knitting project whenever my life's problems were overwhelming. One time I, along with my first son, six-month-old Rick, and our live-in 'femme de manage,' during a move from Paris to the French Riviera, were stranded in a hotel in Nice awaiting the arrival of my husband. Bob, who was driving from Paris with our dog Liza and her newborn puppy, was two days overdue and I was scared to death that something bad had happened. To calm my nerves, I went through my baggage and found the argyle socks I started knitting for him months before. He arrived a few hours later. It was two years later that I finished the socks. One of the worst crises I knitted through was when my husband was dying of cancer in Harkness Pavillion at the Presbyterian Hospital in New York City. I carried my knitting bag to his room everyday. Because he slept most of the times, I would sit in a chair near his bed for hours and like Fanny, my fingers moved swiftly creating an afghan. It was dull brown and beige, like my mood I guess, but knitting away helped sustain me.

And yet one more traumatic period that knitting guided me through. A serious oral cancer operation forced me to stop smoking. If you have ever been addicted to smoking and are trying to quit, you will find your hands unconsciously reaching for a pack of cigarettes. Your fingers fidget and you clench them into a fist. Shortly after the operation, just sitting around brought on urges like this, so I turned to knitting again which made my withdrawal symptoms less painful and it gradually turned into an everyday pastime. (Whenever a little girl sees my knitting, she wants to learn how to knit. I have taught several girls this wonderful craft.)

*   *   *

My Aunt Fanny lived with my parents until she died at the age of 75. Her influence on me is hard to pinpoint, except that her kindness, patience and understanding made me feel good and important. I knew she was different from others; I simply accepted that fact. She was a delicate person, really not in full contact with the world outside our house or the movies. Today she would be classified as "special." My other two aunts, Toni and Marie (Big Marie as she was called—I was Little Marie), were unlike Fanny. They were independent and holding jobs on their own. I never realized it until I matured that my mother and three aunts were remarkable women and how much of them I had in me.

4. AUNT TONI—LETTER WRITING

"AUNT TONI!" I shouted from the car as my father parked our new 1936 Chevrolet in front of Grandma Schaffer's house in Milwaukee. It was summer vacation time again—I always spent every summer with Toni and Grandma. These were happy months. I was growing closer to my full height and in every way was the typical 11-year-old in those days. I loved to experiment with makeup, new hairdos and giggle a lot about boys with my girlfriends.

Aunt Toni, my second aunt, came rushing from the big three-story house, opened the gate smiling and with her arms outstretched, ran toward me for a hug. I gave the hug and a quick kiss on her cheek. Then I spun around on my heels and sniffed the warm humid air. It seemed as if I could smell the kohlrabi, cabbage and other wonderful smells from Grandma's vegetable garden. How good it was.

As my parents unpacked the car, Aunt Toni and I walked the narrow cement path to the kitchen door. We kept hugging each other every step of the way.

"I can't believe you're almost as tall as I," Toni said. Then softly, she whispered, "Marie, try and use the little bit of German I taught you when you greet Grandma, okay?"

I nodded okay, straightened my back, fluffed my hair and walked into the kitchen that was as large as the living room. I walked over to this small, white-haired woman sitting in a rocking chair and bent over to give her a quick hug. "Gutten Dag!" Her bright eyes smiled back. "Was machts du?" I threw out my arms, "Alles is gutt" I replied, laughing and looking at Toni to see if I did well. She nodded.

I roamed around the room and spotted a freshly baked strudel on the counter and a pot of chicken soup boiling on the stove. I could almost taste them. Grandma raised her own chickens and made her own bread as well as the most fabulous pastries I'd ever tasted. I'm sure my being 'pleasingly plump' as a teen was due to the wonderful rich foods I ate during my summer vacations.

Aunt Toni grabbed my arm and led me to the bedroom I always used when I visited. She stood before the closed door, smoothed her long apron, adjusted her small wire-rimmed glasses and smiled, "I hope you like how I decorated your room." I gasped as I looked into the room. It was beautiful. I gave Tony a big hug.

My bed had a new quilt on it that Toni said she made especially for me. On the opposite side of the bed was a tall bureau with a narrow mirror in the center and drawers down each side of it. I gasped at its beauty. Then close to the bureau was a small desk of matching wood. On top of the desk were a cup filled with pencils and pens, a tablet of lined paper, a box of envelopes and a vase full of waxed flowers.

It was my first private bedroom. I slept with my brother, Patrick, back in Los Angeles in one room. We each had our own bureau for our clothes and each a bed and that was it. Here, I would have my own privacy—my own room. I was so happy.

"Enjoy," Toni said, "and Marie, don't forget to write to your parents after they leave and to your Aunt Fanny. That's why I put those papers and things on your desk. Take them back home with you when you leave so you can write to me. I'll send you letters too. That way we'll keep in touch with each other. Okay?"

She always ended many of her sentences with "okay," so I answered "Okay."

I did keep my promise and for years we communicated.

Five minutes later, I did what I always did on my first day of my summer vacation, I ran out of the house and down the street to my girlfriends from the summers before. I felt free and couldn't wait to tell them about my new bedroom.

5. AUNT TONI—WEARING THE PANTS

I'LL NEVER FORGET my 12th birthday when I received a package from my Aunt Toni. I rushed home from school, saw the box on the table and tore it open. In the box were two pairs of halter pants—one navy blue and the other striped white/blue. Aunt Fanny was standing behind me and when I started jumping up and down with joy, she started laughing, "Looks like those overalls Toni sent you are just what you wanted, but I don't know how your Mother is going to like them.

Pants or "slacks" as they called them back then, were the newest fashion, especially with movie stars like Greta Garbo and Katharine Hepburn, but not well received by conservative dressers. I, however, being a movie buff, thought they were just swell and now I had a pair of my own. I tried them on and they fit perfectly. I decided I would wear them to my school's baseball game that afternoon.

I was the designated pitcher for the softball game and it was one of our most important games of the season. St John's elementary (my school) was playing St. Vincent's elementary (our hardest competition) and being the captain of our team, I was in a hurry to get back to the schoolyard to greet our adversaries.

I needed a blouse or some sort of top to wear with the pants. I ran into my parents' bedroom and opened my father's drawer and pulled out one of his t-shirts and put it on. Then I pulled the pants' shoulder straps up, looked in the mirror and whispered to myself, "Perfect!"

As I approached the fenced area of the playground, I could see both teams practicing. The nuns were clustered in a group close to home base. I took a deep breath, put my hands into my pants pockets and walked over to the benches. I could see my teammates staring at me. I suddenly realized I was wearing the pants and wondered what the nuns would say about them. I took my hands out of my pockets and tucked my hair under my "SJ" baseball cap. My knees were shaking. I took a deep breath and waved to my schoolmates.

"Marie," Sister Mary William (the principal) shouted out to me. "Why are you dressed like that, in men's overalls?" I walked over to the stern-looking, black-robed nun. "Sister, these are slacks my Aunt Toni sent me from Milwaukee for my birthday. They're cool and comfortable. I know I can play better in them. My uniform and stockings are too hot to wear—I can't stretch in them."

The other nuns grouped around me. I spread my legs as if ready for battle, folded my hands behind my back, twitching my fingers together. Out of the corner of my eyes, I saw my classmates nearby, huddled together, their faces looking very anxious.

"Go home immediately," Sister William snapped, her finger shaking toward me, "and change that outfit. You are to appear here like a proper young lady, not a ruffian!" I turned quickly on my Keds sneakers and ran toward the street gate. I glanced back to get a glimpse of my team and gave them a quick wave. "I'll be right back," I shouted out.

Tears flowed down my face as I ran up the steps to my house. "I'm mad, mad. What do I do now?" I asked myself. "I don't want to put on that dumb uniform again!" I thought for a second, then rushed to the telephone, found Aunt Toni's number in the phone book and called her. I was nervous because I'd never phoned her before. When she heard my voice, she gasped, "Little Marie is everything all right?"

"No Toni," I replied, "I just got your birthday gift and I love the pants but the nuns say I can't wear them to my baseball game which is about to begin. It's just not fair!"

There was a pause, then a sigh on the other side of the line. "Little Marie, I can't tell you want to do. It must be your decision. I understand it's easier to play in the pants, but it's not a good idea to make the nuns angry. Think about it. Maybe you'll come up with a solution. Now hang up—this is costing your mother money. Bye."

I walked to my bedroom and stared into the box in which the other blue/white striped pants lay folded. I thought about what Toni said. I slipped off my navy blue pants, picked up my uniform from the floor and put it on. I carefully rolled up the long sleeves of the dress to my elbows, pulled on the pants, tucked the skirt of the dress under the pants, bloused out the top and looked at myself in the living room mirror. A blue and white checked top with a blue/white striped halter pants. "Not bad!" I said to myself and dashed out the door.

A few minutes later I was back at the playground. My team cheered me on as I approached the nuns standing around home place. The five stern faces glared at me, black veils flapping in the wind, arms tucked into wide long sleeves.

"I gulped, "Well, Sister, like you said, I've changed my pants and wore my dress."

The women gasped, looked at each other and quickly walked away without a word.

I popped some bubble gum into my mouth and rushed to the pitcher's mound. Our team won 12-2. I had never played better. After the game, my team plus the girls from St. Vincent's rushed over to congratulate me but mostly to see my outfit up close. We all agreed my halter pants would make a great new "play uniform" for our softball games.

No, it would not, at least for now. The next morning when we all assembled in the courtyard of the school for the raising of the flag and singing the National Anthem, Sister Mary William walked up in front of us all.

"Marie Duffy will no longer be captain of the girl's baseball team. She will be replaced by Frances Griffith." I took a deep breath, looked around at my classmates. I couldn't believe my ears. As Sister William walked away, all my teammates, including Frances, rushed toward me, crying "no, no!" and we all hugged each other, sobbing like little children.

A month later I was reinstated for the "celebration" game and wore my uniform and stockings. That June I graduated from St. John's, such a happy occasion that the traumatic baseball experience faded into the past.

*　　*　　*

(Several years later when I was in St. Agnes High School, I walked by my old elementary school playground. A girls' softball game was in process. I couldn't believe my eyes. There were both teams dressed in short sleeve uniforms and wearing knee socks and Keds. I grasped the wire fence and just stared. My standing up for a more flexible baseball outfit seemed to have paid off. The outfit was not pants, but it looked a lot more comfortable than the old one. I called Aunt Toni that night to tell her the good news.)

6. AUNT TONI—MY FIRST ROMANCE!

I WAS 16 years old and spending another vacation in Milwaukee with Aunt Toni. Grandma Schaffer had recently died so it was just Toni and me living in the big house. My parents were busy back in Los Angeles with their new restaurant. I was now allowed to wear high heels but preferred the "groovy" fashions of the early 1940s. In true "Bobby Soxer" fashion I wore long jackets and short skirts, wide-collared white boy's shirts, saddle shoes, white angora socks or knee-highs. Curly hair was in (we would wet it down with sugar water, then set it in pin curls). And red, red lipstick, Max Factor's pancake makeup, Maybelline cake mascara were our prized cosmetics—Lanvin's Arpege our favorite fragrance.

I felt very grown-up and thrived on going to the local movie houses with friends. We loved the romance films—we'd swoon over Robert Taylor, Errol Flynn, Gary Grant, Glenn Ford, Paul Henreid but Clark Gable was the best!

The annual Wisconsin State Fair was held in August for two weeks. The fair grounds were only 15 minutes from my house. My best girlfriend, Helen, and I would run across the Allis Chalmers railroad tracks to walk the road to the fairgrounds. Entry fee was 25 cents and there was always a big band on weekends. I even heard Frank Sinatra sing one night with Tommy Dorsey's band. Hundreds of young people came to dance to the fabulous music of these orchestras.

It was a tradition that the girls would stand against the walls of the ballroom or lean on the rope that circled the huge dance floor. Helen and I preferred the latter. We knew who the best dancers were and awaited their tap on our shoulders.

Hours before the dance, I would primp in my bedroom—choosing the right outfit, styling and re-styling my hair, putting on makeup, deciding which cologne to wear. Aunt Toni would get so exasperated with me she'd practically push me out the door. "Go already," she'd say," but be back by 11.

It was now the third Friday in a row that Helen and I came to the dancehall. We felt like real grown-ups being able to get in now that we were 16. Helen was somewhat slimmer than I so I always felt awkward and afraid that the boys would find me too fat to dance with but the boys outnumbered the girls and I never really had a problem.

We decided to stand against the rope at the edge of the ballroom floor to better watch the dancers. The big band on the stage played so loudly we could hardly hear each other's words. We'd hum and sway with the music. It was like a dreamland with the big sparkling ball hanging high over the dance floor, turning round and round reflecting its colorful lights on the couples below.

A tap on my shoulder awakened me from my daydream. I looked up and saw an older man (he must have been in his 20s) with white-blonde hair and a solemn expression on his face. "Would you like to dance?" he asked. I gave Helen's elbow a nudge. Her eyes when she spotted the man were wide as saucers. "Okay," I said.

The band was playing "In The Mood" and the way he led me into the dance was to be unforgettable. We twirled, did fancy steps that captivated the attention of others around us. Then the band changed to a slow tune, "As Time Goes By," and we glided smoothly on the polished floor. I had never felt so right, so perfectly in sink with anyone else. I looked up at his face that was beautifully tanned which set off the blondness of his hair and light blue eyes. He was so handsome! I gulped. I had the urge to turn my head in "his" direction but I didn't. A few minutes later I felt the familiar tap on my shoulder. There he was. We glided onto the dance floor. I was "in heaven" again. Glenn Miller's band was there that night playing the most marvelous songs. "String of Pearls" was my favorite. Ivan and I danced and danced without talking. We did smile at each other and when one of us missed a step, we'd laugh and hug each other. When a slow number came up, I couldn't resist resting my head on his shoulder—he didn't seem to mind.

When the band broke for a recess, we went to the S & W stand for a root beer. Helen was there with a dance partner but I could see she was not much interested in him because when she caught my eye, I spied the thumb on her right hand turned downward so I knew she wanted to escape. She said it was time we were heading home. Ivan touched my shoulder, "Can I drive you home?" I reached over and squeezed Helen's hand. "Thanks, Ivan, but I always go home with Helen." "No problem, Marie," he said, "We'll all go together. We can drop her off at her house first." Helen shrugged an "okay" and off we three went to Ivan's car. As we climbed into Ivan's white Studebaker convertible, my knees were shaking. I'd never been in a car like his. I sat in the front seat next to Ivan, Helen in the back. The warm summer breeze blew my hair but I didn't care. It was like I was in a movie and when I looked back at Helen she too had a smile on her face like she wanted this to go on forever. Helen jumped out of the car, waved goodnight to us, we waved back and I directed Ivan to my house. This was the first time I was ever alone in a car with a boy. The radio was playing a Frank Sinatra song, "I'll Get By As Long As I Have You." I glanced over to get a quick look at Ivan, then pointed to the big white house on the right. "That's where I live." We stopped in front of the house and Ivan turned off the headlights. I started to take deep breaths.

I glanced toward the brightly lit front windows and saw Aunt Toni's face peering between the white curtains. I felt Ivan's arm encircle my shoulders. He pressed close to me and planted a soft kiss on my cheek. I smiled back at him, my eyes wide open and my heart thumping again like it did when I entered the dancehall that night. I slowly pulled away, touched my hair and arranged my skirt.

"Ivan, do you go to school? Do you have a job?" In my nervousness, I resorted to quick conversation. "Where do you live? What's the last movie you've seen?" My patter came out so quickly—I hardly gave him a chance to answer.

Ivan tossed his blond head backward and started to laugh. "Marie, I like you very much; in fact, I'm starting to feel deeply about you. First, I must tell you something. I believe in free love." Did I just detect a slight accent in his voice?

I sat up straight, looked into his eyes. "Free love?" I asked. What's that?" Ivan softly grasped my hand and placed it on his chest. "It's performing the act of love-making at any chosen moment with a partner who has a mutual attraction to you. That's how they do it in Russia." I pulled my hand away and again smoothed my hair. Looking down and away from his piercing blue eyes, I said "No, I don't think so—at least, not tonight. I have to think about it. Goodnight!" And I got out of the car without looking back.

The front door was partially open. I arranged my skirt and blouse as I entered the living room. Aunt Toni was sitting on the couch and she wasn't smiling. I gulped. "It's midnight, Marie," she softly said as she poked her index finger against the nose guards on her glasses. "Sorry, but Ivan asked to bring me home from the dance. We first dropped Helen off, then we talked for awhile in the car." She nodded. "Toni, he's swell and we dance beautifully together." My face felt flushed, my hands clenched in front of my body and I was bobbing up and down on my heels. Aunt Toni patted the cushion next to her on the couch. "Come over here, Marie, and tell me about your Ivan."

After a half-hour of my babbling about how marvelous he was, Toni stopped me to ask what actually happened in the car. I froze. "Nothing, Toni. We just talked."

She nodded and then settling back against her back pillow, she proceeded to give me a "lecture" about sex, although she never used the word. Rather, she turned the conversation toward my future. "Keep your virginity," she whispered. "You will meet the right man one day and he will probably expect you to be a virgin. You will get married and have children. Now is not the time for a passing escapade that would ruin your chances for a happy life later on. Do you understand what I'm trying to say?"

"Yes," I answered and hung my head. Toni grabbed my hand and squeezed it. She smiled at me and said, "Good. Now, go to bed and we'll talk about this later." She never did.

The next Friday, the band was playing "I'll Be Seeing You," and the dancehall was overly crowded when Helen and I arrived. It was the last evening of the State Fair dances. All the doors were open because of the intense heat inside the ballroom—outside, light rain was falling and the humidity drifted in. The dancers had sweat pouring down their faces but it didn't stop anybody. We all wanted to savor this last night of fun. Tommy Dorsey was back again with his band and Sinatra was the top star.

Helen and I had to push our way through to get close to the dance floor rope. I looked back around the walls trying to spot Ivan, but no luck. I stood close to Helen, feeling alone and lost. A few minutes later, I felt a grasp on my arm, looked up and there was Ivan. I melted. We smiled at each other and he guided me under the rope to the dance floor. They were playing our song again. We danced close, then Ivan pulled back and looked into my eyes. "I'm leaving tomorrow. I wanted to tell you last night but I never got the chance. I've enlisted in the Army." World War II was on its way and I didn't have a clue about what this would all mean to me.

MARIE FENTON GRIFFING

"What!" I gasped. "You mean I'll never see you again?" He nodded, "At least, not for a long time. Come on let this night be our night. I really want you; I want to make love to you. Drive home with me tonight."

I felt tormented as I walked home that night with Helen after refusing Ivan's offer. I sobbed. Helen hugged me. I didn't even say goodnight to Toni as I went to my bedroom. My heart was broken. I truly felt I was in love with Ivan but Aunt Toni's words kept coming and going in my mind. They caused me to say "No." I think it was one of the hardest decisions I had to make as a teen. Later in life, I realized Toni had made the difference . . . and for the better.

7. AUNT TONI—THE AMATEUR CONTEST

I T WAS THE end of the summer. The state fair grounds had closed. My girlfriends and I were bored. We'd go to West Allis and sit for hours in a booth at the local drugstore, sip on cokes or root beer floats. I'll never forget the marvelous scent of that shop—a mixture of sugar and spice and everything nice, and the swirling stools at the ice-cream counter, the fan turning above on the ceiling but more especially the intimate talks my girlfriends and I would have in the booth.

We'd reminisce about the boys we'd met that summer. Occasionally, I'd mention Ivan. Once a week we'd buy the latest pink song sheet at the drug store. It was only five cents. We'd meet in a nearby park every afternoon and do a sing-along, practicing harmony on the latest tunes by the Andrew Sisters, Dick Powell or Alice Faye. Mildred, Helen and I sang well together. We copied the Andrew Sisters' style down pat, so much so, that people sitting nearby would gather around and listen, then applaud us afterwards.

Signs were posted around town about the end-of-summer Amateur Talent Contest to be held in the park over Labor Day weekend. The prize for first place was five dollars which was a lot of money in those days. I knew our singing group could win. My confidence and excitement in entering this contest convinced my girlfriends to go along with me. We practiced and practiced our song, "Three Little Fishes in an Itty Bitty Pool" all week. Aunt Toni was our audience and critic every night in the house. She would criticize our posture, hand movements and word phrasing. We laughed a lot; it was great fun.

The announcer ushered us over to the microphone, then I turned to them, unclenched my hands, smiled at them both and whispered through my teeth "Let's do it!" I could see the fright in their eyes and the stiffening of their bodies. I was standing between them.

We had no musical accompaniment but our voices came through strong, right on key as we started the first chorus of "Three Little Fishes in an Itty Bitty Pool" but when it came to the line "and they swam and swam all over the pool," Mildred flubbed her words and started to giggle. Then Helen stopped singing and started to giggle. I kept nudging their elbows, looking angrily at them as they were bent over, holding their stomachs, with laughter. I stood upright singing the last chorus, a giggling jag. I kept nudging their elbows as they were bent over, holding their stomachs with laughter, but I went on singing the last chorus by myself. Now the audience was laughing too. I was humiliated. I did a quick bow as I finished the song and we all left the stage, thundering down the stairs. I ran back to the big tree, leaning my head on its big trunk and started to cry. Helen and Mildred hid behind the gazebo. I didn't want to see either one of them again.

Since we were the last contestants, the contest manager called for applause from the audience as he read off the names. We ended up with third prize of $1.00 which I accepted, then gave it to Helen without a word.

Toni and I walked slowly home, my head bent, sulking in my embarrassment of our performance. Toni put her arm around my waist and touched her forehead to mine. "Marie, it's okay," she whispered in my ear. "You did fine. At least you carried off the song till the last note, and you did win a prize."

"Yeah, I guess so, but I counted on them. They messed up. We could have won first prize."

When we got home, I slumped in my chair at the kitchen table and Toni heated up some hot chocolate for me. "You know, Marie, I've gone through life not depending too heavily on others to get me through. I think it's fine to ask others for help in a project, but not to expect too much from them in order to meet your goals. Sometimes, you have to go it alone; then you can accept the consequences on your own. Maybe, entering the contest by yourself without your friends might have won you first prize. Think about it the next time you take on a project like this."

The hot liquid slipped down my throat and warmed me all over—or was it Toni's words? "Yeah, I guess you're right." Then I started to giggle, "Anyway, we had a lot of fun getting ready for tonight. What the heck! I can't wait to bawl out Helen and Mildred tomorrow. Toni started to laugh and shook her finger at me.

When I returned to Los Angeles in the fall, America's involvement in World War II was soon to take place. I received weekly letters from Ivan. First, from Georgia, then from a UPO numbered address from who knows where. I kept writing back to him. Then the letters became less frequent. For Christmas, the postman delivered a bottle of Prince Matchabelli perfume along with his proposal of marriage. He asked if I would marry him when he came home after the war. I wrote back "Yes, Yes." Our pictures of each other crossed back and forth over the ocean. I pinned his up on my wall and kissed them goodnight before I went to bed.

Then one day after I hadn't received any mail from Ivan for over two months, I found a bundle of letters (all rubber banded together) in my mailbox. I couldn't believe my eyes—"KILLED IN ACTION" was stamped on each letter. I clutched the bundle to my breast and ran straight to my bedroom. I rocked back and forth on my bed and thought of my beautiful Ivan who was now dead and why? This was my first connection with the horrors of war. But little did I know that another young, beautiful man was fighting in the same war and that his and my path would cross in the years ahead.

I don't think anyone of us ever forget our "first romance."

8. SISTER MARY MARGARET—SHE INSPIRED ME

I WAS IN the last semester of my senior year in Pius XI High School in Milwaukee, still wearing a uniform except this one was more acceptable to me—navy blue pleated skirt, white blouse and yellow cardigan and socks were the rigger as well as saddle shoes or loafers. At least I didn't have to stand in front of my closet for 1/2 hour like my friends who went to public school, figuring out what to wear each day. Even the nuns I'd had through the last few grades were more relaxed and open—especially Sister Mary Margaret. I never realized at the time what a strong influence she had on deciding what I wanted to do in the future.

Sister Margaret was in her 40s; short, heavy-set and a homely facial appearance. She wore thick glasses and the high white neck collar of her nun's outfit pushed up her jowls so she almost had a "squirrel" look. Her heavy wool attire disguised her enormous figure and you couldn't see her shoes so when she walked quickly down the hall, it almost seemed as if she were gliding along on a skateboard. Because there was no air conditioning in the school in those days, body odor scents wafted around. I had just started to use "Mum" deodorant and often thought of giving Sister Margaret a jar but was fearful of embarrassing us both.

I was one of the 18 students that made up Sister Margaret's English class. Her emphasis was on teaching the "work ethic" as she called it. "Learning is work," she wrote every afternoon with chalk on the bulletin board before she started each class. Reading books was the nun's passion and she drummed that passion into us. We had to read two books a week and on Friday we took turns discussing them. If I were called on to talk about the most impressive chapter in a book I was assigned to read and didn't know it—God help me. She would then make me read three the following week. Since then I've always been an avid reader.

She would open our minds to new horizons in other ways too. Unlike most schools today, we had no guidance counselors to help us to plan our higher education or whatever we would do after graduation. Here's where Sister Mary Margaret exerted much influence on most of the students.

She would take the last fifteen minutes of her class once a week and discuss the options we had open to us. She stressed going on to college but with the United States into World War II, most of the boys' minds were on getting drafted or even enlisting immediately. And, we girls just wanted to get jobs so we'd have our own money to buy clothes and things—it was hard for her to persuade us to keep going to school. But she plugged away. She told the boys to continue after the war and to the girls she advised to seriously consider getting a higher degree. "The more you are educated, the smarter you will become and the more money you will receive. The working woman is becoming an important part of our society, especially now when so many men are being taken away from their jobs and going to war. Someone has to fill those jobs; it's a chance for women to prove themselves. Even a Junior College course at night can help."

But she kept drumming into us to keep learning and to look toward a career that we'd enjoy all our lives long. I really thought about that and after seeing Katherine Hepburn and Spencer Tracy in "My Girl Friday", I seriously felt I would make a good newspaper writer and I loved the excitement of the editorial offices. Working with Sister Margaret on the school newspaper this semester enhanced my feelings to go into some sort of writing career.

Most of the students didn't get much backup from our parents. They expected the boys to go into the Armed Forces and we girls to stay home, wait for them to return and then get married and have children. To me that sounded like a bore. Even a Junior College course at night can help.

It was while working with Sister Margaret on the monthly school newspaper when I started to focus on going into journalism. She taught me diligence and persistence when doing research for my articles. Whenever I used a quote, I had to prove it was correct and if the name of a student was spelled incorrectly, she would reprimand me. "People don't like to see their names misspelled, Marie—it's one of the most important journalistic rules. Check and double check to make sure all the names of places/people are spelled correctly."

"Take the stenographic course," she advised, "It'll help you with interviews and you'll be able to record events faster. Continue your typing classes until you pass the 40 words per minute test. And when I give you a certain amount of inches to write to for your articles or columns—keep to that length. I don't want to spend my time editing your copy down to fit." And so it went. She was a most impressive journalism teacher.

MARIE FENTON GRIFFING

She prepared me for my entry into the University of Southern California School of Journalism.

Once a month, the newspaper staff gathered to discuss "ideas." One time Helen came up with an astrological rundown on each of the students. "No," Sister Margaret said strongly, "The Catholic Church does not believe in this type of 'voodoo' belief." Richard came up with putting up a suggestion box in the gym locker rooms on how to improve locker room etiquette. Sister Margaret gave him the go-ahead. Helen suggested doing a column on the different high school clubs. "Fine," said Sister Margaret, "but be sure you get all the names and dates of meetings correct and remember the 5 W's—Who, What, Where, Why, When."

I had thought of inaugurating an annual "Short Story Contest" that offered a monetary prize for the best piece and which would be printed in the school newspaper but was a little leery about approaching the idea to Sister Margaret for an okay. I was thrilled when she gave me the "go ahead." I saw the birthing of my first creative project that would go public and which would be such a success that it was continued every year after I left the school. It took a lot of work on my part.

Today, I realize how important teachers are—they can turn a young person's life around with their guidance and inspiration. Sister Mary Margaret was the one for me. After submitting my very first creative idea to Sister Margaret and seeing it come to fruition, I never hesitated in later years to approach my college professors and even in the 60s and 70s to offer my top editors, subjects that offered imaginative and creative projects which I felt would be successful. Sometimes, I was turned down—other times, they gave me the "go-ahead" like Sister Margaret. She opened my psyche, my creative urges, and my urgency to prove myself.

9. AUNT MARIE—LEARNING THE WORK ETHIC

M Y FIRST JOB since leaving high school was working at a roadside vegetable stand in Milwaukee with my friend, Shirley, where I earned $60 for two months service. Then, I worked part-time as a file clerk for a shoe factory in Milwaukee where I was paid minimum wage and reaped a great sum of $100 for three months service. I didn't enjoy either of the jobs, so when I returned to Los Angeles with my parents in the spring, I had a conflict—find another job or try to get into college. I remembered Sister Mary Margaret's advice, "Get a higher education if you want to make good money later on in life," but I just wasn't ready. I had turned 18 in April; the war was scaring us all, reports of Japanese submarines off our coastline made everyone paranoid. I became a member of the USO, having a grand time dancing and dining with all the sailors, marines and army young men who were stationed nearby. Chuppie and Mary (my childhood friends) and I loved to use our free hours to go to the Hollywood Canteen or the nearby Inglewood USO Center for a good time.

I was into other "patriotic" services—my knowing how to knit prompted me to work with a group, creating scarves, mittens and other items for the soldiers. I even took a job at a nearby aircraft plant as a stenographer, but after three days there, I quit. The noise in the huge building was unbearable and the pace at which I had to work was even worse. There was no time for conversation between my fellow stenographers. When a sharp, loud whistle blew in the plant it was either for coffee break, lunch or starting/quitting time. By the time I left my station to get a coffee or a sandwich, the whistle blew again to go back to our stations. It was sheer bedlam. I didn't have a minute to think for myself, so I left even though the pay was excellent.

Then my Aunt Marie asked if I'd work with her at the bakery. I did need money to buy new clothes, go to the movies and wanted to travel to Catalina Island over the Christmas holidays. It was a fun place just off the coast of Santa Monica in Los Angeles. My friends told me it's the best place to meet guys. So I accepted Marie's offer and the first thing she did when I came to work is wrap a huge white apron around me. She laid down strict rules I had to follow—wash my hands frequently after serving the pastries; smile when a customer approaches; say 'thank you' after a purchase and most importantly, be patient while the customer makes his/her selections (they did change their minds very often and I had to keep shifting the doughnuts, cookies or coffeecakes back and forth). I loved slicing the various breads on the electric slicing machine and the wonderful smells that came wafting out of Uncle Charlie's ovens in the "kitchen."

My Aunt Marie was a couple inches smaller in height than I, but she seemed like a "giant" to me as she handled the business of the bakery. I watched everything she did behind the counter and copied her as best as I could. The moment the doors opened at 9 a.m., Aunt Marie and I had brought in all the fresh bakery goods to the shelves and laid them out in appetizing arrangements. Uncle Charlie had been working since 4 a.m. In those days there were no preservatives used; everything was baked fresh each day.

As the patrons swarmed in, she would alert me to stand at attention and take the customers that she couldn't handle. Most of them asked to be served by her, so I took the ones who were in a hurry. She'd give me a kiss or hug during the early morning busy time and tell me "You're doing good, keep it up." Sometimes I'd drop a "crawler" or a bagel on the floor and Aunt Marie would run over, pick it up and throw it in the wastebasket. Anytime I made a "faux pas" she'd correct me with a smile, sometimes a laugh and a remark like "You've got sticky fingers!" I was trying my best.

Within a week, I had the job down pat; I was learning and better yet, I really liked working with my aunt. She always smiled, kept a sense of humor and was patient with me when I goofed, and she always treated the customers like they were extra special. It was a trait of hers that I admired and have tried to emulate all my life. It was she who taught me the work ethic.

Living with Aunt Marie, Uncle Charlie and their small son, Butch, while working for them in the bakery, was one of best fun times of my life. The house was always filled with music and laughter. Our meal times together were filled with lots of conversations and I learned to love the Mexican food that Charlie prepared—but not the hot peppers which he would gulp down right out of the jar. He insisted I try one which was so hot I had to drink cold water for hours afterwards.

Marie was very tolerant of his urge to spend all Sunday afternoon molding beautiful clay figures. He gave me one, a horse, which I named Black Beauty after my favorite book when I was a child.

*   *   *

(My Uncle Charlie was like a jolly Santa Claus—robust in size, twinkling eyes, a deep musical laugh that was catching, especially when he kidded me about snitching an occasional doughnut or sweet roll for myself as I carried them into the shop area. "Watch it, Little Marie," he'd say, "You'll get so 'rolly-poly' your apron strings will strangle you one day!" I'd laugh, blush and answer, "Charlie, they're so divine, I just can't resist them." He was right. I gained 10 pounds that summer.

My Aunt Marie was the youngest of the four Schaffer sisters. They all came over "on the boat" with their mother. Marie was only three then and was educated in Milwaukee, went to secretarial school after high school. She had no Austrian accent like her other sisters. She was petite—only 5 feet tall and with a slim figure, unlike her sisters.

When my parents moved from Milwaukee to Los Angeles (I was only 3 years old), Aunt Marie moved with them and stayed with us. She got a job as a bookkeeper at a vocational school where she met and fell in love with Charles Ortega who was from Mexico, had become an American citizen and was taking two very diversified subjects (bakery & sculpturing) at the vocational school where Marie was working in the office. The bakery course offered him a chance to make a living and eventually open up his own bakery shop. The sculpturing course provided him with a creative outlet for his artistic talents. Grandma Schaffer was not happy with Marie's choice of a husband—she didn't like Mexicans. Marie proceeded to overcome and married Charlie. I was the flower girl. The other sisters welcomed him into the family. Aunt Marie's marriage to Charlie was an indication of the "mixed" marriages that were just starting to occur in the United States in the early 1900s.

Little did I know at that time, I, too, would confront a somewhat similar situation in the future and Aunt Marie would be there to support me.

10. WOMEN MOVIE STARS—MY DREAMS & HOPES

THERE WERE FIVE movie theatres within walking distance from my house in Los Angeles and three from Grandma's house in Milwaukee. During my teens in the late 1930s and early 1940s, I was an avid movie buff. There wasn't a weekend that went by when my girlfriends and I didn't go to one or more of the theatres and oftentimes we'd sit through two or three times to watch the same movie. Each movie house had its own price—10, 15 or 25 cents—depending on the newness of the film. At first we couldn't get enough of the wonderful musicals starring Ginger Rogers and Fred Astaire, Nelson Eddy and Jeanette McDonald, Mickey Rooney and Judy Garland. We would leave the theatre in a happy mood, tapping our toes down the street, singing the songs, dancing all the way home. I so badly wanted to become a dancer/singer that I convinced my mother to enroll me in the Meglin Kiddie School in Hollywood where I took tap dancing lessons. I never reached my goal there because my parents couldn't afford it any longer. I was devastated.

About the age of 16, I focused on the romantic movies and the beautiful actresses who portrayed the sirens in the exciting dreams of the early 40s, like Betty Davis, Rosalind Russell, Joan Crawford, Ann Sheridan, Greta Garbo. My girlfriends and I would spend hours manicuring each other's nails, experimenting with pompadour hairdos, using "rats" to produce the look, applying bright lipsticks and rouge. We had a lot of fun doing all these things and our parents didn't mind a bit. Of course, we never went to school or even on the street with our "movie-star" looks. But it all proved to be good beauty training for later life.

We were all carried away with the tender love scenes, the lovers who finally discovered each other and the romantic theme of the films. These new movie idols, like Katherine Hepburn and Rosalind Russell, gave me food for thought. I began to form a strategy for my future. I had been writing little verses in my diary over the years but now I was reading the Los Angeles Times every day and making up news stories. I even used some of the money I'd earned at Aunt Marie's bakery and bought a small portable Royal typewriter. Thanks to Sister Mary Margaret's advice "Take a typewriting course," I was ready to set my course toward a career in journalism.

One night my mother asked why I was always writing on my typewriter. "I know what I want to be, mother—a newspaper woman."

"How are you going to do that?"

"I'm going to college. Is that okay? You put Patrick through Marquette University, so I want to go to UCLA or USC. I know it takes a lot of money but I promise I'll pay you back and I'll work real hard."

She shook her head at me and walked away. I was glad I said it but I was scared my parents would refuse me. They didn't. A year later I went to college.

CHAPTER TWO

MY MATURING YEARS
(1944 to 1950)

1. ROSEANN—MY MENTOR

I FELT GROWN up at the age of 19. I was getting a sense of myself—what I wanted to do with my life, how important friends and family meant to me, recognizing my own good points. But I was still unsure on how to achieve all my goals.

World War II was slowly coming to an end. The German threat was diminishing and there was talk about using a nuclear bomb on Japan to bring "the Nips" to their knees. Because of the distance between where the war was going on and where I was living, I didn't feel much impact from all this. Yes, we had gas rationing, sugar rationing and collecting newspapers, cans, aluminum foil from gum wrappers, on and on. The worst for me was finding nylon stockings and for others, standing in line for cigarettes. I felt bad for the friendly Japanese gardener who worked for my Aunt Marie. He with his family were taken away and placed in a camp for the duration of the war. The news on the radio said that they were rounding up all the Japanese because of the fear of them being spies. I could never believe that but there was nothing I could do.

My parents agreed they would pay for a few courses for me at the University of California in Los Angeles (UCLA) and if I proved myself, they would allow me to go full time in a year. I was thankful for that and enrolled in two early morning classes—one in English Literature and the other in Creative Writing. Because I needed more money than I'd been earning at Aunt Marie's bakery to pay for my transportation to school, for books and new clothes, I started reading the want ads in the Los Angeles Times for part time work. After several different interviews, I was finally accepted as a secretary for a district salesman who sold brake linings for a big company in Detroit. It seemed I was just what he was looking for—a girl to come into the office at 1 p.m. and leave at 5 p.m. I was thrilled to get the job. It paid $25 a week which was more than I received working full time for Aunt Marie, so I accepted immediately even though it seemed boring—writing invoices, dull letters, answering the phone and being alone in the office for many days while my boss, Mr. Abrams was on the road.

I had to get up early to take the two different buses to UCLA, attend my morning English classes, grab a bite in the Student Union, then take two more buses to Pico Blvd. in central Los Angeles where the office was located, then after five p.m., board two streetcars back to my house. During the quiet time in the office after I'd done a few invoices, answered a couple of phone calls, I'd do projects for my classes, writing silly romantic verses or just leaning back in my desk chair and daydream.

After a couple of days on the job, a woman walked into the small office and announced her presence—"I'm Roseann Sherman. I do Mr. Abrams bookkeeping and I'll be coming in every Wednesday and Friday afternoons. I hope we have a good working relationship, Marie." Then she went to her desk across from mine and started to shift through all the invoices I'd placed there.

I hid the verse I'd been writing under my blotter and started to straighten out little things on my desk. She smiled over at me, "Marie, it would be nice if you 'd go to Sy's Deli on the corner and get us both some coffee and a piece of apple pie." She handed me a dollar bill. I took a deep sigh of relief and went flying out of the office to the shop. I knew I could get to like this woman.

Roseann was a tall, elegant, statuesque woman in her 40s. Her clothes were fashionably tailored, her nails impeccably manicured, always painted the same shade of bright red with white "moons" and tips. The French fragrance she wore lingered in the office even the day after she was there. She wore her salt/pepper hair pulled back from her classic-featured face, styled in a neat bun on the back of her head and she always had exquisite earrings that matched her dress. But it was the shirred beaver coat she wore no matter the temperature of the day that stunned me most. One day she let me try it on, and as I ran my fingers over the soft fur, I swore I'd have one, too, some day.

I was in awe of this remarkable woman. She had all the qualities of my favorite female movie stars—a little bit of Kate Hepburn, Rosalind Russell, Bette Davis. I started to look forward to Wednesdays and Fridays. Just before quitting time, she'd take off her glasses, lean back in her chair and strike up a conversation with me. Our talks at the first were non-personal then she started to ask me questions about my family, my schooling and my ambitions. I really enjoyed our conversations especially when she'd recount to me her past experiences about her bit parts in movies made ten years back, amusing stories about her three husbands and sad accounts of her aging mother whom she was caring for at the moment. When Mr. Abrams would pop into the office without notice after one of his selling trips and Roseann was there, I thought it so romantic how quickly they hugged each other. I never did find out, but I fantasized that they were lovers and did write a verse about it. I remember the title: "My Man Has Come Home," (still thinking of Ivan and what we could have been.)

Every Friday night after I cashed my paycheck at the bank, I'd give my mother $10 for room and board—something we agreed upon. On a couple of those occasions I'd tell her how impressed I was with Roseann.

"Mom, you'd be amazed at this lady I work with," I told my mother one Sunday at the dinner table. "She's kinda like a movie star and she's a great story teller. Her voice is always soft and quiet. I don't know how to describe her except I think she's fantastic." My mother just nodded, patted my hand and kept on carving the roast beef.

Roseann became even more friendly as our relationship began to grow. The late day talks continued. I began to reveal my feelings and ambitions, how I felt stymied that my college expectations were on hold, told her how much I wanted to be a journalist and even let her read some of my short stories and verses. She kept urging me on to further my education and suggested I check out the University of Southern California that had a good journalism school. USC was a private school that cost a lot of money and I told her I didn't think my parents could afford to pay for it. She said not to worry about that, to just apply, be accepted and then go from there.

We also talked about my present boyfriend, Carl, who was a corporal in the army, stationed in Inglewood, nearby where I lived. I saw him on weekends when he got a pass. I told her I liked him a lot and how much fun we had together.

"Marie, think very seriously about this; don't rush into marriage if he asks you. You're young and you have a whole life ahead of you. I made a mistake many years ago at your age. I dropped out of the acting business that I loved to get married and have the little white cottage with children playing outside. I never got the cottage or the children but in the meantime I lost my chance to become an actress. First, pursue your ambitions to become educated in journalism, get started in your career. In time, marriage and children will follow."

I would lay awake at night thinking about what she had said, finally put in my application and was accepted at U.S.C. Now came the hard part—asking my parents to pay my tuition—it was only $350 a semester but in those days that was a lot of money. When I approached them, they said they would see if it was possible.

Then I had to tell my boyfriend, Carl, of my decision and that I might not be able to see him as often. He wasn't happy about it but said he'd wait it out.

During my last talk in the office with Roseann, I told her what I had done and she seemed pleased. "Good, Marie, I don't think you'll regret your decision. I've read your writings and I feel you have the talent to go forward. Remember, be the best you can be in your work. Don't be afraid—go forward. If you make some mistakes along the way, use them to better your work, your life. It's important that you do what you like to do—work you enjoy and have fun while you're reaching your goals. There are a lot of young women out there who want to achieve but there's the old saying, "It's a Man's World." Don't believe it—in time, it's going to be "A Woman's World." One day you may even see a woman President in the White House."

Sometime later I terminated my job with Mr. Abrams. Before leaving I thanked him for his kindness and for the job. He said he was glad I could go to college. Roseann came up to me as I was putting on my jacket. She slipped an envelope into the pocket.

"Marie, take this to help pay for your schooling. Keep in touch."

Then she gave me a hug and I ran out the door to catch the next streetcar back home. I didn't open the envelope until later. The sun was just setting and the flower garden in my back yard was in full bloom. Aunt Fanny was picking bouquets for the house. I tore open the envelope and found a $500 check. My mentor had suddenly turned into an angel!

2. MY GIRLFRIENDS—URGING ME ON

M Y DREAM HAD come true. I was going to college full time, moving into an important transition in my life, learning new things about the world and myself. I had classes from 8 a.m. 'til 4 p.m. My brain was flooded with all kinds of new facts and ideas. I met fellow students who came from not only different parts of the United States but from other countries. World War II had ended and the campus was filled with loads of young men who had served and were taking advantage of their GI Bill of Rights to further their schooling. It was so different from the year before when I attended UCLA part time and the girls outnumbered the boys ten to one. I was lucky to get acquainted with two friendly girls: Clare from my English class, and Mary from my Astronomy class. We hung out in the Student Union whenever our classes broke up. Clare was from Des Moines, Iowa and living in a dorm on campus. Mary lived with her family in Beverly Hills. We became very close during our first semester. On the weekends we liked to go to the Paladium Ballroom in Hollywood. We became like sisters, thick as glue. I swore them to secrecy over the story how my bowling instructor (it was required that I take an athletic class each semester) tried to hit on me. I refused his attentions. He said if I walked away from him, he'd give me an F in the class. I walked away but he still gave me an A. (In those days there was no such term as "Sexual harassment.")

I bid farewell to my boyfriend, Carl, who had been stationed in Inglewood and was leaving for his home back in Oklahoma. My feelings for him had dampened after my new experiences in college. I wrote him letters time and time again but he never responded. Roseann's advice came to mind—to pursue my education first and then consider marriage and children later on.

It was 1946. The end of my first year at SC was coming to an end. Spring fever had sprung on campus—the girls were wearing pretty pastel dresses with billowy skirts and long, curly hairdos. Some of the young men just out of the service still wore their casual military garb, mainly because they were surviving on a small income from the government. They were serious and earnest students working to finish up what they had started before being drafted into the war. They wanted to get their degrees and start their lives all over again. They were not like the frivolous college kids of the late 30s. Social fraternities didn't interest them nor did proms or even dating. They just wanted their diplomas and a good job. They knew a job might be hard to find because so many companies that had flourished during the war were now cutting back. But we who were in the School of Journalism had high hopes. With five thriving daily newspapers in Los Angeles, most of us felt we could get some kind of job.

I was lucky to find a summer job at a "throw-away" newspaper that was circulated in the area that bordered the university. This four-page paper was given out free to about 10,000 homeowners—actually thrown on their doorsteps twice a week. The main offices were in Redondo Beach—the company owned about five "throwaways" around Los Angeles and thrived on local advertising. The front page was all editorial—news about each particular area; then social news was interspersed with advertising on the other pages. After two lengthy interviews, I was given the job as Editor. What a thrill for me. Clare, Mary and Chuppie (my girlfriend from my childhood) were excited for me—said they'd act as my reporters if needed.

It was late in May and the Journalism class was throwing a hot-dog fest at Zuma Beach near Malibu. Students were allowed to bring friends, so I invited my three childhood girlfriends, Clare, Mary and Chuppie but when the day arrived I was in a "blue" mood. I still hadn't heard from Carl in Oklahoma, my mother was bugging me about my low-paying job at the "throwaway" newspaper, comparing me to my brother who just got a high-paying job as an electrical engineer at Richfield Oil Company. Getting my period that Sunday didn't help either.

I called my friends and said I wasn't in the mood to go to the party and if they wished, go on their own and mention my name. I lay down on the couch in the living room that morning and dozed off and on. Aunt Fanny tried to revive me with a cup of tea, my parents kissed me goodbye as they went off to an American Legion barbecue. I thought of Garbo—"I want to be alone."

Suddenly, out of the blue, three pretty faces were staring down at me, jiggling my legs. "Get up, Marie! We're going to the beach party. Put on your bathing suit." After fussing with them, I said okay, but I was not myself. We all piled into Clare's 1938 Chevy and drove to the beach.

My friends kept cheering me up, singing songs along the way. When we finally parked and found the group at Zuma Beach, I was beat. We found a place on the sand to spread our towels. I looked around and waved to a few students from my journalism class. The girls ran to the ocean to take a dip. I just laid face down on my towel. The warm sun on my back felt good and I was glad that I'd been urged to get out of the house and into the fresh sea air. I took deep breaths and fell into a deep sleep.

Suddenly, I felt a thump on my back. I sat up and saw a basketball rolling along the side of my towel. I picked it up, then looked up and saw a handsome dark-haired young man looking down at me with a broad smile on his face. "Hi, I'm Bob!"

He grabbed hold of my hand and pulled me up.

"Come play some volleyball with us. You'll get burned lying on your towel and by the way, I like your suit."

"No, I can't—I'm not a good ball player and anyway I have to wait here for my girlfriends. They're in the ocean."

I looked down at my white latex swimsuit and pulled down the tight front skirt. I hoped my pad wasn't leaking any blood. I checked and it hadn't. Then I remembered what Aunt Fanny had told me years before when I got my first period—"go for it." I told Bob okay, I'd play one game but that he shouldn't get mad at me if we lost. He grinned—he had the nicest smile and deep green eyes. He was tall and muscular. He looked familiar but it wasn't until half way through our game that I remembered where I'd seen him before. It was in our journalism class that had more than 50 people in it. He sat in the back of the room and when I turned my head sideways, I could see him looking at me but I always pushed my bangs aside and glanced elsewhere. He was a Junior and I was only a Freshman.

After the game, he insisted we both go into the ocean. The waters were very rough and I was frightened because I didn't know how to swim very well even though I had taken a class the last semester. He held me around the waist and lifted me up every time a big wave crashed in. I screamed every time a wave approached and shouted "Oh, God!" Finally, looking and feeling like a drowned rat, I told him I had to go back to my girlfriends and we walked back on the beach. I introduced him to Clare, Mary and Chuppie who were stretched out on their towels. I fell down on my space and said, "Thanks, Bob. That was fun." He said he had to go and help the other guys set up the barbecue. "You're coming, aren't you? We're going to have a songfest too. John brought his guitar." I nodded.

"He's cute, Marie! Who is he?"

"His name is Bob something. He's in one of my journalism classes. He's okay."

"Come on, Marie," Chuppie responded, "He's so handsome and he liked you. I could see that. Let's change and go over to the barbecue. Maybe there are a couple of other guys there for us."

"No, I don't want to."

That started a barrage of protests toward me: "Stop feeling sorry for yourself; forget about Ivan; you're a big girl now, so act like one and stop sulking like a child; do it for us, we're friends, aren't we." All their remarks came at once until I held up my hands and said, "Okay, Okay—but you've got to promise that we'll leave as soon as we eat our hotdogs." They laughed and nodded. We all grabbed our towels and totes and ran to the beach bathroom to change into our shorts. The aroma of barbecue wafted around. Oh, heck, I thought, 'what's the diff'—I'm starved.

It turned out to be a fun evening. The weather was perfect, even the usual fog didn't drift in that night. The food tasted wonderful. I ate three hotdogs, more than I should have because I was trying to keep on my diet but couldn't resist. Bob never left my side, even wiped up the mustard that I had spilled on my shorts. He put his arm around my shoulders as we were singing songs. I glanced over to my friends who indeed had met some guys—they winked at me, gave me thumbs up. I blew them a kiss. I realized what good friends they were, so supportive and thinking of my best interests. It would be a long time before I'd find three great "buddies" like them. (One of the relationships still holds true today even though miles separate us.)

Everyone decided to go to Venice Pier and take on the rides. Bob urged me to come too; he'd drive me home. "Let's do it, Duff." When he learned my last name was Duffy, he asked if it was okay if he called me "Duff" instead of Marie. "It seems to suit you better." he said as he grabbed my hand and squeezed it. I told him I didn't mind, in fact liked the idea. I'd been called "Duffy" by the boys on the block when I was a kid. It didn't please me but it made me feel like "one of the guys." "Duff" sounded kind of cute and from then on for the next 23 years, Bob Fenton called me "Duff"—but no one else.

I thought it would be fun to go to Venice Pier so I checked with my friends if they were going too. "No, Marie, we're heading home but you go—it's okay." I didn't want them to get mad at me so I said that I'd go home with them.

"Absolutely not!" Clare responded. "This is the best medicine to get you out of your doldrums—go, go and have fun. I'll see you at school tomorrow." I hugged them all, picked up my towel and tote bag and left with the gang.

I don't know if it was the roller coaster ride, the Ferris wheel or what I went on with Bob, but my stomach felt rather queasy. I liked feeling close to him, his arm around me when we went on the rides and how he offered me to share his ice cream cone as we strolled the boardwalk. It was a new feeling to me—different from when I was with Ivan. I felt safe and warm.

We drove home in his 1934 Chevy. He turned off the motor as we rounded the corner into Victoria Avenue and we slowly coasted to the front of my house. It was very quiet. He kissed me and I liked it and smiled. He kissed me again and we started to neck. I don't remember how long we kept necking but I suddenly sat up and opened the door and got out of the car. As I ran up the walk to my house, I turned and waved goodbye. Bob waved back and smiled. What a day . . . and night!

As usual the door was open and I tiptoed through the living room. So as not to wake my parents and Aunt Fanny (it was 2:30 a.m.), I didn't even brush my teeth, just slipped out of my shorts and top and plopped in bed. That queasy feeling was still in the lower part of my stomach but it wasn't an ill feeling. I lay there thinking about Bob and realized that a special chemistry existed between the two of us.

Slowly drifting off to sleep that eventful night in my life, I thought about Clare, Mary and Chuppie and how nice they were to me. I suddenly realized what a "pain" I must have been to them all day and they were so supportive and understanding and encouraging to me. I said a short "Thank You" to God and fell asleep smiling.

*　　*　　*

The summer of '46 kept me busy working part-time at the "throwaway" newspaper, taking classes at SC so I could move forward toward a degree and dating Bob at least three nights a week. I was literally burning the candle at both ends but felt exhilarated by it all. I lost 10 pounds, changed my hairdo, bought some new clothes and knew within me that serious, new experiences were taking me into another world.

My girlfriends and I would discuss our lives and feelings openly. Our get-togethers at the diner near my newspaper office on Adams Ave. were like group therapy sessions held today. We talked about sex, religion, our futures—things we could never discuss with our parents. They helped me make decisions like the time I did a front-page article on the city shutting down the bus service on Adams Blvd. even though the elderly relied on the transportation to take them to doctors' appointments, shopping, etc. Being an idealist, I editorialized it by voicing my objection. That incident took me back to the day I wore the halter pants to my elementary school baseball game and the nuns rebuked me. I had to give up my place as baseball captain but I stood up for my convictions.

The day the newspaper came out the publisher called me to her office, ranted and raved about the article and how I did not have the right to editorialize in a front page news story. I knew, journalistically, she was right but the idea of the old people who would suffer from this cut-off of their only transportation was the bottom line for me. She fired me on the spot. I picked up my last check and in sad spirits went home to tell my parents. They weren't happy about it but said I could always help Aunt Marie in the bakery. I told them no, that I didn't want to gain weight back again, and I'd look for a new job. My girlfriends helped me out and got me part-time clerical work in Clare's father's insurance office. Here again, my "buddies" came through for me.

My close relationship with Bob and my "buddies" continued through the summer. I was always with Bob during my free time, and every Sunday morning after Mass, Chuppie, Mary, Clare and I would get together in Inglewood Park, near my house, for a talk session. They had steady boyfriends now and we'd discuss them. One Sunday, Mary came all red-eyed and started to cry—she was pregnant. We all gasped and asked, "Mary, what are you going to do?"

"I guess I'll have to marry Charles. My mother would kill me if she knew. So we're eloping to Las Vegas tomorrow."

We all sat on the blanket in the park and mourned Mary's departure from our group. None of us said much to Mary except wish her luck and asked her to keep in touch. I was curious how she got pregnant—I was absolutely ignorant of the sex act but I didn't impose on her. After she left the group to go meet Charles, I started to ask Chuppie and Clare. They laughed and started to detail intercourse for me. I listened and shook my head, "never, never for me—that sounds awful—animalistic! I like necking with Bob and his caresses, but to do THAT—NEVER!" In that era, no sex acts were ever shown on screen, how-to sex books were not even thought of and in my environment we never had access to "naughty" pictures or magazines.

When I look back at myself at the age of 21, I am absolutely amazed at my naivety when it came to sex. But one day, my girlfriends who were a couple of years older than I, gave me a crash course on it. They took me to the library and we paged through biology and other kinds of medical books, giggling so loudly that the librarian finally came over shaking her finger at us.

Then there was Larry who was in my German class that summer. I thought he was flirting with me because he'd buy me coffee at the Student Union, asked if he could take me to a movie. I always refused because I didn't want Bob to think I was cheating on him. He never touched me or even tried to kiss me which I thought was strange since he was so attentive to me.

One day Larry told be about a casting call being held on campus for the upcoming Andy Hardy movie starring Mickey Rooney and Judy Garland. We both went and were chosen to jitterbug in a high school dance scene. One of requirements was that we had to be no taller than five foot four inches. Larry and I just met the height requirement as did 49 other students. I was so excited to be in a real movie. We arrived at 8 a.m. at the studio in Burbank, but we had to wait around until 1 p.m. for Mickey Rooney to show up and even then he was on the set for only an hour. Meanwhile, all of us dancers had to jitterbug over and over again until the director called the final cut. It turned out to be a long day and not as exciting as I thought it would be, but we were paid over $100 which was a good day's pay. Larry and I laughed a lot throughout it all and I began to think he was a real nice guy.

When I mentioned him to my "buddies," they roared with laughter and rolled their eyeballs upward, shook their head at me.

"What? What's so funny."

Then they proceeded to tell me that everyone knew Larry was a "fairy."

"What's that?"

More laughter and finally when I stamped my foot, looked at them angrily, they pulled me close to them and whispered "He's a boy but he wants to be a girl."

"What? I don't believe you. I never heard of such a thing! You're kidding me."

They assured me they weren't and then continued to explain it all to me.

I liked Larry and felt sorry for him. I welcomed him to be my friend and never let on what I knew. I then realized why Bob never seemed jealous when he saw Larry and me together. He must have known too.

That was the last summer my friends and I would ever be so close. Clare quit SC and went to work in her father's company. Chuppie got a new job and was dating a man she met there. Mary was married. For the first time in my life, I felt really alone.

3. AUNT FANNY—THE WIND BENEATH MY WINGS

THE FALL, WINTER, spring seasons of 1946 and 1947 went swiftly. I was busy from early morning to late evening with my studies but especially enjoying and having so much fun with all our journalism friends at SC. We had silly holiday parties like Halloween when we all dressed up in costumes that depicted people we admired or would want to be. I chose to be a Egyptian Queen and Aunt Fanny made me a short, white toga. I bought a paper gold crown for my head and gold cord to drape around one shoulder, between my breasts and tie around my waist. It was very fetching. I also had her make a long brown one for Bob and I created a green ivy wreath for his head. We won first prize as Caesar and Cleopatra.

The football games kept us busy on weekends. There were times we all drove up to Berkley or down to San Diego to root for our Trojans; drank a lot of beer; wore funny little beanies on our heads and just got high on laughs and having fun. It was a whole new world for me. Little by little I realized I was falling in love with this exciting, talented, energetic young man—Bob.

Because my parents were busy from early morning to late night, they were unaware of my "goings-on." They went to bed around ten p.m. and I would sneak into the house around midnight almost every night. They thought I was occupied with my studies and never questioned me about things, except at Sunday dinners when we all gathered around the table. I would simply tell them about what grades I had received (they were good, thank God) and a few remarks about Bob, a nice boy I had met at college. They said they would like to meet him.

But Aunt Fanny knew better. She had seen Bob's old Chevy pull up in front of the house every morning and at midnight. She never said anything to my parents.

I knew my parents were getting anxious to meet Bob, so I arranged for him to come to a Sunday dinner at my house. He was nervous—so was I, but it turned out to be very pleasant. I think they truly liked him.

My father brought out his bottle of Scotch from the closet which he only did a few times a year for guests (he and my mother were teetotalers) and offered a drink to Bob. My mother and I were not even asked. Aunt Fanny served the dishes and I caught her eye when she was passing Bob the gravy—she winked at me. Bob and I left the house late that afternoon. As we climbed into his car, we both breathed a sigh of relief.

"Honey, I think you passed with flying colors." He answered," Yeah, where do we go from here?" I looked at him quizzically—what did he mean by that remark?

One morning a few Sundays later after we had attended Mass, my parents asked me Bob's religion and nationality.

"Fenton, is that an English name?" my father said. I hadn't even given thought to Bob's religion or nationality. "He says he's American." They shook their heads.

When I saw Bob that night I brought it up.

"Bob, my parents asked if Fenton is an English name?"

"Yes it is but it's not my original name. My parents had our name, Feinstein, legally changed during the war. My family is Jewish but I acclaim myself a non-denominational American. I don't follow the faith anymore. They don't like it, but that's the way it is."

I was confused with what I had just heard and then started to realize what a problem this was—he of Jewish background and I a Catholic! We were very much in love and had even talked about getting married. Now I didn't know what to think.

We didn't discuss the subject any more after that. We were busy with exams. Bob would be graduating in June; I would become a Junior. I was planning what job to look for during the summer plus we had become very social with our colleagues—playing Poker at Boyd's house, dancing at Venice Pier, fun nights editing the SC newspaper, Trojan Owl, with Neil, Gilda, Joyce and others. Bob was the Editor and he took his job seriously. He'd drive me home every night and we'd spend an hour sitting in his car talking about all sorts of new adventures we were having. We'd do a lot of kissing and "petting" but never "went the whole way." Aunt Fanny always kept the door open for me and when I passed her pullout bed in the living room, she'd sit up and ask if I had a good time. I knew she could keep a secret.

One morning early in May 1947, I was bathing and Aunt Fanny was pressing a blouse and skirt I needed to wear for interviews at the five newspapers in Los Angeles.

"Fanny, I'm scared. I don't know what to say."

"Marie, you'll do fine. Tell them what you want and be persistent. Say you'll take anything they have available. Tell them you're good and you'll work hard. Don't give up and don't get discouraged."

Off I went—first to the Herald then the Examiner. I went straight to the City Editor of all the newspapers but each editor only smiled, shook his head. The interview was over. In those days, we didn't prepare resumes, we just spoke our story. After four rejections, I decided to try my last source, The Los Angeles Times, the most prestigious newspaper in Los Angeles. It was already three p.m. I was tired riding the streetcars and walking the hot pavement but I shrugged my shoulders, took a few stretches, tried to un-wrinkle my skirt which looked as tired as I, and took my last try.

Ed Strong was a short, heavy-set man who sat behind a large, paper-strewn desk with his name on it. He was the Sunday Editor. I had made a three p.m. appointment with him. I already was a half hour late. Ouch!

I don't know what I said, although remembering Aunt Fanny's advice, I came on strong and emphasized how important a summer job at the Times would mean to me. Mr. Strong listened and then picked up the phone to call someone. He was calling Personnel, kept nodding his head, then hung up and smiled at me. "Okay, Marie, there's an opening in editorial."

My heart started to beat rapidly. "My God, editorial," I said to myself. "I'm going to be a real reporter."

"You'll be working as an assistant to Lydia Lane, our Beauty columnist. You'll help her answer correspondence, test the newest cosmetics, give her reports on them and when she's away or on vacation, write some of her columns. Do you want the job? It pays $65 a week?"

It wasn't what I thought it would be but I couldn't refuse so I thanked Mr. Strong and went to Personnel to fill out all the forms. Then it began to sink in—I was working for one of the biggest newspapers in the country. When I told my parents, Aunt Fanny, my friends and Bob, everyone congratulated me. I had my first important job!

The position turned out to be fun. Lydia was a nice lady and once she had told me what to do, seldom interfered with my work. Testing and learning about the different products was exciting. After a month I realized I wanted something more so I'd go to Mr. Strong once a week and ask him if there were any other new openings in editorial—especially on the news side.

During this time, Aunt Fanny was so helpful. She made sure I had freshly pressed blouses and skirts to wear for each day of the week, helped me set my hair in pincurls every night. She urged me to forget my job on weekends and spend time with Bob and our friends. "All work and no play, makes Marie a dull girl," she would remind me.

The week after Bob's graduation, Mr. Strong called me to come to his desk and said there was an opening as assistant editor to the Society Editor. I grabbed it and started as Christy Fox's helper. I got a ten dollar raise. I was now earning more than I ever had before. I not only was able to pay room and board to my parents, but bought a lot of new clothes, paid for Bob and my dinners out and had enough left over to "share my wealth" with Aunt Fanny. I'd give her five dollars every payday to buy yarn and go to the movies.

One night in late July, my relationship with Bob came to a head. Our physical attraction to each other and our love for each other was leading into dangerous territory. We both wanted to get married but couldn't figure how to do it without bringing pain to our parents. Neither of us felt strongly about our faiths, but there was the difficult task of my being excommunicated from the Church if I gave up the faith plus the embarrassment to my parents—and likewise for Bob. Neither one of us could come up with an answer. After talking about it while sitting in his car in front of my house, we decided to break up. I ran sobbing into the house and straight to my bedroom, threw myself on the bed.

The bedroom door creaked open and Aunt Fanny in her flannel nightgown, her silvery hair tumbling down her back, came in and sat on the edge of the bed, stroking my back softly. "Shush, Shush," she kept murmuring. "What's wrong, child. Tell me."

I turned, sat up and hugged her. I smelled lavender on her—the scent took me back to my childhood and all the times she had comforted me in my time of need. I took a deep breath, wiped my eyes on the collar of her nightgown, and began to tell her about my dilemma.

"You're young, Marie. You'll meet another man. Lena and Pat would feel so bad about all this. You're Catholic—you cannot marry a Jew."

"But I love him so and I know he's the one I want to marry. What can I do?"

"Think about it. Go to church and search your soul."

"Aunt Fanny, the church means nothing to me anymore—too many restrictions. I've grown up. I'm my own person now."

"Take your time and think carefully about what you want to do, Marie. I have had a lonely life all these years. They tell me I'm crazy but I know I'm not. I have never been brave enough to go out on my own. Do you think I'm crazy?"

I looked at her and smiled, "No, Aunt Fanny, you're not crazy." So began our talk that lasted over an hour. I slept heavy that night and awoke to Fanny's call to come have breakfast and catch the eight a.m. streetcar to downtown Los Angeles.

Three weeks went by. I waited for Bob to call me, but he didn't. My heart ached to tell him I loved him, to kiss him, to feel his touch. Meanwhile, Mr. Strong was very happy about my work with Christy. She assigned me stories, like covering the opening day at Santa Anita where I went with a photographer to shoot pictures of the society people. I had to write all the captions plus a three inch story for the Society page. Then one night she had me cover the opening of the Los Angeles Symphony. Aunt Fanny made me a long black skirt and I topped it with a white ruffled blouse. It was fun but I thought of Bob every minute and missed him so much. Little did I know he was missing me too. I kept thinking of our decision to split and would lay awake at night trying to figure out what I should do.

Every time the radio played the popular song "You'll Never Know How Much I Love You . . . You'll Never Know How Much I Care," I was hoping that Bob heard it too. I kept my energies up by going to bed early and focusing on the important demands of my job as assistant Society Editor. Christy could sense that I was distracted but my work satisfied her. Then one morning in late August, 1947, I got a phone call from Bob. My blood pressure must have gone up 100 degrees. Just hearing his voice again made me swoon. "Duff, lets get together tonight and talk this all over again. Can I pick you up at the office?" "Yes, yes, yes!"

His old Chevy was waiting outside the Los Angeles Times building. I jumped in, looked straight ahead as he drove away. After driving five blocks, he pulled over to the curb, grabbed me in his arms and kissed me passionately. I kissed him back, then we hugged and I started to cry. "I've missed you so much, I love you so much," I sobbed.

"Me, too, Duff. Let's get married. I talked it over with Boyd and Fern and they said if we drove to Tijuana, we could get married tonight. They'll drive us and be our witnesses. I love you and want to be with you forever. Please?" "Yes," I said.

I couldn't resist his proposal but I needed some time to make plans so we agreed to meet at eight a.m. Meanwhile, we spent the rest of the evening parked high on one of hills surrounding Los Angeles where you could see the whole panorama of the city lights. We kissed, touched each other and affirmed our love for each other. At midnight I was in my room, thinking of what to do. I first wrote a letter to my parents explaining my actions and begging their forgiveness. I packed a small suitcase with a few clothes and then chose a new gray suit and white blouse to wear as my wedding outfit. There was one more important thing to take—my savings account book. The $500 my grandma had given me years before would come in handy now. Finally, at 2 p.m., I fell fast asleep. I had wanted to talk to Aunt Fanny but this night she was sleeping so hard she didn't even wake up.

I awoke shortly after my parents left for work at their restaurant and suddenly realized what I had committed myself to. I was so scared and sat upright in bed staring out of window. "Marie, are you sure you want to go through with this?" I asked myself. I looked at my suitcase on the floor and thought of the sealed envelope on my bureau. I must have sat on my bed for 20 minutes, thinking. I glanced at the clock—seven a.m. I nodded my head, rushed to the bathroom for a bath (we had no shower in those days), brushed my teeth, and put on my underclothes. I kept staring out the window as if looking for an answer. Bob said he'd be by at eight—what to do?

I always find it amazing how the early morning can give you qualms about an incident that occurred the night before. The light of day seems to sober the mistakes, even the glory of the preceding evening—one seems to have a different perspective on decisions made. I was going through this trauma . . . should I, shouldn't I?

I heard Aunt Fanny calling me from the kitchen—"Marie, your eight o'clock streetcar will be coming soon—breakfast is on the table. Hurry up!"

Here I was 22 years old and Fanny was still calling me to breakfast. I knew then it was time to break loose and find my own life, even if I were to hurt those I loved. I straightened my back, pulled down the jacket of my suit, slipped on my white pumps, tossed back my short brunette hair, grabbed my suitcase, picked up the sealed letter to my parents and walked toward my fate.

My cornflakes were on the table, a bottle of milk and sugar next to the bowl. I saw Fanny peering at me through the kitchen door. Then she

MARIE FENTON GRIFFING

closed it. I placed the envelope addressed to Mother and Daddy on the mantle.

Suddenly there was a knock on the door.

"I'll get it Fanny," I shouted.

Thinking it was Bob, I rushed to the door and there to my surprise was Bob's older sister, Ruth, whom I had met only twice. She asked me if I could come out to her car to talk. I started to shake. I nodded and followed her down the porch steps, closing the door quietly so Fanny couldn't hear me leave.

In the front passenger seat sat Bernice, Bob's sister-in-law. She smiled and waved hello to me as I got into the back seat of the car. I knew what was coming.

"Bob told us you two were off to Mexico to get married," Ruth said in a low, calm voice. "Bernice and I beg you not to do this. My parents will be devastated and I'm sure yours will be too. Wait a little while and maybe we can all work this out. Bob is Jewish and he cannot marry a Catholic. Don't you understand?"

"Did Bob tell you to come here?"

They both shook their heads—"No, but because Bobby is the youngest in the family, we felt he needed our help," Bernice interjected, "and we felt we could convince you both to hold off getting married until the families could get together and decide what was best for the two of you."

I unclenched my fingers to open the car door, smiled at both of them, said goodbye and ran into the house. I peaked through the lace curtained front window and saw them drive away, then breathed a sigh of relief. What to do now?

I walked over to the mantle, grabbed the letter and started to tear it up, but suddenly stopped. "No," I said to myself, "I'm going through with it." Then Aunt Toni's advice that she gave me when I was 16 and had a crush on Ivan came back to me—"Someday you will meet the man you want to spend the rest of your life with—" I replaced the envelope on the mantle.

Bob's horn was tooting outside. I grabbed my suitcase, looked back at the kitchen door and shouted, "I'm going, Fanny, bye, bye!"

4. AUNT MARIE—MY GODMOTHER SUPPORTS ME

AUGUST 27, 1947 was the most exciting, wonderful day I had ever experienced in my young life. It was my wedding day. It seemed the minute Bob and I met Fern and Boyd, got into their new Cadillac to drive to San Diego, all my conflicts of the morning vanished. Bob said we had to make one stop at his house so he could tell his parents. Sitting in the back seat waiting for him to come back seemed like an eternity. Fern and Boyd tried to quiet my fears, but I wondered if his folks would change his mind—but they didn't—he came running back to the car, jumped in, gave me a hug and kiss "Okay, Boyd—we've got a wedding to go to. Step on the gas!"

When we stopped at a gas station along the coast, I made a phone call to my Editor, Christy. I told her what I was doing and said I would use the personal days I had coming for a short honeymoon. She understood, said okay and wished me happiness. I breathed a sigh of relief—my last hurdle was completed.

What a night it was. We arrived in Tijuana around 3 p.m. Bob and Boyd went shopping for a wedding ring for me and Fern and I went looking for a "Justice of the Peace." The ceremony took about three minutes and we received a small printed white sheet that said Bob Fenton and Marie Duffy were legally married. They said our real wedding license would arrive at my house a month later from Mexico City. Bob carefully folded the white slip into his wallet and then we all took off for the Rosarita Hotel that was right on the ocean a few miles away. The place was old and beautiful. Our room overlooked the ocean and we could hear the surf thundering in. The night was mild and the marihajoes were strumming their guitars in the bar. I felt like I was in paradise. I was now a married woman. The next day with Bob and me still necking in the back seat, Fern and Boyd drove us back to Santa Monica where we rented a room at a plush hotel on the beach. We called our friends, Neil and Gilda, to join us at the pool. Neil brought his camera to record our honeymoon. It was a glorious four days.

Reality finally set in when Bob and I returned to Los Angeles and I had to go back to work. We rented a small motel room on Figueroa Street near Boyd and Fern's apartment which made it easy for me to catch a streetcar to the Times building. Bob had brought his typewriter with him and while I was away, he worked on an article for a national magazine, a piece he had started before our elopement.

We ate dinner at a local diner, saw our friends and were passionately in love with each other. I was ecstatically happy but I had qualms about how to come to grips with my parents. I knew they were worrying about me; I loved them but I just couldn't face them right then. Bob sensed my stress and suggested I call my Aunt Marie first and see which way the wind was blowing.

"Little Marie, it's so good to hear from you. We've all be wondering where you are and how you are. Are you okay?"

"Yes, Aunt Marie. I'm fine. I'm married and so happy. Can Bob and I come over and talk with you?"

I held tight to Bob's hand as we rang the doorbell to Aunt Marie and Uncle Charlie's house in Beverly Hills. She embraced me, smiled and gave her congratulations, then did the same thing to Bob. I walked down the steps that led to the sunken living room, looked around, breathed deeply—I was in friendly territory, a house I loved and lived in while working for Aunt Marie—it brought back many carefree and fun memories. We sat down on the plush couches and Marie offered us some coffee and Charlie's famous cookies. Charlie never appeared.

At first she was cheerful, not judgmental, just asked us about our honeymoon—a lot of small talk that slowly led us into a more serious discussion—the reason we were there. I first asked her how Mother and Daddy were taking this.

"Listen, both of you. You have a lot of barriers in front of you. Even though it's a well used cliché "love can conquer all." It does and can happen. Your conflicting religious backgrounds are foremost now because of your families' objections."

"Aunt Marie, Bob and I don't put importance on religion—in fact, organized religion is no longer for us."

"That's fine for you but what happens when you have children?"

"We've agreed not to have a baby now. We each want to work on our careers. If and when we decide to start a family, we'll raise them according to our own moral values, not the strictness and rigid laws that organized religion demands. We consider ourselves good, moral people and that's all we want our children to be."

My chin was held high but I could feel my eyes wallowing up with tears as I tried to convince Aunt Marie that we knew what we were doing. She sat back on the facing sofa, folded her arms around her waist, took a deep breath, and nodded at us.

"Okay, I can see you've got it all planned out—that's good. You know, your situation reminds me of my dilemma when Charlie and I decided to get married. Your Grandma objected strongly, even though he was Catholic. It was that he was Mexican and she didn't like that. But we stood fast and in time she came around. Marie, even your Mother had a hard time convincing your grandma she wanted to marry your Father. She was a tough lady."

Bob and I laughed. I suddenly recalled the image of this tiny grey-haired lady, sitting in a rocking chair in her Milwaukee house and how I as a little girl used to have a strange sense of fear of her, yet respecting her every wish like running to the corner store for her rock candy which she sucked on all day.

Recalling the sense of fear and wanting acceptance and approval from Grandma Schaffer, suddenly made me aware that I was reliving these same feelings with my own mother, but thanks to Aunt Marie she helped put my fears to rest.

"Now, Marie, I think the first thing we have to do is get in contact with your parents—and that means yours, too, Bob—to come to terms that you are legally married and they must recognize that. If they do that, then that's half the battle. Next, you must see them face to face in a friendly atmosphere. Don't have a serious discussion—put yourselves on a different level—like it's done and over with—you just want to be back in their graces again, you love them, want to keep seeing them and you can bring up all the different work you're doing and how busy you are making plans for the future. Marie, you call Lena and Pat and invite them to come to your new apartment in Hollywood, and Bob, you call your parents and do the same—but not on the same day, for heavens sake. Meanwhile, I'll call Lena and Pat. Bob, maybe your sister, Ruth, can call your parents and calm them down. How does that sound?"

It felt like a weight was lifted off me—Aunt Marie's plan sounded perfect to me. Bob agreed. I gave my aunt a hug and wiped my eyes. Uncle Charlie suddenly walked in from the kitchen, carrying a bottle of champagne and four glasses. "Here's to a wonderful warm, happy married life!" He said, his face glowing,. "Okay, come on you newly-weds, let's drink a toast to the beginning of a new and beautiful relationship." Now it was Bob and I who were glowing.

5. AUNT TONI—THE PEACEMAKER

A MONTH HAD gone by since Bob and I had our meeting with Aunt Marie. I still hadn't called my parents because of my work at the Times and moving from our motel room to an apartment in Hollywood, I just didn't have the time to set up a get-together with them. Plus I was so excited about our first new home. It was an ingenious plan of Bob's that resulted in our getting a studio apartment in the heart of Hollywood—on the corner of Franklin and Gower, just a block or two away from Hollywood Boulevard. We were lucky to get it and at $45 a month. Because of the war just over, apartments were still scarce in Los Angeles.

It was Bob's ingenuity that got us the apartment. Being an alumni now of SC, he was able to get tickets to all the school's sports events at a low price and first pick of seats. The Notre Dame-SC football game was scheduled for late November 1947. He bought a pair of tickets, then ran an ad in the Times stating two tickets to this popular sports event in exchange for an apartment. We received five replies and picked the one in Hollywood—$45 a month.

The place was sparsely furnished. I bought some new drapes and the first weekend after we moved in, Bob and I tried to make it homey with little touches like a small desk for his typewriter and a couple of pots and pans for the kitchen. I didn't even know how to boil water so we ate most of our meals out. I'd have coffee and toast for breakfast and a sandwich for lunch in the Times cafeteria; Bob would go to the nearest diner for his food, then in the evening we'd pick up a steak, a can of peas and some lettuce at a nearby grocery store. I tried my best to prepare a tasty dinner but most times I'd burn the steak and overcook the potato. But fancy eating was not important then. We were young and in love and that satisfied us.

Finally, one night I called my parents. My mother immediately started to cry and asked me all sorts of questions. Aunt Marie had told her I was okay and what I was doing so I was relieved for that. After she quieted down, I asked her and my father to come to dinner on Sunday. "Yes, yes," she replied.

I called Aunt Toni who had just come to live with Aunt Marie after selling Grandma Shaffer's house in Milwaukee.

"Toni, make sure Mother and Daddy come on Sunday. Okay?"

"No problem. They're so anxious to see you. What are you going to have for dinner? Can I help? I so want this occasion to come off right. Your Aunt Marie and I have been talking about it, and I will do anything in order to make peace between you and Lena and Pat. You're their only daughter and you mean so much to them. They are hurt by what you and Bob did, but I have been trying to convince them to just accept what has happened and come to terms with it. I really feel, Marie, that they are trying to, but it's not easy for them. I'm sure Bob's folks are going through the same thing."

"Oh, Toni, I'm so nervous about seeing them. I feel so sorry I hurt them, but I had no recourse. I'm so happy with Bob. I hope I can get back in their grace again. But what should I make for dinner. What's easy to cook?"

"Marie, I'll tell you what I'll do. I'll cook a roast chicken, some boiled potatoes, peas and Charlie will give me a coconut cake from the bakery. How does that sound?"

"You'd do that for me. Oh, Toni, you're the best. Okay, but you'd better bring it over before they come. I don't want them to know you did it."

"I'll be there at five, and we'll put it all on the stove just like if you'd cooked it yourself—how's that?"

On Sunday morning Bob and I were rushing around the apartment, vacuuming, dusting, making up the wall bed and setting the small round dining table. I used a sheet for a tablecloth, picked out the least chipped plates. I had bought a small vigil-like candle in a glass, a little bouquet of violets for the centerpiece. We were both trying so hard to make the place look nice that we didn't realize we weren't even showered or dressed and my parents would arrive in an hour. Toni arrived just on time and I helped her bring in the food from her car and we set it up on the stove. It looked great and I thanked her so much. She said she had to hurry out and wished us good luck.

Bob put on his only suit, the one he wore on our wedding day and I put on my only party dress—a pink tight-fitting sheath. We were as nervous as two kids going to a party. The doorbell rang and we were off and running from that time on.

There were a lot of hugs and tears. My mother came with a huge brown bag of groceries. We sat on the couch and drank Coca Cola, nibbled on peanuts. Bob and I remembered what Aunt Marie had advised and kept the conversation on my job, Bob's writing and stories about the new neighbors we had. My mother said she had talked with her priest and he would perform a ceremony for us. I brushed that off by saying, "We'll see." Fifteen minutes later I rushed to the kitchen and started to put the food on the table.

"Marie, this chicken is delicious. Lena, see, our daughter has turned out to be a good cook. She must have got it from me." praised my father.

"Pat, I taught her everything she knows about cooking. The potatoes could have been boiled a few minutes more, don't you think?"

The entire mealtime conversation centered around food. My mother gave me tips on how to make chicken gravy and my father explained how to prepare one of his favorite dishes, rice pudding.

Bob helped me clear the table and in the tiny kitchen we both started giggling so hard that we had to turn on the faucet so my parents couldn't hear our outbursts. Little did they suspect that Aunt Toni had helped us through. As we said our goodbyes, my mother started to cry again and I tried to comfort her. My father said he would go to work on making us a bookcase and a coffee table. "You can't have those books sitting around on the floor and you need a table to set your dessert and coffee on, not juggle them on your knees." Then my mother squeezed a fifty dollar bill into my hand—she always was a generous person. That's one of many good traits I inherited from her.

The next weekend was set up to meet Bob's parents. I had never met them before and was more nervous about this meeting than with my parents. Bob reassured me that his sister, Ruth, had quieted them down and they were able to accept me as their daughter-in-law but I sensed that it wouldn't be as easy as with my family.

Again I called Aunt Toni.

"Toni, what do you think about having a baked ham and yams? I have a good recipe for it?"

"No, Marie, God forbid! Most Jewish people don't eat ham, bacon or pork."

"But, Toni, Bob eats them all."

"Okay, that's Bob—but not his parents, I'm sure. Go for a pot roast with potatoes and vegetables and lots of gravy. Listen, I'll cook it all and

MARIE FENTON GRIFFING

bring it over like we did last week. Charlie will give me a pound cake and I'll buy some strawberries. You buy some seltzer and you'll be all set."

Toni was like my guardian angel. She was always there when I needed her.

One night while I was sitting knitting and Bob was editing one of his articles for US magazine, he turned in his chair and said, "Marie, what do you think about going to Paris?"

I was shocked. I knew Bob had passed through there when he was in the Battle of the Bulge but I never expected this from him. I didn't know how to respond. I tried to explain that we didn't have the money to go there and I really didn't want to quit my job at the Times. He nodded and then said, "Think about it. Art Buchwald just went over a while ago and he already has a job on the Herald Tribune. Maybe you could get a job over there too. I figure I'll attend classes at the Sorbonne that the government will pay for plus I'll get a $100 a month from them that we can live on."

Art had gone to school with us and edited the humor magazine there. Bob and he were close friends. It did sound exciting but scary too.

The subject wasn't brought up again. I stopped worrying about Bob's plans to take off for Europe and just concentrated on my job and happy times I was experiencing as a married lady. Bob and I were so much in love. We enjoyed each day to the fullest, even though we didn't see each other except for an hour in the a.m. before I went to work and in the evening. I still wasn't into cooking, so we ate simply but whenever I had a small dinner party planned, Toni would come to my rescue with some sort of wonderful dish.

The months flew by and on August 27, 1948 we celebrated our first wedding anniversary. Toni brought us a beautiful cake and gave us $10. She was always there for us. We would make occasional visits to see our parents and things were going along fine without any conflicts. We had all of our close friends from school and would spend weekend nights playing poker or dancing at the Navy Officers Club where Boyd and Fern were members.

Then at a Christmas party at my brother's, Bob told me he had booked two one-way tickets for May on the Queen Mary, sailing from New York to France. He said he had sold an article and used the money for the trip.

"Bob," I gasped, "Why didn't you tell me before buying the tickets? I don't think I'm ready for this. It's not fair."

I was angry with him for a few days, but when I saw the confirmation of the tickets on his desk, I started to get excited. I'd never been anyplace but back and forth to Milwaukee, a few trips to San Francisco and Catalina Island. Just thinking of seeing New York and then Paris revved up my adrenalin. I almost felt like I was in a movie. We talked every day about our preparations for the trip to Europe. Bob agreed with me that we'd only spend six months there. He said, "Duff, wait 'til you see this city. It's beautiful. I know I can do good writing there. You'll fall in love with it and the people too."

And so we prepared ourselves for this adventure. We sold our car which gave us extra money for a six-month leave of absence from the Times. My boss accepted that and then surprised me with an offer to be the Times' women's representative in Europe. I was to send back articles about the couture collections in Paris, the Parisian women and any other type of feature pieces for the Women's pages.

"I'll pay you a one dollar per inch of printed copy. Send your pieces in every Monday and we'll mail you a check at the end of month. I'll write you a letter so you can get yourself accredited over there with the American Ambassador's office. They'll issue you a press pass so you'll have entry to special events."

I thanked him for this opportunity. It eased my anxiety over financial security.

May, 1949 came quickly. There were a lot of farewell parties and dinners with our families and friends. Tears flowed all around and at times I had thoughts of dropping the whole thing, stay home and let Bob go by himself. When I told Toni about these scary feelings, she said, "If I were you I would go with Bob, help him and consider it an adventure—after-all it's only for six months and you'll be back home again." Toni's encouraging words made me less nervous. I was ready now.

Dozens of friends and family came to the train station to see us off to New York. We had decided since there was no rush to get to New York for our sailing, we'd take the train and see the country. Our new luggage was filled with clothes and pages of Bob's first novel. Of course, our little portable typewriter came along too.

After a lot of hugs and kisses, we were ready to board. Toni came running toward us carrying a furry-looking thing on her arm. She approached me, breathless. "Sorry, I'm late, Marie but I had to dig this out of my closet. I want you to have it. It's my fox jacket that I used to wear in Milwaukee. It's yours now. I know the fall and winter in Europe can be very cold, so wear this for warmth. It'll bring you luck." I grabbed the coat and rubbed my fingers over the soft fur, thinking of the time Roseann had let me try on her beaver coat and I swore I'd have one like it someday. I took a deep breath and hugged Toni so tightly she had to break away for a breath. "Be happy, Little Marie. Take care of yourself and write me often." I said I would—after-all she was my first pen pal. Little did Bob or I ever imagine that our stay in Europe would last for six years instead of six months.

CHAPTER THREE

MY CREATIVE YEARS
(1949 TO 1960)

1. LILLIAN TRIDOUX—MY FRENCH "TEACHER"

ARRIVING AT THE Paris train station in the middle of the night was the culmination of five days of fantasy aboard the Queen Mary. For me, a young woman, who had never traveled much, it was all overwhelming, especially at the station. There were loud horns tooting, taxi drivers were shouting, people were rushing back and forth, pushing, some being plain uncouth. Bob made me sit on our baggage while he rounded up a taxi.

I reflected back a few hours when we disembarked at Cherbourg, France. During the train ride from Cherbourg to Paris, I got my first taste of blue cheese and French bread and a glass of wine. I could still taste the tangy flavors. I suddenly heard Bob's voice. He had hailed a taxi to take us to a little hotel on Rue Merivoux on the Left Bank.

I held tight to Bob's arm and looked around at all the bright lights. "See, I told you, Duff, this is the place to be. Aren't you glad you're here?" I smiled and nodded "Yes," sensing he was trying to put me at ease.

The weeks to come were a matter of adjustment for Bob and me. We had all sorts of stomach problems due to the new food and water. We were told to drink the wine instead of the water which we did but that only put us to sleep in the middle of the afternoon. Little by little our heads and our bodies got adjusted to the newness of Paris. At the American Embassy I showed them my accreditation letter from the Los Angeles Times and received a press pass. I followed up with the couture public relations people and was given entry to all the fall/winter collections to be held in August. Bob was in his glory, exploring all the book outlets on the Seine and visiting the art shops on St. Germaine de Pres. Getting used to the subway system and how to read the maps was a lesson in itself as well as the money exchange. Most Americans bought francs on the black market; cheaper than the bank. We'd spend our evenings at the Dome or other outdoor cafes on the Left Bank. Bob entered the Sorbonne University as a GI vet and took classes in the French language. I was trying to learn French by ear. Meanwhile, I was sending articles back to the LA Times on my impressions of the French women, their dress and their feelings about the position of women after the war. I did a lot of "on the street" interviews. My editor at the Times seemed to like them, asked me for more. Fortunately, my monthly checks for writing the articles kept arriving on time at the American Express office where we had a mail box.

After a couple of months, I was in love with Paris as much as Bob was. We saw some of our college friends. Art Buchwald tried to get me a job as fashion editor of the Paris Herald Tribune, but some woman got it just a day before my interview. Summer was coming to an end and both of us were tired of living in the hotel even though the owner and everyone there were marvelous. We started to scout the newspaper for apartment rentals. No luck. Apartments were hard to find. Then one night at a local street cafe we found our new home.

It was at the Deux Magots on St. Germaine De Pres that we met up with an American photographer sitting next to us. Apparently, he heard us discussing the search for an apartment and saw us with the newspaper ads. He started up a conversation. We struck gold! He offered us his rental apartment as he was returning to the states for an emergency. His father who was in the Hollywood film industry had been accused by Senator McCarthy of being a Communist. He was upset by this wrong doing and needed to leave immediately for the states to stand by his father's side.

We were behind the times regarding the McCarthy era in Washington, but this account brought it close to home. We gladly accepted the offer and in a week had our new home.

It was located on 26 Rue de Plante on the sixth floor of a building built after World War I. The concierge said this was young for a building. It was a studio-one room with a tiny kitchen and bathroom with a tub. It was sparsely furnished with antique pieces. To us it looked perfect.

The next morning while I was overlooking Paris from our open window and breathing in all the smells that wafted in from kitchens below, there was a knock on the door. Bob answered it and there stood a woman whom we had met in the elevator the day before when we were loaded down with groceries. She welcomed us to the building and seemed so happy that we were Americans. It seemed everyplace we went, the Parisians couldn't be nicer or friendlier—one exception. When you were in a rush to get into the subway car, they would fight you to the death to get through the door first.

"Je suis Lillian Tridoux. Bonne chance a votre nouveau maison."

She held a bouquet of flowers in one hand and a large soup bowl in the other. We greeted her and welcomed her into the apartment. Bob took the things out of her hands and we both thanked her for the offerings. Bob spoke his broken French—she understood.

"Ooh, la la. Il faut que vous avoir a femme de menage," she acclaimed after walking through the apartment. "Ja'i quelcon pour vous."

Lillian took the flowers out of Bob's hands, found a tall vase in the kitchen and placed them on the Louis XVI table. Both Bob and I were so surprised by this hospitable visit, we didn't know how to react. This petite brunette, so full of energy, giving us directions not only about having a housekeeper (one dollar for once a week), but instructing us to tip the concierge (the apartment manager) every month for keeping our mail and how to handle the elevator when it broke down . . . take the stairs.

The concierge lived on the bottom floor and every time you came into the building, he would peer out his window to see if you lived there. One time we walked into his apartment and met his wife—the place smelled awful. They kept over ten cats. But he was always gracious to us because we were Americans and as I said before, the French loved the Americans.

The soup Lillian brought that afternoon was our best meal since we arrived in Paris. I would soon learn the recipe from her. I would also learn much more from her—how to shop the little stores for groceries, enjoying hours of stimulating conversation at a gracious dinner, how to enjoy Paris' bookstores and art galleries. She spoke no English, so it was necessary for me to learn French quickly, and that I did. Shopping helped, as the shop owners would speak slowly so I could understand and learn different words. Lillian opened up another world for me, one I would never had found if I were just a tourist. Plus she became my first new friend here

One morning while we were still in bed, there was a knock on the door. Bob answered it—it was Lillian again. She said I had to hurry down to the bakery to get the croissants while they were hot.

It was like a command from the nuns when I was a child. I jumped out of bed and quickly threw on a pair of slacks and a sweater. Bob, meanwhile, sat on the kitchen sink and waved goodbye, a wide smile on his face. "Duff, I'll put on the coffee."

Those croissants (or, sometimes. petite pains) I bought every morning from the bakery were the best. We spread them with sweet butter and dunked them in our "cafe-aux-lait" in large bowls. Today, I still love it at Dunkin Donuts but of course it's not the same.

That afternoon, Bob went over to the Embassy to talk to one of the American consuls about what job opportunities were open. I was dressing to leave for an interview with Jacques Fath, a well-know couture designer who had his shop on Place Vendome. There was a knock on the door. It was Lillian again.

"Bon Jour, Marie." She invited us for dinner at her apartment below.

From that time on, Lillian and her husband, Raymond Tridoux, became our closest friends. Their two young girls, Claude and Noel, were darlings. We had found a safe place to begin our adventures in Europe.

I, who never thought of cooking as a creative art, learned it could be by watching Lillian prepare meals in her tiny kitchen. I would stand along side her and with a pad and pencil, write down all of her preparations for such fabulous dishes as Coque St. Jacques, Bouef Burgignon, Blanquette de Veau and more.

Bob took off to the Sorbonne every morning for his French lessons. Lillian would drop in either to take me shopping for groceries at a nearby marche (outdoor market) or teach me more French cooking (I never knew there were so many delicious soups to make for almost pennies). We would walk together along the banks of the Seine river, browsing at the book and art stands. My French was improving quickly.

Time seemed to fly after we were settled down. We suddenly realized that the six-months period we had set for our stay in France was over. We decided to remain for another six months. I was receiving my pay from the Times. Bob helped me seek out new article ideas, so I kept writing away and my editor seemed pleased. Bob was getting a monthly check, too, from the Army (GI Bill of Rights) for his schooling. We had no financial worries; everything was so cheap. And to boot, we bought a used Volkswagen for $450.

Lillian alerted us to a litter of Boxer puppies just born to a thoroughbred dog owned by a friend of hers who lived in Nuilly—a wealthy section on the edge of Paris. I'd hadn't had a dog since I was a child and felt this was a good time for a pet again. We drove to Nuilly on the outskirts of Paris with Lillian and Raymond and home we came with the cutest Boxer puppy. We named her Liza.

One of our favorite evening or Sunday afternoon pastimes was sitting at an outside cafe on St. Germaine des Pres. Like most Parisians, we became people-watchers. We couldn't get over how the little children who walked by with their parents were so neatly dressed—little girls in starched pinafores, white gloves, and pretty hats; pressed short pants, shirts and perky caps on the boys. I don't know if it was this scene or what, but suddenly I wanted to have a baby—it was time. Bob said, "Okay, Duff, whatever you want—it's okay with me. We'll have our very own Parisian!"

Two months later I was pregnant. Lillian and Raymond were thrilled. Lillian put me in touch with her doctor when I wasn't feeling well. I kept bleeding off and on during my second month. To make a long story short, I lost the baby. I was devastated, but Lillian talked me through my depression, and I started writing again. Our love for Paris grew stronger. We agreed not to return to the states for another six months.

A number of our college friends began arriving in Paris. They'd come over to our apartment for dinner (I was getting to be a good cook by now), or we'd meet them at one of the cafes for an aperitif. Bob was doing some articles for a magazine called Intercourse (we laughed at the name) that the Embassy put out for the Marshall plan. We traveled to parts of France, Spain, Belgium, Germany and Holland where Bob did interviews and I found subjects to write about for the Times. Our dog, Liza, traveled with us wherever we drove in our car. Sometimes, when we couldn't get her on the train, Lillian would take care of her for us until we got home. She gave us a small, shiny, copper kettle and filled it with a bouquet each time we arrived back home after a trip. Flowers were so cheap in Paris that every housewife who shopped always bought a bouquet home. I loved that because it reminded me of Aunt Fanny and how she would fill our house in Los Angeles with flowers from the garden.

My doctor told me it would now be okay for me to get pregnant again, so I put my diaphragm away and Bob and I decided we'd try again. This time it worked!

On June 8, 1951, our son, Rick David Fenton, was born in a Paris hospital. You couldn't imagine any happier parents then Bob and I. He weighed in at a 8 lbs. 6 ozs, with lots of light brown hair—he was perfect. They had him all bundled up like a papoose when I took him back to our apartment. Lillian had found me a used bassinet and when I laid him in it on arriving home, I immediately unwrapped his bundling. He instantly kicked his legs and flexed his arms. I had read Dr. Spock's books on infants and he said not to bundle them. So I set him free!

I kept staring at this little creature all day long—couldn't believe I had carried it in my tummy for nine months. Lillian showed me how to fold the cloth diapers, how to wash them daily in the bathtub (the femme de manage came in handy), how to lay on the bed while breastfeeding him and gave me a little steel tub to bathe Rick in. She was such a help to me—I don't know if I could have weathered those first few weeks without her. She even went out to do my shopping and prepared most of our dinners. All of our friends dropped in to see our baby. Almost every Saturday night they brought food and wine and we played poker all night. There were times I had to drop out of game to breastfeed Rick, but when done, back to the table.

Bob and a few of friends from the Journalism class started a newspaper called "The European Traveler." It was directed toward American tourists who were starting to vacation in Europe. Bob made up a "dummy" issue and took it to various companies to interest them in advertising and they climbed on the bandwagon. Lillian was very excited about this project and talked Bob into her being an advertising salesperson. She turned out to be terrific. Meanwhile, all of the editorial meetings were first held in our apartment. Aside from my taking care of our baby, Rick, I was writing articles on fashion and beauty for the paper, fixing food for the crew when they came over, shopping three times a day for fresh fruits, vegetables, bread, wine and whatever we needed. I quickly lost the 40 lbs I had gained during my pregnancy. It was about this time that Lillian taught me how to make a French salad dressing. Bob and I had always exclaimed about her marvelous salad which of course was traditionally served after the main course, along with a tray of cheese, fruit and bread and naturally, red wine.

Lillian took me through the salad making process, step by step. First, wash the bib or Boston lettuce, place leaves in a metal basket with handles on it. Then she walked me from the kitchen to the French windows, opened them and while I was leaning over the low wrought-iron balcony, she told me to twirl the basket which shook out all the water. "Keep twirling, Marie—back and forth!" I laughed as I saw the water drops float down to the courtyard and fall on the concierge's cats below. Then, I followed her instructions on making the special dressing. It's the recipe that I still use today and on which I always get compliments.

The European Traveler progressed; Bob got an office around the Place de Opera where our people met and worked. Bob had quit classes at the Sorbonne because he was so caught up with this new project. Again, I had to write my parents that it would be another six months before we'd return to the states. I sent them photos of Rick and in return I'd get "care packages" of baby clothes and cans of baby foods. There were so many people in my life at that time that I sometimes wondered how it would all end.

Months flew by and then like out of the blue, the world's economy went downhill.

The Vietnam War was costing France and our big advertisers like Cunard Lines and American Express cut us out of their budgets. It wasn't long before we had to give up the office and let our staff go. Everyone was so sad. We were sure we had a good thing going and would have if it weren't for the war.

Then to top it off, our landlord wanted his apartment back. It not only rained on our parade—it poured!

It was October, 1951. Inflation took over and we found ourselves with less money to live on. Bob wrote to several American governmental agencies operating in Europe hoping to find a job. Friends suggested we move down South where food and rental prices were lower, so we advertised in the daily Nice newspaper. Surprisingly, we received a few answers and chose to rent the top floor of a villa on the Mediterranean in Roquebrune St. Martin, just between Nice and Menton. Meanwhile, we moved to a small chateau in Houilles, a small town outside of Paris. We stayed there for a month before leaving for Nice. It was there we met Simone who would become our femme de manage, baby sitter, cook and bottle washer. At only 16 she came to us pleading for a job, said that her family had thrown her out of the house and all sorts of horror stories. We said we could not pay her a salary; she said okay, that she's work for room and board. We couldn't say no and she adored Rick. We also had another addition to our family—Liza surprised us one morning with a puppy, a beautiful little boxer. We had bred her a few months earlier but thought it had not taken because she never looked fat. No wonder, she only had one pup.

When it came time to leave for Nice, Bob took off in our Volkswagen with Liza and her pup in Rick's bassinette in the back seat plus our belongings and priceless typewriters and Nikon camera. The next day I left with Rick and Simone on the train to Nice. Lillian was there waiting to say goodbye. I was carrying my fur coat that Aunt Toni had given me and which I hadn't worn at all.

"Here, Lillian," I said, "I want you to have my coat. I'll never use it on the Cote de Zur."

She thanked me profusely and said I should remember that "something good always seems to come out of something bad!" Those words have stayed with me throughout the years and proved themselves many times over. She said she and Raymond would come visit us soon. Unfortunately, that never happened and I never saw Lillian again until one day in 1963 in New York we received a call that she was coming to see us (Raymond had died).

Lillian was my teacher, my friend, my confident and I will never forget her. Here I was going to yet another strange place, with a few dollars in my purse, a baby to take care of, a teenager who was a runaway and a husband someplace on the road, god knows where. I began to wonder if I was the same Marie who left the good old U.S.A.

2. LUCIE—MY "TEACHER" IN GERMANY AWAITS ME!

IT WAS EARLY in the morning when I received a call from Bob. He stopped at American Express in Nice to cash a check and said would be at the hotel shortly. He had car trouble, something about the wheel rolling off into a field at night and how he stayed at a farmer's house until the sun came up, then searching the field until they found the tire, put it back on the car—plus no telephone there so he couldn't call me. I was relieved and so glad to see him. It's amazing the things that go through your head during a situation like I was in. I thought maybe he crashed or ran out on me. Everything turned out okay.

We immediately drove from Nice to Roquebrune—Cap St. Martin in Southern France to see what our new house looked like. The old car barely got us there. Just a skip and a jump from the ocean was a lovely villa with a huge eucalyptus tree in front. An aging woman and her daughter owned the place but since the war, couldn't afford to keep it up, so they decided to rent the second floor. They lived on the first floor. Our floor had three bedrooms and one bath, a kitchen and a living room with high French windows that looked out to the most spectacular view of the Mediterranean. I immediately opened them and breathed in the fresh, balmy air. I'd never seen anything so beautiful. Over to the right, I could see Monte Carlo, only 15 minutes away, and off to the left, the rocky ridges that bordered the Italian coastline. I felt like I was in heaven and I could stay here forever.

Our landladies were most generous. It seemed they would do anything to help Americans—"You liberated us and now it's our turn to pay you back," they said. Their neighbors graciously donated a crib, highchair and playpen for Rick. The rooms were well furnished and had everything else we needed. They even accepted our dog, Liza, but didn't know we had a puppy, too, so we sneaked her up while they weren't around. Our first job was to find a new home for the puppy. The landlady told us that the market place in Menton was open twice a week. Immediately Bob and I thought this was the ideal place to look for someone. The next day we walked the two-mile trek to Menton and pleasantly rested with the baby dog on Bob's lap at an outdoor café near all the vendors.

While sipping on an aperitif we heard English being spoken. At a table near us, was a young couple about our age, also holding a baby that looked about the same age as Rick. Immediately we identified them as Americans and waved to them. This is how we met our lifelong friends, Stan and Nancy. During our conversation, we mentioned we had to find a home for our puppy. They said they knew someone.

They took us down on the dock and introduced us to a friend of theirs who had a huge sailboat and to our surprise loved Boxers. The moment he saw our pup, he grabbed her out of Bob's arms and said he'd take care of her. Well, to say the least, we were thrilled. When we arrived back at the villa that night, one of the landladies knocked on our door.

"Oh, we heard the pitter-patter of little feet on our ceiling—is Ricky already starting to walk. Amazing, he's only nine months old!"

We didn't know quite what to say, because we knew what they heard was the puppy running around the house. So, we just nodded.

Stan and Nancy lived in a huge villa a few blocks inland. We spent most of our time together, playing poker, drinking coffee at the cafes in Menton, gambling at the casino in Monte Carlo, having quiet gourmet dinners discussing "life." We learned they were from Northern California and like us came to Europe to enrich their lives. Stan was a writer, too. He loved poetry. They had a wonderful MG convertible and we'd drive the corniches along the Mediterranean with the top and windshield down. Our little boys played together. Life was fun again!

It was now the summer of 1952. Rick was starting to walk, thriving in this wonderful climate. Liza loved the ocean and swam with us before breakfast and before dinner almost every day. We had no phone, no car anymore (we sold it to a mechanic in Roquebrune for the same price at which we bought it). We did have a radio, but all in all we were cut off from the outside world. We had never felt so free and relaxed.

Although Bob did a little writing for Time Magazine as a stringer, we realized that our financial scene did not look promising. I wasn't able to find any "meaty" pieces to write up for the LA Times. It was time for one of us to find a steady job otherwise we'd never get back to States. Bob wrote to his friend at the American Embassy in Paris and asked him for help. Late that summer after Nancy, Stan, Bob and I were attending the Cannes Film Festival, we came back home to find a letter from the Consul.

The news was bittersweet. Bob should report to the Commander of the U.S. Army Post Exchange in Nuremberg, Germany. A position was open there that paid very well and they would provide us with housing, etc. To celebrate this good news we went out to dinner with our friends—a small Russian restaurant in Nice where I had my first taste of vodka—chilled in a shot glass and served with caviar and black bread. Vodka was not a liquor that most Americans drank in those days. Bourbon, scotch and gin were in—vodka was too expensive. The local wines and an inexpensive bottle of "Mother's Gin" were our usual cocktail hour drinks. I discovered many new recipes during our stay on the Riviera—all sorts of seafood dishes like calamari (squid), macarel, smelts, Tomatoes Provence (fried tomatoes) and marvelous soups like bouillabaisse, even crepe suzettes.

It was late October and time for us to leave this marvelous place and move to Germany so Bob could begin his job. Luckily, we found an elderly American couple who took on Simone as a housekeeper. She was sad to leave us but now she would receive a salary and that made me happy. We didn't want to leave. Stan and Nancy didn't want us to leave—the parting was heartbreaking. They came to the train station to see us off. Stan noticed Bob had no socks on (I had forgot to leave a pair out for him when I packed). Stan took his off and passed them on to Bob who quickly put them on minutes before the train pulled out (Bob kept those socks forever). We waved goodbye as they called out "Go for the Gold, guys!" Again, tears streamed down my cheeks. It just seemed like I'd been saying "goodbye" to good friends for years. I hoped this time we'd stay put for a while.

After a long train ride, we finally arrived in Nuremberg and checked into the Grand Hotel as we were instructed to do. The place was very nice and we had a lovely room. The next morning Bob went to meet with his boss. Meanwhile, I had only 50 cents in my purse and no food for Ricky. I went down with Rick to the fancy dining room with him and ordered an egg and toast. I, too, was starving but sat and fed Ricky his breakfast—licked his spoon when he was done. Bob returned later smiling and holding cash in his hand. He was now a civilian employee for the Army. We all went down to the dining room and had a great dinner.

A week later, we were assigned to a huge three-story house in Furthe-Dambach on the outskirts of Nuremberg. It was a lovely house on a large fenced-in property, totally furnished with everything we needed. It was one of the many houses that the Army had confiscated from the

Germans for U.S. personnel. I often wondered about the people who owned and lived in this house. I felt sorry for them, but there was nothing I could do about all this so I accepted my new home and was so glad to be settled down again. The Army not only supplied us with the house, but with a caretaker who stoked our room heaters with coal each day, a gardener and a live-in housekeeper whose name was Lucie—a woman who like Lillian would help me find my way through the next few years we would spend in Germany

*   *   *

Lucie was a well educated woman from Berlin who had lost everything during the war—her husband, her home, her money. She came to Nuremberg looking for employment and found us through the Army civilian employment agency. In her middle fifties, she was robust in physical appearance. She was full of energy and never seemed to tire during strenuous housekeeping tasks. The Army paid her $50 a month, plus room and board with us, and every other weekend off. She spoke perfect English and a day or two after she moved in I realized this was an impressive woman who would become an important person in my life.

*   *   *

There were so many bedrooms in the house even Rick has his own room. The huge kitchen reminded me of my grandmother's in Milwaukee when I was a little girl; a dining room, living room with lovely curved window overlooked the garden below. We decided to live only on the second floor because of the view and you could see the local train pass by once a day which was a treat for Rick. The large entry was the size of a room, where Rick could run about and play with his toys. We had shipped our dog, Liza, in a truck bound for Nuremberg from Nice and she arrived in good shape a week after we did. Europeans love animals and they took good care of her. We were all delighted to see her again—even Lucie, especially since boxer dogs were German bred. At last, we were all together again, a family. Things were really looking up.

Bob had a nine to five job at the Post Exchange headquarters, with his own office that handled purchases for the Post Exchange—it was a "sweet" position that paid a great salary. Our only expenses were for food and clothes. All medical was free; gas for our little English car which we bought cheap, was only a few pennies. We began to build a nice savings account from Bob's pay checks. I wanted to get back to America and this was the only way I could see to do it. It was now four years since we left the States and my parents were anxiously awaiting our return. It seemed like every time I wrote them during those four years, I kept saying—soon, soon. But I did keep in contact with them, sent them photos.

At first I had a hard time working out arrangements with Lucie, our new live-in housekeeper. She had strict rules—dinner exactly at 6 p.m., Ricky's bath at 4 P.M., shopping chores in the a.m., etc. etc. I had never lived with strict rules since a child and wasn't going to begin to do so again. Over coffee with Lucie one morning I asked her to relax the rules and let our daily routines flow as to our own needs. She said her former employee, a high ranking officer liked a strict routine. I could understand that but she was more than happy to go with my wishes.

Little by little Lucie became more open and friendly toward me. She was marvelous with Rick, pampered Bob—brought him his slippers every night when he arrived home from work, offered him hors-douvres, a scotch before dinner. She advised us to learn more about Nuremberg. We took the little train from Furthe-Dambach to Nuremberg with Rick, walked the promenade around the park in Furthe every Sunday, bowing and greeting passing German couples and families. This was a German tradition. She brought in neighboring German children to our garden to play with Rick. Plus she taught me many German dishes she cooked for us—Wiener Schnitzel, Sauer Brauten, tomato and cucumber salad in sweet, vinegar sauce. I was learning a lot about German life and it reminded me of my grandmother and aunts even though they were Austrian—the cultures were very similar—especially the wonderful strudel at the local bakery. I missed Paris and the French Riviera but this new "territory" was interesting too. I felt like a pioneer—energized!

I often wondered where Lucie went on her weekend offs. She was a private person and seldom revealed anything about herself or whereabouts when away from us. But little by little and the longer she lived with us, I could see she was opening up to me. One afternoon while we were sitting together in the garden watching Ricky play in his sandbox, I decided to get personal.

"Lucie, do you visit friends or relatives when you have your days off?"

"I have no relatives—no children. My husband is dead in the war." She sat up straight on the bench and kept looking at Rick. There was a minute of silence, then she started to talk to me.

"There is a man I've met in Nuremberg—he's a doctor at the hospital, about my age and he is very good to me. We plan to go skiing in Garmish this winter."

I had broken the barrier. From then on, from time to time, she'd tell me about what she did with her boyfriend on weekends. I thought it was wonderful that at her late age she had found a lover. Never too late, I said to myself. I thought about all this many years later when at age 49 I would meet my second husband.

I came to respect this energetic German woman who even though was highly educated needed to be respected at her menial job as housekeeper—and I, too, wanted to give her that respect. She soon became an important part of the Fenton family. She spoke French fluently and always conversed with Rick in that language. He had learned some from me but she spoke it better than I so I asked her to continue while Bob and I talked to him in English. He was now learning two languages at the same time. A couple nights during the week, she would give Bob and me German lessons. She was an excellent teacher. The only negative thing about our learning German was that we never were able to converse outside the "classroom." Whenever we shopped or dined out, the Germans spoke English because they wanted to learn the language so we didn't get much practice.

We found new friends through Bob's work and it didn't take long before we became very comfortable living in Nuremberg. The city had been terribly destroyed by the war but restoration was being done day and night. Within a year since we had arrived, the change was amazing . . . much of its original old-world architecture had been restored—a beautiful city again.

With the small English car that we bought from an American going back to the states, we took side trips with Rick and Lucie to Garmish and Bertschgarten, gorgeous mountain resorts and often drove the fabulous Audubon to spend a day in Munich, just three hours away. With our friends, Joe and Beverly Howland, Al Hix and his girlfriend, Siw, we fell in love with Germany. When Oktoberfest came, Munich went wild. The bratwurst & beer was fantastic. We got to practice our German by singing songs in the Bauhaus's, sliding back and forth on the long dining table benches, arms linked to strangers next to us. It was hard to believe that after such a terrible war, here we were, Americans and Germans, living, singing together as if nothing had happened.

Lucie never talked about the war only to say that part of her life was over. She bought Ricky a small pair of Lederhosen (leather shorts), an Alpine jacket and green Bavarian hat. He looked so cute in it that Bob went out and bought himself an outfit too. I went along and bought a dirndl dress with apron but it made me look too fat, so I didn't wear it much.

Now that we were pretty much settled down—our financial crisis was over, we had a lovely home, and Rick was being well cared for by Lucie. I got the urge to go back to my newspaper writing again. When I contacted my Editor, Ed Strong, at the LA Times, he gave me the green light to send him any articles I felt would make good feature pieces for the Women's pages. I dusted off the old portable typewriter we had carried from LA, to Paris, to the Riviera and now still with us in Germany.

I told Lucie about my intent to get back to my writing and that she'd have to take care of Rick while I was busy with my work.

"No problem, Madam (she never called me Marie even though I asked her). He is a darling and I like taking care of him. You do your work."

And so I began to write again. It felt wonderful to put on my "thinking cap" and get back to the job I loved so much. I didn't know quite where to begin but Lucie suggested several outlets. She gave me the name of the head of the German Red Cross in Nuremberg that was helping refugee families escaping from East Berlin and I did a couple of articles on this subject. I even traveled to Berlin and got permission from the American Embassy to cross over to East Berlin. I visited refugee camps set up in huge warehouses in West Berlin and interviewed some of the German women and children who had risked their lives, left everything behind to come to the West. It was an exciting assignment.

Lucie seemed to get caught up with what I was doing and gave me all sorts of sources to peruse like the top dress designer (a woman) in Germany, a famous woman poet who had fled from East Germany, a gypsy woman who owned one of the most popular restaurants in Munich's Left Bank. I also was doing pieces on the wives of important American military personnel.

My mother became my biggest fan and would clip out my articles from the LA Times and mail them to me. She was so pleased to see my name in print that her anxiety about me was lessening and that made my own urgency to return to the States quiet down, so I put that need on the "back burner" for the time being.

Rick was into the "terrible twos". I enjoyed him so much, I felt it would be a good idea for him to have a sister or brother, yes, time to have another child. As usual, Bob said "Whatever you want, Duff, is okay with me." And so my diaphragm went back into its case again.

When I told Lucie I was pregnant, she didn't seem too happy about that.

"Madam, I will help take care of Ricky, cook and clean for you, but I do not want to have anything to do with your new baby."

I accepted that and agreed I would be in full charge of the baby when it arrived. Heidi Fenton was born July 5, 1954 and what a beautiful baby she was—different looking than Rick when he was born. She had lots of blonde curly hair, blue eyes and weighed in at 9 pounds 6 ounces. I was so hoping she would be born on the 4th of July but not one baby was born in the Army hospital in Nuremberg on that date—on the 5th, five women delivered. The German nurses went wild when they saw Heidi, especially when they heard we had named her Heidi (a popular Bavarian name and title of a famous children's book). They tied pink ribbons in her hair and pampered her in the nursery. Bob and I couldn't believe how we could have had this beautiful blonde, blue-eyed baby—both of us had dark hair and brown-green eyes. "Duff, are you sure you never invited the milkman in?" Bob teased me.

Using my past experience of caring for Rick and recalling the advice that Lillian had given me when he was born I sailed through my first months of caring for Heidi. The new paper diapers I got from the PX, the availability of a pediatrician nearby—all the amenities of American products and clothes that were now accessible to me, made my life a pleasure. When Heidi was about three months old, I noticed Lucie was starting to get attached to her.

"Madam, you can go take a nap and Ricky and I will watch over Heidi." I welcomed the offer. Not only did I get in some naptime but was able to give more attention to Rick. He was three years old now and I sensed he was feeling neglected because of this new baby that had come into his life and had taken away some of his importance with Bob and me. I wanted to make that up to him we began to take him on shopping trips, short weekend jaunts to Garmish or other lovely places nearby.

One weekend we flew to Paris so he could see where he was born. Meanwhile, Lucie was becoming more and more attached to Heidi—she called her "my little Heidily" and bought her a little German dirndl dress just like mine. It was now two years that she was living with us and the insular demeanor she had when she first arrived had changed drastically. Even though she continued to call me "Madam," she'd give me a hug when Bob and I would come home from one of our many short travels on weekends. She'd help me decorate our Xmas tree—bought tiny white lights to string around—"Here, we only use white lights, not colored." Even though I liked the colored lights better, I opted for the white. "When in Rome, do as the Romans do" I told myself.

When I received a beautifully framed print of a woodcut "Cherry Blossom Time in Nuremberg" by a famous German artist, from the then President Heuss of Germany in appreciation of my articles written about the German Red Cross, Lucie was so excited and told me what an honor this was. She immediately took it upon herself to hang the large print on the wall in the entrance hall. I could tell that she was happy and I expected she'd be with us for a long time. But I was wrong.

I sensed that Bob was anxious to get back to the States. He had started a novel about the PX but his job took up most of his time and I knew he was itching to get into American television. Letters from friends in California told us there was a demand for TV scripts. Even though I felt comfortable in Germany, in a way, I, too, wanted to get back home. I was tired of being a "nomad" and I wanted our children to see their grandparents. So it began—we started to formulate out plans to return to the United States.

I wrote my mother and asked her if she could find a rental apartment in Los Angeles that would accept children and a dog. We had just mated Liza with a thoroughbred German boxer but the vet said it didn't take so that was one thing we didn't have to worry about. We planned to ship her via a Dutch airline to Phoenix where Bob's sister, Ruth, lived, and then we would pick her up when we got to Los Angeles. We were booked to leave by boat from Bramerhaven, Germany to New York. There I would fly with the children to Los Angeles while Bob would drive our newly purchased Mercedes car across the country. This all took us three months to finalize but finally the day of departure came. Because of the Army's generosity our expenditures were nil. I felt financially secure with the "nest egg" we had saved up during Bob's tenure with the government. I so desired our own home and a stable environment to raise my babies.

The day before we left, Lucie was helping me pack clothes for our voyage. Quietly she asked, "Madam is it possible I go with you to America? I pay my way."

I felt so sorry telling her it was impossible at this late date but maybe after we were settled in Los Angeles I could send for her. She accepted that and continued to lay the clothes in the suitcases. I told her how much I appreciated all her hard work and caring for all of us. She hugged me and with tears in her eyes she pulled a ring off her finger and offered it to me.

"Madam, this is for you to remember me by." I looked down into her outstretched hand and saw the beautiful silver ring she always wore and which I always admired.

"Lucie, I can't accept this—it's a keepsake of yours." I was taken back by the offer. She had told me one time the story behind the ring: her mother had it made especially for her, a replica of the famous sculpture of Queen Nephrite's bust in the Berlin Museum of Art. The sculpture was removed during the war and just lately returned to the Museum.

She insisted I take it and said it would always bring me good luck. I slipped the ring on my finger, smiled down at it and suddenly remembered the day that my Aunt Fanny had given me her ring when I left the house to elope with Bob.

The rain was pelting down outside. It was a gloomy day, but inside I saw a wonderful light. The six years I had spent in Europe had taken on such meaning—I had experienced and learned so much, made so many new relationships. I knew I was ready to go back home more enriched and mature than I could have ever hoped for. I brushed away my tears of joy, gave Lucie another hug, wished her a good life. I knew then I would never see her again, but what she said came true—every time I slipped the beautiful silver ring on my finger I thought of her—and, yes, it did bring me luck.

As our ship was leaving the German port, Bob, the children, and I went on deck even though it was drizzling. Bob held Rick in his arms, I held Heidi sleeping in my arms. Bob and I stood very close to each other, didn't talk, just gazed out at the fading landscape. "Duff, we're going home!" I looked at him and nodded. We kissed with both kids in our arms.

MARIE FENTON GRIFFING

3. MY MOTHER—GETTING TO KNOW HER, AGAIN

I REALLY HADN'T paid much attention to the Statue of Liberty in the New York harbor when we left New York over five years before, but as we arrived on the ship, it was the best "welcome home" greeting I would ever have. We all stood on the deck to get a close glimpse of this magnificent statue and like many of the immigrants of years past who had seen her, we too felt her impact—America, the land of freedom and opportunity. Bob and I clasped hands; there was a special feeling passing between the two of us. We explained to Rick the meaning behind this fabulous statue, standing strong and welcoming to those who reached the shores of America many years ago and even now.

We disembarked in Brooklyn, took a taxi to Manhattan. There a room was reserved for us at the Hudson Hotel on West 57th Street. I was to fly the next morning to Los Angeles where my family was to meet me. Bob would pick up our Mercedes at the port and then drive to Phoenix where his sister lived, pick up Liza and from there to Los Angeles. Meanwhile, we had a night to spend in New York. With "babes in arms" again, we walked the streets of Broadway with all its glittering lights above and all around us. We had never seen such a spectacular sight in our lives. We ate at a small restaurant and had our first real hamburger in years. I even ordered a chocolate malt and Bob had a doughnut. Rick wanted a hot dog—unlike the Bratwurst he used to have in Germany. I brought a bottle for Heidi. It was a memorable night for us all.

Early the next morning, we took a taxi to the airport. I wouldn't see Bob for 10 days. As I waved goodbye, it reminded me of the trip I took alone to Nice with six-month-old Rick while Bob drove from Paris to meet me there. Like then I was trepidatious about our separation. As the plane flew from New York to Los Angeles (a 14 hour trip in those days), I began to contemplate what was going to happen when I arrived—who will be there to greet me? Did my mother find an apartment for us. She never gave me a definite answer, only said everything was arranged. Will I be able to cope without Lucie's help. I was really on my own now. I looked down at my two sleeping children and knew I had to come through for them, no matter what. I laid my head back and fell asleep until we arrived in Los Angeles.

I walked down the stairs from the plane and saw arms waving at me from ahead. My parents, all my aunts and brother and sister-in-law were smiling and crying. I had more hugs than I had had in over five years. My mother quickly grabbed Heidi out of my arms and my dad lifted Rick up into his arms. It was a wonderful welcome home. We immediately drove to my parents' house on Victoria Avenue in Southwest Los Angeles—the home I had known for 21 years. As we turned the corner off of 63rd street onto Victoria, I spotted the house. It was a strange feeling because the house seemed to look so much smaller than I remembered. The palm tree was no longer there, nor the fruit trees all around. A paved driveway went back to a large two-story apartment building that towered over the little house in front of the property. It all looked so different. I had a sinking sensation in my stomach. My parents never told me about their apartment house. I guess they wanted to surprise me—and they did.

I saw that a lot of things had changed since I'd been away for six years, yet I realized that I had changed too. My mother said that she and my father had retired from the restaurant business and had built the apartment complex in the back acre. Her face was flushed with excitement over our return. I was so tired by the time we walked into the house, all I wanted to do was sleep—which I did, with Rick on one side of me and Heidi on the other side.

Heidi awakened me with her familiar cries a few hours later and I knew she was hungry. My mother took over and prepared the bottle for Heidi. Rick and I went to the bathroom to wash up. When we came out to the living room, my three aunts and my parents were having coffee and cake—little Heidi was lying back in a lovely stroller, smiling and waving her arms about. I was aghast—where did they get this thing? Then I peered over to the dining room table and saw a dozen or more decorated gift boxes. Everyone was looking at Rick and me. I caught my breath and said, "Hi, what's going on here?"

"Welcome Home, Marie," my aunt Marie said and came over to hug me.

"We're glad you've come back," my aunt Toni said and gave me a hug, too.

"Now, you're finally home," said my mother, "and we've got everything ready for you. Open your presents—then we'll have dinner."

Aunt Fanny waved from the kitchen and smiled but said nothing. I went in and gave her a hug. Looking around the house, I realized that nothing had changed within—everything was the same. I smiled.

Box after box I opened filled with beautiful clothes and toys for the children. It was too much for me. I started to cry. I never expected a homecoming like this. I had left not only hurting them all because of my marriage to Bob but also I hadn't returned in six months like I said I would. But I knew now I was forgiven.

I was taken aback by all this attention but relieved that I was so warmly welcomed. I think it had a lot to do with the children. Even when I announced that Bob would be arriving in a week or so with our dog, Liza, everyone seemed delighted.

"Mother, did you get an apartment for us?" I asked while Rick was opening up all the presents—it was like Christmas all over again for him.

"Yes, Marie, and in a little while I'll take you over to it."

I expected to drive someplace to see the apartment, but instead she led me out the back door toward her building in the back of the property where there used to be loads of fruit trees; her garden was still there, but smaller. She went directly to a first-floor apartment, opened it up and ushered me in. "Marie, this is your home now. Your father and I want you to stay here as long as you like until you can find the house you want to buy."

I was astonished by all this generosity. It was a newly furnished two-bedroom place. She had bought it all for us, right down to the crib for Heidi, small single bed for Rick and a double bed for us—bureaus, lamps in the bedrooms, a lovely couch, coffee table, end tables in the living room, a large table/chairs in the kitchen, linens, dishes, pots/pans, silver wear. It was absolutely unbelievable to me. I realized it must have taken her months to order and prepare all this for us. Again, I started to cry but it wasn't because I was happy—I can't quite explain my feelings then but I believe I felt like a charity case. And the thought of living so close to my mother whom I really never knew because of her busy work schedule during my childhood, gave me qualms about how my relationship with her would turn out.

"It's okay, Marie," she said as she hugged me during my tearful outburst. "You're home now and that's all that counts." She then called for the kids to come see their new home. Aunt Marie and Aunt Toni came running to the apartment carrying the children in their arms. I gave a sigh, said "Thanks" to my Mom but wondered what "paybacks" I'd have to exchange for all this. I really wished Bob were with me—how would he accept this?

While I awaited Bob's arrival, my mother and aunts were very supportive to me. They stocked the fridge with all sorts of foods. Every morning, my mother would bring over fresh breads she had picked up at Aunt Marie's bakery; Aunt Fanny delivered flowers from the small garden; Aunt Toni would take Ricky for a walk so I could attend to Heidi's bath. I was beginning to feel smothered by love and protection. I couldn't wait for Bob to come. He had called me from Phoenix where he stayed overnight with his sister, Ruth, and picked up our dog, Liza. I explained to him about the apartment. "I'll see you tomorrow—and do I have a surprise for you!" he laughingly said. I wondered what it could be.

As I was feeding Heidi her lunch in the highchair the next day, I heard a car pull in next to the front door, the horn honking away. I grabbed Heidi out of her chair, called for Rick who was playing in his room, and we all rushed out to greet Bob. Hugs and kisses all around. Bob looked tired but he was smiling. "Oh, Duff, I'm so glad to see you." "Are you kidding!—I am SO glad to see you."

"Daddy, Daddy, did you bring me something?" Ricky had been so spoiled with all the gifts he had received from my folks, that he was expecting more from his father.

Ricky and I went wild about the puppies (Heidi giggled as she petted them). As we placed them in one of the open garages behind the apartment house, I kept asking Bob how this came to pass. "I'll tell you all about it later—right now I'm pooped and I think we better give the dogs some water and food." Rick ran immediately to the kitchen, filled a bowl full of water and sat watching them drink it down. My parents were out to a Legionnaire meeting so at least I had time to prepare myself on the announcement that not only did I bring in two children, but four dogs to her apartment complex which was off-limits to the likes of my family. I knew her tenants wouldn't approve of us and wondered where we could go from here.

I made a quick spaghetti and salad and after a short nap, Bob, came smiling to the table, giving us all extra hugs and kisses. It was so great to see his handsome face again. With Heidi sitting in her highchair, Rick and I at the table with Bob, I waited until dessert to ask again, "What happened with Liza? How did she ever give birth to those puppies? She wasn't pregnant when we put her on the plane to Phoenix."

MARIE FENTON GRIFFING

Bob leaned back on his chair, sipped his coffee and started to tell us the whole story about this extraordinary happening. Rick and I were all ears and Heidi was sitting very still as if she knew she was going to hear something important.

"Apparently, Liza was pregnant when we put her on the plane," Bob began the long saga. "The vet in Germany had misdiagnosed—whatever. Anyway, when Ruth picked her up at the airport in Phoenix, it happened to be "Dog Week" there, and the TV cameras and newspaper reporters were on this story. Liza became a celebrity because here was a dog flown across the Atlantic to come live in America.

Ruth was so excited. She noticed that Liza seemed awful fat and wondered why. Ruth, Jack and the kids welcomed Liza into the house and everything seemed okay. You know how well trained and behaved Liza always is. Ruth said she was a delight to all. A few days later, Ruth and Jack went out to a dinner party nearby and left the kids and Liza with a baby sitter. Liza had been very lethargic the last day or two and just kept sleeping on Barbara's bed.

"Barbara was four when we got married—but I don't know the other two kids. Come on, Bob, keep telling us what happened."

Bob sat up straight on his chair and started to fold and unfold his paper napkin.

"Well, Ruth and Jack received a call from Barbara. She told them that Liza was having puppies on her bed and please come home right away." Ruth and Jack grabbed their coats and left the party immediately, as did the other guests—they wanted to see this birthing. When they arrived back at the house, Liza was mothering the four puppies on the stained quilt. Everyone marveled at all this and one of them called the newspaper to report the incident and it was on the front page of the Phoenix newspaper the next morning.

"When I arrived, the puppies had been born and I was as surprised as you are today. So, now, Duff, what do we do with all these animals?"

My head started to clear as soon as Bob came to the end of his story. I slowly started to laugh, Rick picked up my giggle sounds and he started to laugh, then Heidi probably didn't know what she was laughing about but seemed to want to join in on this funny situation. Bob got up from the table, came over and hugged us and with all eight arms entwined, we kept giggling and giggling.

What a story! And now my parents were coming home soon and I would have to introduce them to their new "tenants." Give me strength!

Rick kept going out to the garage to play with the puppies. When my mother and father drove to their garage they saw him. "Grandma, Grandpa, come look and see what my Daddy brought from Phoenix."

I peeked through the kitchen window and saw my parents approaching Rick. I called Bob to the window. We both took a deep breath and hoped for the best. Then I saw my mother pick up one of the puppies and cuddle it close to her while my father bent over her and petted the dog. Meanwhile, I could hear Rick begging them to let the dogs stay. I saw them nod their heads. Was I relieved!

Since I had arrived, my mother seemed like another person—not like the one I had known all my life—disciplined, a workaholic, distant. She had mellowed out which I couldn't understand but accepted with delight. I figured it must be because she had less stress now that she was "retired." Anyway, she had made our adjustment of living again in the States much easier than I had anticipated.

"It's all right, Marie, to keep the puppies here until they can eat by themselves, then you must find homes for them. And you must clean up after them in the garage, otherwise my tenants will get upset." I agreed—so happy she wasn't going to ask us to move out but I knew she wouldn't because she was so pleased to have us there. Sometimes, however, she became a pain in the neck like when she'd just walk into our apartment (she had her own key) unannounced, bringing a cake from Aunt Marie or a prepared dinner for us for that day. Or the time she took both kids to her church on the corner to show them the inside and all the statues, introduced them to the priest—something I didn't know about until Rick told me. I let that slide. but when she came in with rosaries, medals and prayer books for Rick and Heidi, I stopped her short. "Mother, I'd appreciate your not giving these to the children. Bob and I have decided not to raise them in an organized religion. We will give them spiritual guidance on our own—teach them our moral values. Please take these things back."

This didn't sit well with her but she accepted it. I breathed a sigh of relief after she left but I knew this wasn't the end of it and it wasn't. For years to come she would sneak little religious items to the kids which I would find and instead of returning them to her, let Rick and Heidi keep them but explaining that Grandma thought this would bring them closer to God and then telling them God loved them because they were good. I did teach them a nightly prayer I had made up and more uplifting than

MARIE FENTON GRIFFING

the prayer my mother had taught me. Before bed each evening as I tucked them into bed, we'd all say it out loud.

"Thank you, God, for a lovely day. Keep me healthy, happy, safe and strong tomorrow in work and play." Later on we prayed for certain loved ones. I bought a large modern version of the Bible and often read them passages from it as a diversion from the regular bedtime stories. I tried to give them a sense of a background for all religions, When they became adults, they could make their own decision about organized religion. As for me, I couldn't possibly go back to the strict adherence of the Catholic code. My new lifestyle had changed that forever and I felt I would be a hypocrite if I raised my children in a religion that I didn't believe in anymore. I believed in Heaven, but not Hell, nor Purgatory—the church's teachings said that non-baptized people were sent to Purgatory (a desolate place) because they were not allowed to enter Heaven. To me, God is a loving spirit not a fearful one who punishes innocent human beings. I wanted my children to know that was my belief. One day they would make up their own minds about religion.

On the other hand, Bob's family was not trying to influence us to raise the children in the Jewish faith. I heard from a friend that in an inter-marriage like Bob's and mine, the children born were not considered Jewish unless the mother was Jewish. It seemed weird thinking to me, but I accepted it. I was just glad I only had to deal with my mother's fanaticism.

We found homes for the dogs—Bernice and Sam (Bob's brother and sister-in-law) took one, we easily found owners for the others. The people didn't mind paying good money for them because they were thoroughbreds; we even had Kennel papers for them. Everyone was happy.

Television was a whole new experience for us. We would sit glued to the screen the first few weeks. We couldn't believe seeing movies and all kinds of programs right in our own living room. Television was why Bob decided to come back to States. He immediately contacted some friends who were already writing scripts for TV shows. He set up a card table in the living room and with our faithful typewriter that had traveled back with us, he started to work on ideas for this media. No money was coming in and I didn't want to dig into our money that we'd deposited in a bank—that was for our future home. But I didn't want to bug Bob about our mounting bill problem.

Meanwhile, I enjoyed taking care of the kids, cooking and cleaning the apartment and going shopping with my mother. I was expecting some sort of confrontation with her about Bob writing all day and not earning a penny. I always supported Bob's work and I was prepared to do so now. To my surprise, my mother didn't give us any problem—in fact, she even mentioned how talented Bob was.

"I just hope he gets something soon because we need the money and you have given us too much already." I mentioned to clear the air.

I began to look at my mother in a different perspective. Here was a woman who had worked hard all her life to keep a roof over my head and instead of using her savings for herself and my father, she generously gave much of it to Bob and me. Plus she gave so much of her time to caring and playing with the children. I had never seen her smile or laugh so much. Even with her intrusions into our day-to-day activities, she and I got along very well. I was beginning to know this extraordinary woman and discovered many formable qualities about her—her on-going energy, her diplomacy in getting people to do things her way, her love of flowers, music, good cooking, the caring for her sisters, dedication to her religion, her "mind-over-matter" attitude when her arthritis kicked up, her sincere love for me and the children. The six months I spent living next door to her after we returned from Europe gave me a chance to really get to know my mother. Today, as I look at myself, I can see that I'm somewhat like her. I think that I chose to copy many of her good strengths to imitate, and refused to acknowledge her negative side. Mothers and daughters are a strange breed.

With the help of friends and Bernice, Bob's sister-in-law, we finally found our dream house. It was a rundown estate of two acres in Tarzana in the San Fernando Valley that had a main house, a guest house, a small stable and a fabulous pool. It was owned by the Edgar Rice Burroughs family and since their father's death in 1950 his children were trying to sell this house where their father, a famous writer, creator of the Tarzan book series as well as popular Tarzan movies did some of his writing. When we first came to look at it, we wondered if it could be salvaged. Nobody lived in for the last five years. It needed a lot of repair, but I fell in love with it the moment we opened up the eight-foot grape stake gate that ushered us into a Spanish-style courtyard complete with trees, a fabulous barbecue pit, and a rustic-style house in the background. Beyond that was a charming two-story chalet-type of guesthouse. On the left as you walked in was an incredible jungle-like pool with a rock waterfall, a tiny rivulet that flowed into a large womb-shaped water area. There were pepper trees swaying in the afternoon breeze. Sloping down from the main house and courtyard was an acre of alfalfa in full bloom. Surrounding the whole two acres was an eight-foot grapes fence bordered by almost 100 eucalyptus trees. It was breathtaking.

Bob and I told Bernice to immediately alert the agent for this place. Yes, we would buy it right away, even though we might have to go in debt for it. It seemed that the family wanted to get rid of the place fast, so the $24,000 agreed upon was a pleasant surprise for us. The $6,000 we had stashed in the bank not only paid for the down payment but left us with a couple thousand extra to use for repairs and living expenses. Our monthly payment on the loan was $120.

My parents weren't too happy about us buying this devastated place instead of a new track house. At that time, we could have bought a nice tract house for the amount of our down payment. But there was nothing they could say that would change our minds.

As for me, I was ready to be on my own again without my mother being "underfoot" all the time. I felt free like when I left for Europe. Bob and I couldn't wait to get settled in, but it took almost two months painting the place, putting on a new roof, buying a new stove and fridge for the kitchen plus getting the pool in running order. Each day, we'd leave the kids with my parents, work all day in the new house, then return back to the apartment to collapse. My parents and aunts were so supportive for us during this period—even my Uncle Frank came over to help paint. I finally had my own home!

4. MARY LENSING—MY NEW FOUND FRIEND

THE KIDS WERE as excited as Bob and I with the move to our Tarzana home. The paintings, dishes. precious crystal, silver and other precious things we accumulated in Europe arrived. We immediately bought a hi-fi system and another TV for the den. Finally, we transported all the furniture, lamps, etc. from the apartment. Now we were settled in. At first we never seemed to run out of things to do.

We cleaned out the stables in case we got a horse, swam every day in the pool, arranged the guest house, cooked marshmallows in the living room fireplace, ate many of our meals outside in the courtyard. We went shopping to antique stores and bought beautiful oak tables and chairs. My father redid an old bench that looked great in the living room which was paneled in rustic-looking worm-wood. Bob and I would take early morning walks down a path on our property, in our pajamas, our arms around each other and just marvel that all this was ours. The air was clean and crisp. We could see all the way across the Valley below to the purple-tinted Santa Susana Mountains far away. It was paradise!

A few days after we moved in, Rick came running to me in the kitchen and said there was a little boy about his age, peering through the fence from the house next door. I went out to look.

"I'm David and I'm your neighbor. Can I come over and play with your little boy?"

I was pleased that there would be a playmate for Rick. "Sure, come to the front gate." I welcomed him in and introduced him to Rick who immediately led him to the brick-enclosed sand box (Burroughs built it for a fish pond—we turned it into a sand box for the kids). Heidi was just starting to walk and as I peeked from the kitchen, I saw her approaching David & Rick. With just her diapers on, Heidi waddled over to the sand box. Rick and David shooed her away, then I heard her start crying. I rushed out of the back door, grabbed her up in my arms and looked sternly at the boys. "Ricky, the sand box is for everyone to play in—I'd like you to share it with Heidi."

Suddenly, I heard the big cowbell ring on the gate and with Heidi in my arms, I walked over. "Hi, I'm David's mother. It's time for his lunch. I have come to get him." I could barely see this woman's face through the fence, so I opened it and let her in. "I'm Mary, your neighbor next door. Welcome to Tarzana. I know you just moved in recently and I have been intending to come see you. I guess our boys made it happen." We laughed and she smiled at Heidi, "What a beautiful little girl. I only have David and he gives me much joy—but little girls are something special." I hugged Heidi tight, "Yes, they are special."

Her warm greeting made me feel comfortable, so I ushered her into the kitchen for a cup of coffee while we left the boys playing outdoors. Little did I know then that this lovely person would become an inspiration to me and one of my dearest friends for years to come.

*   *   *

Mary had moved to Tarzana from Chicago two years before, bought the house next door with her friend, Eva. They were both nurses. They started a nursery school on Ventura Blvd., minutes away. Mary's husband, a doctor, had been killed in an automobile accident which left her devastated, a widow with a young son. In order to make a new life for herself, she moved to California with David and Eva.

*   *   *

As we sipped our coffee, I was in awe of this pretty blonde-haired 30ish woman just a few years older than I. I thought she had so much courage to go off on her own like this and start her own business. Mary talked about it all with such confidence. I couldn't wait to tell Bob about her. He was on the second floor of the guesthouse where he had set up an office. I didn't want to disturb him.

"Marie, why don't you come over tonight for coffee and dessert with your husband and bring the kids—they can watch TV in the den" was her invitation as I shut the gate. "Okay, thanks. Is seven all right?" She nodded.

After that first encounter, Mary and I became fast friends. Bob liked her too. He was already thinking of some of his college friends who would make a good husband for her. Even though it had only been two years since her husband's death. I knew her biological clock was ticking down and she didn't have too many years left to get the baby girl she so wanted, so I too kept thinking of a possible mate for her.

We'd see each other every day during the week, usually after 4 p.m. when her nursery school closed. Since she took David to the school, the only time that he and Ricky could play together was late afternoon. I took Rick and Heidi over to her house and while the kids played, she prepared her supper (I had set mine up earlier so it would be ready when Bob came down from his office at six.).

Our daily ritual was to first pour ourselves a glass of red wine and then as we gabbed about our day's happenings, she'd make dinner. Those two hours before I went back to my house with the kids for dinner, were the best therapy I'd had in years. Her Irish humor seemed to coincide with mine. We laughed a lot over little daily frustrating things the kids did. It was wonderful. She also clued me into the best places to shop for food, inexpensive clothes for the children, and all sorts of other outlets I never knew about. She was great!

Our Mercedes was giving us trouble so we sold it at a good price—twice what we had paid for it in Germany. The monies were very welcome since Bob hadn't as yet been able to sell his TV projects. When I confided in Mary about our financial dilemma, she suggested I contact my old Editor at the Los Angeles Times and maybe I could get some freelance assignments. The kids and the house were taking up so much of my time, I couldn't see myself working again but I knew something had to be done in order to meet our mortgage payments. I called Ed Strong. He was pleased to hear from me and asked if I could drop in to see him.

Bob drove me to the Times building in midtown Los Angeles (We had just bought a cheap Ford station wagon—you can't get around in LA without a car). When I met him after the meeting, I was all smiles. "Honey, guess what? Mr. Strong said I could contribute articles for the Sunday Home Magazine section. I'll work out of the house and drop off my work. He said I would have to include photos to go with the writings. Do you think you can take the pictures?"

"Of course, Duff." In fact, if you take notes and research the story, I'll even help you write it—we'll work together. Okay?"

And so it came to pass. While Bob took care of Rick and Heidi in the morning, I interviewed people who lived in the Valley, Hollywood, LA who had interesting homes, gardens, collections, etc. which I felt would make exciting and informative articles for the Home Magazine. Then Bob and I would go to the homes while my mother watched the children and we'd take the necessary photos to go along with each article. At night when the kids went to sleep we would type up the stories and Bob would drop them off at the Times. Our system worked beautifully and we were able to stop borrowing money from my parents. Things were looking up again but it took a lot of energy for me to handle the kids and the house. Bob still found time to keep up his own writing. We decided to "close up shop" over the weekends for some R & R and fun with friends—and what fun we had!

We loved having parties for our dearest friends and relatives. They started in the early afternoon and lasted until late in the evening—children were invited too. Everyone brought their own drinks. The food was potluck and we always had lots to eat. The pool was the watering hole and the courtyard was the gathering place for food and drink. The barbecue was well used. We piped music into speakers hung on the trees, the kids swam with us all in the pool, played in the sandbox or ran around the fenced-in property—everyone was free, relaxed, enjoying the outdoors.

It was like Shangri-La. My parents and aunts loved to come to our parties. They never stayed long because of the loud music and people milling around—they'd get nervous and leave after an hour. Still it was a good change from their dull routine. Oftentimes, my mother would bring a huge baked ham or roast beef, German potato salad and strudel. That was a treat!

We always invited Mary and her friend Eva. Since many of our male friends were bachelors, Bob and I were still trying to be matchmakers for the girls. Mary was very considerate and always stayed after the parties to help me clean up. It gave us time to gab about all the happenings that went on. We'd talk about the guys she liked and didn't like. Within a couple of years, we were as close as two peas in a pod. There wasn't a day that went past that we didn't see each other.

I'll never forget the time we went to a farm nearby and bought a baby lamb for the children. When we brought him home, he was so small that he still needed to be nursed. I quickly called Mary and asked her what I should do. She brought over a baby bottle filled with milk and showed us how to bottlefeed him. He took to it right away and Heidi and Rick took turns feeding him. Our dog Liza didn't take to him right away but with training she accepted "Babe." They both got along after a few weeks—Babe even started to behave like a dog and would Ba-Ba whenever Liza barked at someone approaching the front gate. The visiting children loved to play and pet him. When he got to be a ram and grew little horns, he would playfully buck Heidi. She got scared of him and wouldn't leave the house. Finally, we gave him back to the farm that had sold him to us. They were thrilled to have such a healthy stud. He had feasted not only on the alfalfa on the knoll, but most of my ivy in the courtyard. I wasn't too unhappy to get rid of him.

A few months later, Mary almost freaked out when she heard a burro baying away in our stable and came running over. "Marie, what have you and Bob done now—a burro?" We both giggled but agreed he would be fun for all the kids. "You can't keep him in the stable all day long," she said. "Tie him up down at the fence in the alfalfa field so he has room to roam. Marie, I think you are asking for trouble with this animal."

The next month would prove how right she was. The kids rode him up and down the long driveway and named him Poncho. He was the main attraction at all the birthday parties. Kids loved riding him as Bob lead him around our trail. I think Poncho enjoyed it too because he had been in a carnival and was used to being around children.

Bob was now working part time for an advertising agency in Reseda, a little town nearby. Our funds were again getting low. He had had little success with his TV ideas—did sell a couple of scripts but not enough to keep us going and my freelancing didn't pay much.

One afternoon while he was away at work and the kids were napping, Poncho had torn loose from his rope and came up to the courtyard on his own, onto the porch by the kitchen and was trying to push the door open with his nose. I tried to scare him away. "Go Away, Poncho!" I screamed from the kitchen sink. I picked up the phone and called Bob but he was out of the office. I dialed Mary at the nursery school and frantically told her what was happening. I shouted, "What should I do?" She calmly told me to get one of Bob's belts, put it around Poncho's neck and lead him back to the stable. "Marie, he's a tame animal and he won't hurt you—he's just trying to get attention; probably wants to see the kids. Call me again if this doesn't work."

I did what she said and led Poncho back to his stable behind the guesthouse. I was in my bikini swimsuit because I was hoping to get in a few laps in the pool before the kids woke up. I was feeling so confident and proud of myself when suddenly Poncho whose head was about my height started to push me to the sidewall of the guest house and backed me right into it. I held onto the belt around his neck; his nose came down and he started to rub it on my midriff. I screamed and shouted "Stop,

Poncho." Then I looked down and saw his huge, red penis. I was terrified but I kept my calm, crawled down under his head, swiftly led him down to the stable and locked him in. I was shaken. Mary's prediction came true.

Quickly, I ran back to the kitchen, phoned Bob. Thank God he was in his office. "Robert, you come home this minute and take this animal off our property!"

"Hold on, Duff. What are you talking about. What's wrong?"

"Poncho tried to rape me!"

"Duff, calm down. Tell me what happened. This sounds crazy. Are you okay?"

I took a deep breath, then explained to Bob what had taken place. I knew he didn't believe me. "I'll be right home. We'll work it out." We did and that evening the original owner of Poncho came to pick up this horny animal. We made up some excuse to the kids, "the circus needs him." I was still in shock.

When I recounted the experience to our friends; not many of them believed it either. We laughed a lot and I realized how funny it turned out to be.

There was always something new going on in the Fenton household that made the "Tarzana Era" one of the most fun periods of my life. When Heidi was about three and Rick was six, Mary's son, David, had come over to play. The three of them wandered down into the alfalfa field. I was able to keep an eye on them from the living room broad front window that overlooked the "pasture" as we called it. I would occasionally peek out to see if they were okay. Suddenly, I saw them running up the path, all three of them caring a huge object. I rushed outside and met them on the driveway next to the guesthouse.

"Look, Mommy, look what we've found—a head!" Rick shouted out.

I looked at this object, covered with moss and weeds. I could barely see what it was. After scraping away some of the dirt, I saw a pair of eyes and a broken nose. I gasped and told the kids to just leave it on the ground and go into the house to watch TV. Then I ran to the phone and called Mary next door. In my usual hysterical voice, I screamed, "We just found a human head; come quick!" In her usual calm way, Mary said she'd be right over.

I opened the front gate to let Mary in. She entered waving her arms and laughing, "Marie, what's this about a human skull?" "Should I call the police?" I questioned. "No, no, Marie not now, let's look at it."

I led her to the object on the driveway. She started to scrape moss off the "thing" with her hands, then picked up a fallen branch nearby and removed more stuff. She asked me to turn on the hose and she sprayed water on it. Suddenly a whole face and bust appeared. The face looked somber, hollowed eyes, closed lips and a long neck. From where we stood, it looked like the real thing. We both stepped back in amazement, afraid to touch it. Mary approached slowly and softly spread her fingers on the "thing" then breathed a sigh of relief. "Marie, come look. It's a head made out of clay or something, but it's not human."

When Bob came home he looked at the head which was standing outside on the barbecue table. Because he had been researching the Edgar Rice Burroughs and Tarzan saga for a possible book, he immediately recognized the bust as that of Johnny Weissmuller, one of the most famous movie Tarzans. Bob checked it out with the manager of the Burroughs estate who was helping Bob with his research, and discovered the bust was sculptured by Burroughs' son. Apparently, he must not have liked his own work and dumped it into the field years before.

We cleaned up the bust and placed it on a mushroom-like cement table that overlooked the pool. It always drew a lot of attention and wonderment from guests and definitely reminded us all that we were living in a house built by a very exciting and creative person.

Some months later, doom crept into our happy household. Bob's brother, Sam, had come down with Hodgkin's disease Disease and my father was diagnosed as having Lou Gehrig's disease—(Lateral Sclerosis)—both were terminally ill. Our weekend partying came to a halt. Both Bob and I tried to keep up a normal scene for the kids but we were both so distraught about our loved ones, that we had to push to keep our own work going. Bob kept up writing his Burroughs biography in the guesthouse (the advertising agency went defunct; he was out of job). I did my articles for the Home Magazine, but it wasn't easy with trips to see our sick relatives, keeping up the house, caring for the kids. I didn't even have time to visit in the afternoons with Mary. She came to me during these trying times and helped me handle my anxieties. We'd sit by the pool talking late into the night.

Even though Mary was a devout Catholic, she knew that I no longer practiced the faith; and she never forced her religious thinking on me. I was grateful for that because I had more then I could handle with my mother's continuous nagging to get me and the kids into Catholicism—even blamed me for my father's illness. Instead, Mary

MARIE FENTON GRIFFING

offered me spiritual guidance through these difficult times. With her nursing background, she knew all about the two different but deadly illnesses and would truthfully tell me about their progression and what I should expect. She comforted me when I had a bad day and took care of the kids when I went to visit my father. She urged me to get back to our normal lifestyle. "Marie, it's important, especially for the children, that you and Bob resume your relationships with other people. These illnesses will probably go on for a year or more. Take off on a vacation with the kids or have a party for no reason at all, just to have friends over." I took her advice and started to feel better because of it.

Mary had been dating a nice guy, Dean Lensing. One late summer day in 1957, she called me and said I should prepare to go to a wedding—hers and Dean's. I was so excited. The church ceremony was small and the reception was held at her house next door. Eva, her live-in friend and business partner, was her maid of honor—no bridesmaids. Eva had just moved out and had her own apartment nearby. The day was perfect. I whispered my vows all over again during the ceremony—Bob and I held hands and I think he was saying them, too. When we walked back to our house and put the kids to bed after the reception, I was feeling so romantic, I shyly asked Bob, "Honey, would you like to make a baby tonight?" He laughed and said his usual, "Duff, whatever you want is okay with me." And so, that night, Todd Samuel Fenton was conceived.

A few months later when I was visiting at Mary's house while she was preparing dinner, I told her I was pregnant. She grinned, hugged me and said "Marie, this is unbelievable—so am I." Well, we laughed and toasted each other with our wine glasses. I told her my due date and she told me hers—they were just a few days apart. Neither one of us could fit into most of our clothes anymore so we went to a special store that Mary knew about where they sold used maternity clothes—even swimsuits. We decided to stop the afternoon wine drinking and I gave up smoking again just as I had done when I was pregnant with Rick and Heidi. Dean and Bob kidded us both about getting fat and making them run out for special foods we craved. The four of us shared a wonderful experience together.

Somehow, my being pregnant and bringing a new life into the world was helpful to me during these times. I announced my pregnancy to my family on Thanksgiving day when I invited them for dinner. At first my mother was astonished "How can you afford to have another child? You can barely make ends meet now." But when she saw my father smile, she just sighed, shook her head. "Pass the turkey, please Marie. I guess we can always feed another mouth."

Mary and I kept comparing notes as to our physical condition. Her son, David, and my children, Todd and Heidi, couldn't really understand what it was all about. Sometimes, we'd call them to us when we felt the babies kicking and let them feel the thumping in our tummies. Our dual sharing of this experience made us even closer friends.

As Bob's brother and my father were failing, I was sustained by the thought of a new child coming into our lives. Just four days before Rick's seventh birthday, Todd was born—June 4, 1958. He was perfect. I couldn't wait to get him home to show Rick and Heidi their new brother. I had prepared for Rick's birthday party. Mary had helped me arrange everything—presents, decorations, even order the cake before I went to the hospital. But she wasn't able to be at the party because two days after Todd was born, she was rushed to the hospital, too, and gave birth to a daughter, Janet. Her wish had come true.

Even though I was a little weak—it had only been four days since Todd was born—I wanted Rick's party to go off perfectly which it did with Bob's help. My parents came as well as Bob's relatives and many of Rick's schoolmates. I didn't want Todd's birth to overshadow Rick's special day. The only cloud that darkened that party was to see my ailing father hobbling around and Bob's brother, Sam, looking thinner and weaker than I'd ever seen him. I put Todd in his bassinet out in the living room so everyone could look at him. Seeing my father pick him up and cuddle him, gave me comfort. It turned out to be a happy day for everyone but I was hurting inside to see two men whom I loved dearly deteriorating right before my eyes. I knew it wouldn't be too long before I would have to go to a funeral.

Mary and I became closer and closer after the birth of our babies. Her husband, Dean, built a swinging door onto the fence that separated our backyards. Now we could pass back and forth to visit without opening the front gate. On weekends, the Lensing family would come over for a swim in the pool and the Fenton family would go over to the Lensings' for dinner. We were one big, happy family.

Mary and I would occasionally take an afternoon off, share a babysitter for Todd and Janet (the other kids were in school), dress up for lunch out in Beverly Hills—a rare treat! This time together gave us a chance to talk and compare notes about the babies. It was funny, though, because by the time we drove and parked at the restaurant, we were anxiously looking at our watches. Trying not to show each other our worry about leaving two babies alone with one babysitter, we'd rush through our salads and race back home. It's interesting how we female human beings are so much like animal or fowl females who feel stress when leaving their young.

I remember one day I went to a small beauty salon on Ventura Blvd to have my hair cut. My mother was with Todd and Heidi. Again while I was away from the children, I got nervous and told the hairstylist to hurry up. I quickly drove back to the house and when I walked in I saw my mother frantically shaking Heidi. I screamed, "Mother, what are you doing?" "I gave her a candy and it got caught in her throat—what should we do?" I looked at Heidi and her eyes stared at me, she was gasping for breath. I threw my purse on the table and remembering Mary's advice she had given me one day about kids getting things caught in their throats, I grabbed Heidi in my arms, turned her upside down and held her around the waist with one arm. With the other hand, I tapped hard on her back. In a split second the hard candy spilled out on the floor and she breathed normally. She was crying and I hugged her tight. "It's okay Heidi. You're fine." When she ran off to play, I asked my mother kindly not to give her those candies again. She was crying too. I hugged her and said it was okay—"An accident, that's all, Mother. It happens but everything is all right." I was happy that I arrived back home early—I didn't want to think about what could have happened if I had come later.

Within a year of each other, Bob's brother, Sam, died and my dear father, Patrick. I had never faced death before in my life. I was young, I was immortal. But when I experienced laying these two dear persons to rest, I suddenly realized how short life is and how you never know what the future holds. It reminded me of I had lost my baby in Paris and how my French friend, Lillian, lifted me out of depression; now Mary was helping me through yet another crisis. She came over with her daughter, Janet, every afternoon and we talked while watching Todd and Janet play in the courtyard. They were getting big now, running around, building mounds in the sandbox, riding tricycles up and down the driveway. "Marie, it's okay to grieve for awhile, but it's time you let it go," she firmly said to me one afternoon. "Get on with your life with Bob and the kids. Listen, Labor day holiday is coming up soon. Let's you and I throw the party of the year. You invite all your friends and I'll invite some of mine and all the children, too. It'll be like the old times, okay?" I said I'd let her know.

When Bob came down from his office in the guesthouse, I mentioned Mary's idea to him. "I think it's a great idea—let's do it."

The crowd started coming at about 4 p.m. The weather was perfect. They came carrying towels and their swimming gear. They used the guesthouse to change and shower. Mary and I had prepared a great buffet for dinner. Bob and Dean made two huge punch bowl drinks—one with rum and fruit juice, the other with gin and fruit juice. Then we had loads of soft drinks for the kids. It was a party to outdo all other parties. I dug out a white linen sheath I had worn years before and amazingly still fit me. It came with a yellow chiffon cape top and a ruffled yellow skirt that I wrapped around my waist. My shoes were high-heeled sandals with ties around my ankles. I felt so glamorous—even my children thought so. "Mommy, twirl around again," said Todd. I giggled and twirled—he applauded. It was a long time since I had a big party. I was nervous.

Bob invited our college friends; some I couldn't remember. One man in particular was Charles (Chuck) Laufer who had just started publishing a new teenage magazine called 'Teen'. I was interested in this tall, good-looking guy who looked familiar but couldn't quite remember him. While Chuck was talking with Bob, I purposely interrupted their conversation by passing around some hors-d'oeuvre. "Hi, Marie. Do you remember me? We were in astrology class together; you sat across from me. Remember the time you gave me all your notes from the classes I never attended. Because of your help, I got an "A" on my finals." Then I recollected Chuck Laufer—the handsome guy with a smile that made all the girls' hearts melt. I laughed and said, "Of course I remember you" (the light bulb suddenly going on in my head). But how come I got a "C" and you got an "A?" "Way to go, Duff," my husband said. I gave Bob a nudge on his arm and looked up at him sternly. Thank goodness, he was distracted by Mary calling him to fill up the punch bowls and I was left alone with Chuck. I asked him what he was doing and he explained all about this new promising magazine he had started. He stood back and looked at me, scratched his head and asked if I would be interested in working for him. "Most of our articles are on teenage celebs, but we need a Beauty/Fashion Editor—that would bring in more advertising. Would you be interested?" The idea sounded exciting to me. "I don't know, Chuck, I'll have to talk it over with Bob."

And so without my knowing, I would be launched on a new, glamorous career, different from the journalism work I had been involved with off and on for the past 10 years. However, the Paris fashion collections which I had covered were a good background for what was to come.

The next morning, we all slept in until noon—the kids too. It was quite a party—ending up way past midnight with skinny dipping in the pool (we turned off the lights). The Lensings wandered over in the afternoon and we all went swimming. I cornered Mary in the kitchen while we were cleaning up more party crud. "Mary, you met Chuck Laufer last night—well, he wants me to be the Beauty/Fashion Editor of his magazine. Should I? Bob says to go for it but I'm nervous about leaving the kids."

"Marie, I think you would be perfect for it. You've been so close to your children for years. How old are they now?" she asked.

"Well, let's see—Rick is ten, Heidi is seven and Todd is three. Why?"

"You've given them your best throughout their formative years, plus Rick and Heidi are in school all day and you can put Todd in my day care school," Mary answered. "And maybe you could start out working part time to see if it is right for you?"

Because of Mary's sensible advice, I was confident and comfortable in taking the job.

So the next day I called Chuck, "Okay, I accept." It was like deja vu—when my aunts urged me on to new challenges.

CHAPTER FOUR

MY NEW CAREER YEARS
(1960 TO 1967)

1. MRS. DIAZ—MY RIGHT-HAND HELPER

IT DIDN'T TAKE me long to get used to sitting behind a desk and organizing my new job at 'Teen' Magazine. The setting was completely different from my Los Angeles Times work experience—not so fast paced—no daily deadlines. I liked being in charge. Chuck gave me every opportunity to use my own ideas; the art director and other members of the 'Teen' staff welcomed me into the fold. They gave me all sorts of input to the magazine business. Two days a week I drove the freeway to Petersen Publishing in Hollywood. There I spent my time contacting public relations people in the New York beauty/health fields, announcing my appointment as Beauty Editor and introducing them to 'Teen' magazine. Slowly the news releases came flowing in, together with great photos to go along with my articles on teenage beauty subjects—like acne, hair problems, nail care, etc. We had a staff photographer with whom I worked on "shoots" to illustrate my articles. I was learning a whole new area of communications—magazine style writing. I found it exciting and challenging, plus the weekly checks were most welcome.

I had to juggle the house, the kids and doing my job at the same time but I was getting used to that by now. Bob was a big help. However, I could see he was getting irritated spending much of the day with the children, hardly finding enough hours to work on his Tarzan book. It was difficult for both of us but we knew our only means to survive financially at this time was for me to stick with 'Teen' magazine.

One day while I was shopping for groceries at Safeway, a young Hispanic man who worked there and always helped me out with my groceries, asked me if I needed a housekeeper or a gardener. I said, "perhaps—why?" He explained that his parents had just arrived from Costa Rica but they couldn't live with him because he had a tiny apartment. He said they were good people, had come to the U.S. to be with him, find a new life and they would work free just for room and board until he could afford a larger place. It was like manna from heaven—the guesthouse would suffice for them, plus they could help take care of the children while I was on my job. And I thought, most importantly, Bob could get back to his daily writing routine and not worry about domestic chores. I told Andre to bring his parents over that evening.

Bob and I met Mr. and Mrs. Diaz. They were very gracious and spoke only a little English but all in all they seemed like they would be able to solve our recent crisis. The two story guest house, or as we called it "our chalet", had been used a lot over the last couple of years—our friend we met in Europe, Eddie and his two children, Suzzane and Ronald, stayed in it for about two months when Eddie came back from Europe and was looking to find a job and a new house. Vernon Scott, a college friend of ours who worked on The Hollywood Reporter, lived for a couple weeks in it when he was estranged from his wife. Stan and Nancy, our friends from the Cote d'Zur, stayed a few days on their trip back to San Francisco. A couple, Dutch—Jewish immigrants, Bob met in Holland during World War II lived in the guesthouse for weeks. Then there were always "sleep-overs"—friends who got too zonked at our parties and rather than drive home, we convinced them to stay in the "chalet" for the night. By now it had been well lived in. We set it up for our new occupants. When Mr. and Mrs. Diaz saw their new quarters, they said, "Oh, mucho bonito, Senora." They loved the little house. For the next two years, the Diaz's became a part of our family.

Mr. and Mrs. Diaz were loving and caring people. Bob and I and the kids became very attached to them. They were in their late 60s and very soft-spoken, handled their domestic duties with ever so much ease. Mr. Diaz enjoyed and took much pride in keeping the courtyard and pool clean, pruned bushes and small trees—never complained or quit his work because of the intense heat or the ache in his back. He did small repairs around the house whenever I asked, and liked to sit with the children while they watched their late afternoon television programs.

But it was Mrs. Diaz who amazed me most. She would always hum softly as she cleaned the house, even while waxing the wood floors on her knees. She never disturbed me while I was working at my desk in the master bedroom except to bring me a sandwich and iced tea for lunch. She did the same for Bob working on the second floor office of the chalet.

I always made it a point to quit my work in the late afternoon after Todd's nap and Heidi and Rick's arrival home from school to swim with them in the pool. Bob would come down too. The whole arrangement seemed to be working out beautifully. We had lucked out.

As the months went by, I could see a change of behavior with the children. There was less sibling rivalry; they accepted their menial chores without their "sassing back." On Sunday mornings when Bob and I usually slept in late, they'd run back to the guesthouse to have tortillas and beans for breakfast with Jose and Theresa (as the kids called them), then take a long walk with the Diaz's up the lovely tree-bordered path that ran from our road toward the Tarzana hills where sheep and horses grazed.

I began to closely observe the ways Mrs. Diaz handled the children. She'd quiet Todd when he got cranky by taking time out from her job to rock him back and forth in the hammock by the pool. When Heidi got bored, she'd ask her to help hang up the wash—Heidi would pass her clothes pins. Or she'd urge Rick to finish his painting he was working on, play dominoes with him, even listen to his new records. I observed how easily she interacted with the children.

One day I asked Mrs. Diaz, "You work wonders with my children. You must have raised a big family?"

"Oh, yes, Senora," she replied in her poor English," ten children of my own. Andre is the baby—others all in Costa Rica—grandchildren, too. I miss them very much but Andre promises that one day soon they will too come to America. Now, I like being with your babies—they remind me of my own."

"Good, Mrs. Diaz—but what is your secret of getting my kids to so easily do what you ask of them—they're not so cooperative with me."

She laughed, brushed her gray hair back behind her ears. "No secret. Speak in a soft but firm voice—smile. Give a lot of hugs and kisses when they do a good job—sometimes I give them each a chocolate cookie, too. One more thing, Senora, it's good to become like a child again. What is the word—"childish?" Yes, be silly. That's what Ricky calls me "Silly.""

Those words gave me food for thought. Throughout each of my children's first three formative years, I was totally involved with each of them during that growth period—playing, frolicking, reading to them—but lately my new work with 'Teen' gave me less time to be with them and I realized that maybe they were rebelling toward me. Mrs. Diaz made me focus on knowing how to handle the delicate balance of being firm and when to loosen the reins as the kids grew older. I started to concentrate on their needs—like when to allow them to stay up longer to watch a special TV show or to excuse them from the dinner table when they weren't hungry—little but important things—things I wouldn't have done before because I felt I was being too permissive. Mrs. Diaz's life-experience advice helped me feel more relaxed and I especially took to heart her ability to act "childish". I looked in my Dr. Spock book and found the clue—"Do not be afraid to be childlike when interacting with your children—this attitude will put you into closer contact with your youngster." I kept that in mind and acted on it for years ahead—even now as a Grandmother and friend to many children I meet today.

It had been over a year that I'd been working for 'Teen' Magazine. My weekly paycheck was getting us through. We even refurbished our kitchen and built on an extra bedroom for us which gave the children their own bedrooms. My mother would pay her regular twice-a-week visits. She enjoyed being with the children and got along very well with Mrs. Diaz. I was pleased that she was overcoming the grief of my father's death but we did have occasional bouts concerning my going back to the church and having the kids baptized. These discussions always upset me, but little by little I learned to keep calm and appease her with such remarks as, "Okay, Mother, we'll see later on when the kids get older." But she still kept bringing holy cards and medals.

One day in early May of 1960, my Editor, Chuck Laufer, came into my office and congratulated me on my work. He said that the advertising revenue had risen and that the publisher, Bob Petersen, had agreed to open up Editorial Offices in New York City. I said that was great. "Yeah, Marie, it is—we want you to go there and start our editorial scene." I was shocked—"You want me to move to New York?"

"Duff, just think, we'll be closer to the publishing field. I can visit editors in the big houses face to face." Bob said, when I told him about Chuck's offer. "My Tarzan book is coming along—I still have more research to do, but this new opening for you is a big break for us." Chuck told me that 'Teen' will pay all our ways, put us up free for three months until we find a house—even transport all our furniture, everything. Bob's reaction "And they even gave you a big raise. We just can't let this go, Duff!"

I was distressed—it seemed like the time Bob urged me to go to Europe in 1949, not that I regretted the move, but it did cause me anxiety at first. And it happened again leaving our safe shelter in Germany to return to the states because Bob wanted to go into TV writing. I knew he was working hard on his writings but he wasn't getting anyplace. I asked him to take a teaching job so we'd have more income but he didn't even want to consider that. His writing was his life. I understood because I

MARIE FENTON GRIFFING

had read his works and they were wonderful. Maybe moving to New York would help him. I was confused and scared again but felt I must and I wanted to support my husband.

There were other concerns I had too—the changing of schools for Heidi and Rick; taking them away from their friends in Tarzana, leaving all our good friends in Los Angeles, especially Mary Lensing, and being separated from both our families. Hardest of all was having to sell our beautiful Tarzana home—my dream house. Rental houses in LA in the early 60s were not doing well. The real estate agent said it would be better to sell—especially since we would be living so far away. After a couple of weeks of difficult decision making, I agreed with Bob and told Chuck that I would make the move. My mother didn't take it so well but I said I'd give us six months and if the situation didn't work out, we'd be back.

"Yes, Marie, like you told us when you left for Europe—instead of six months, you stayed six years." I sighed, patted her arm and answered, "Okay, Mother, you're right—I can't promise. I don't know where this new road in my life is going to take me, but Bob and I have made the decision to travel it." I bent down and gave her a hug—I could see the anguish in her eyes. A week later, Bob and I started to prepare for our departure.

Our main concern was how the children would accept this move. Bob talked to them about all the exciting things they would experience in New York—visiting the Statue of Liberty, the Empire State Building, go to Radio City Music Hall and to Broadway plays. He made it sound like fun which helped put them into a positive mood. Ricky was the most enthusiastic because he knew he would be close to real theatre—something he had recently become involved with. I had started him in an acting class after school and he loved it. He had just turned 12—Heidi was eight and Todd was four. I felt guilty about uprooting my kids to pursue Bob's and my careers but I knew we had to realize our financial situation—we still had many debts. They had to be paid and this looked like the answer. The sale of the house would solve those problems and my job in New York would secure us for a while. It was like a new beginning—again.

Mrs. Diaz was a big help to me over the next month. She assisted me in arranging Rick and Todd's birthday parties; Todd's on June 4 and Rick's on June 8. My friend, Mary helped too—even took Todd into her nursery school to make it easier on us while we were packing up—she never charged me. I gave Mrs. Diaz a lot of stuff from the house that I couldn't take with me. Her son, Andre, had found a place for all of them to live in, so that put my mind at ease. Every time I would start to cry while sealing up a box of dishes or whatever, she would softly brush the hair atop my head. "Nina, it will be good. You will have your husband and children with you. Try to be happy." I thought back to when I left my dear friends, Lillian in Paris and Lucie in Germany. I knew like with the others that I would never see Mrs. Diaz again. In the last 10 years so many lovely people were lost from my life. I felt sad. I had a feeling that it wouldn't end here but was at least pleased that they all had crossed my path and helped in my growth as a woman.

Bob and I decided to throw a party to outdo all parties—it would be our farewell celebration. We arranged it to be the night before we'd take off for New York. We will have cleared out the house by then and sent everything away on a huge truck. Our dog, Liza, had died and Jake our other dog ran away—it seemed he sensed that we were leaving. All the transactions for the sale of the house had been done. We paid off the mortgage, signed checks to pay off our debts, sold our station wagon to Mary—she would drive us to the airport in it. We were almost on our way except for the last "Hurrah!"

The party was fantastic. Over 100 of our friends and family came to the house for hors d'ouvres and drinks. The living room was bare except for our old hi-fi which we had bequeathed to a friend in need, a lot of our records, too. The music filled the empty house. People arrived by the droves. Mrs. Diaz came to help serve the snacks which I ordered out from our favorite Chinese restaurant on Ventura Blvd, a few blocks away.

The party started at 6 p.m. and at 8 p.m. the guests were instructed to drive to the restaurant for dinner. Everybody was totally surprised because they thought it was only going to be a cocktail party. We had arranged with the manager of the Chinese place to set up for 100 people. He closed down the restaurant to outsiders and arranged it for us only. What a feast and good time we all had. There were speeches and farewell jokes by our friends—I even had few words prepared. I tearfully got through them okay but it was hard to say goodbye.

We asked everyone to return to the house for more drinks and a last skinny dip in the pool. Even our actor/comedic elderly friend, Jack Oakie, joined in on all the fun. It was a night to be remembered.

On our long plane trip to New York's Kennedy Airport, I held Bob's hand, dozed off now and then, thinking about what I had left behind and how much I would miss Mary—we had hugged and cried at the airport.

I wondered what was ahead for us. Again I was scared. But the moment we started to descend for the landing and I looked out the window, saw the millions of lights, the thousands of cars traveling the highways, I knew this would be one of the most exciting adventures of my life. I was going to work in this fabulous city of seven million people—me, with my own office in a huge building on 60th and Lexington just across from Bloomingdale's. I could feel my heart beating faster. I pulled my chair to an upright position, smiled back at the kids behind us, holding my right thumb up. "Here we are everyone—in New York, New York."

We immediately took a cab to Teaneck, New Jersey which is a suburb across the George Washington Bridge, an hour from Manhattan. It was impossible to find a rental in the city so my dear friend, Joanne, who I knew from Tarzana and with whom I had worked in a co-op nursery school where I had enrolled Heidi, came through for us. She had moved back to NJ and found us a small charming house in this quiet town. The owner was there when we arrived and graciously welcomed us. Everything we needed was meticulously arranged. As the children were running around choosing which bedrooms they wanted, I walked out on the porch and smelled the wonderful aroma of freshly cut grass from the public park just across the street. How wonderful, I thought—a place for the kids to play for the summer. The greenery all around filled my eyes. When we left Tarzana, all the alfalfa on our knoll was brown and dry, as was almost everything in California but here all the trees were still green. On that first night in Teaneck there were thunderstorms and the rain pelted against the windows—new sounds I hadn't heard for years. It hadn't rained in Los Angeles since December. The children were a little upset with the storms but Bob and I quieted them down after awhile. We were all exhausted from our trip and fell asleep soon. It was July 2, 1962. We had arrived! I awoke a few hours later. The rain had stopped and through the open bedroom window I smelled the warm humid air drifting in. The sweet pungent scent reminded me of my childhood vacations in Milwaukee. I started to reflect on how far I had come from those wonderful days in the 30s and 40s. Here I was in the 60s and even with all the ups and downs, I was truly happy with my life so far. I wished I could see ahead—know what would evolve but knew it was better that I didn't. "Let it surprise me," I thought. Softly, I reached over and squeezed Bob's hand so as not to awake him. His hand squeezed mine back. I smiled and slowly drifted off to sleep again.

2. JOANNE—MY NEW YORK GUIDE

THE MORNING AFTER we arrived, my friend, Joanne, from Tarzana who had found the rental for us came over to see how we were getting along. Bob and I were still unpacking—the kids were already over at the park. She brought her two girls, Andrea and Pauline who were the same ages as Heidi and Todd. It was wonderful to see an old friend again. Her girls quickly ran to the park to play with our children.

"Well, Marie, you are a long way from home. What do you think?"

"I don't know, Joanne, it's very different so far—the style of the houses, the huge green trees all over the place and those storms last night were like nothing we'd ever had in Tarzana. I don't even know how to work the dryer in the basement."

We laughed as we strolled out to the porch. "I've never had a big porch like this; I like it. You can see what's going on up and down the street—look, I can even keep an eye on the children playing in the park," I said as I put my arm around her shoulder. It made me feel secure to have someone who I knew living only five minutes away. I thanked Joanne for finding us the house and asked if she and Oscar and the girls would like to come out to dinner with us. She declined but wanted us to come to their place the next night for a barbecue to celebrate the 4th of July.

"That'll be great, Joanne. I'll bring a cake—it's Heidi's birthday on the 5th and it would be nice if we could make it like a special party for her too."

*   *   *

Joanne was a real New Yorker—born and raised in the city. She had attended the best private schools there and with all her intelligence and good breeding, she was still a down to earth person. She seemed more worldly than I and there was a self-assurance about her that I envied. I told Bob, "Joanne is a real classy woman. She's like the ideal chic New

Yorker." I wondered if some of that would rub off on me now that I, too, would become a New Yorker.

Her husband, Oscar, worked for the New York Times. He had been assigned to do a Hollywood movie column in Los Angeles two years before—they rented in Tarzana and that's where Joanne and I met at the local co-op nursery school. Since then we became good friends. Now Oscar was called back to New York to write a hunting and fishing column for the Sports Page. Joanne was glad about the move and I was glad that she was there for me. From the very first, she became my guide to New York, advising me on what to wear the first day on my job, where to sightsee with the kids, what type of transportation to get to Manhattan—and much more. I don't think I could have made it without her.

*   *   *

Joanne alerted us about the traditional 4th of July parade down Main Street in Teaneck. I had to go to the supermarket to get food and a cake for Heidi anyway, so the next morning, Bob, I and the children walked the mile to Main Street. It was very hot and I put on a pair of my short-shorts that I always wore in Tarzana. The kids wanted to go barefoot—I said okay—they hardly wore shoes back home—except for school. Bob wore his tattered jean cutoffs and his favorite wooden clogs that our friend Eddy had brought him from Sweden.

Main Street was very crowded that July 4th morning—everyone was waiting for the parade to start. Looking around at the natives, I realized there was a different dress code here—most wore slacks or Bermuda shorts to the knees (no short-shorts), everyone had on shoes or sandals. As we walked into the market, I could see eyes appraising us. Oh, dear, I thought, they don't approve of what we're wearing. I knew then that there were going to be changes we'd have to make to adapt to this new territory.

I don't think I'd ever felt more like an American than I did watching the parade down Main Street. We'd never had anything like that in small towns around Los Angeles. Someone came by as we were standing on the curb watching the marching bands and gave us all small American flags to wave. The kids really enjoyed it and tears came to my eyes as I saw the elderly veterans march so proudly—I thought of my father and how tall and straight he used to march down Broadway in Los Angeles as a World War I veteran in the American Legion parade each Memorial Day.

When I described our morning's experience to Joanne, she smiled and said that the lifestyle in the East is a lot different than out West. "We're more conservative here, Marie and we tend to be more critical of outsiders than you are back in LA. It'll take you a little more time to adjust and learn all the ins and outs."

So true but thanks to Joanne's orientation, we soon became acclimated. Bob threw out his cut-off jeans and I did the same with my short-shorts and we both bought Bermudas. The kids started wearing sandals to the park.

I was to report for my first day at my job with 'Teen' on July 15th. That gave me enough time to set up the household. Joanne found a piano teacher for Heidi. I had this desire to expose my kids to music early in life. I had missed that in my youth and regretted it to this day. Joanne suggested that I enroll the kids in the summer programs held in the park, which I did immediately. She came over one afternoon before I was supposed to report for work and clued me into all the bus lines, subway trains, and taxis. that would take me to 60th and Lexington Ave. Joanne put herself out for us, drove us to the best rental car dealer in New Jersey—we finally had wheels again. Plus, she had us over for dinners during which our two families became closer and closer. Joanne was a prize.

The big day arrived. Bob walked me to the bus stop a block from the house, gave me a kiss as I boarded the bus. I knew I was leaving the kids in good hands. Bob had set up a small table in the bedroom for his typewriter so he could work on his book and begin a new project he started on the side with my Editor, Chuck Laufer,—"Teen Features Syndicate" they called it—a series of columns relating to teenagers that they would try to sell to newspapers around the country. I thought it to be a good idea but was a little worried about how the financing of this new project would be handled. I didn't want to go in debt again yet I didn't want to bust Bob's balloon either.

As I crossed the George Washington Bridge from New Jersey to Manhattan, I couldn't believe the splendor of the New York skyline. It took my breath away and at the same time gave me strange feelings in my stomach. I suddenly realized I was into the big time! From the bus that left me off at the terminal in West Manhattan, I followed the crowd to catch the A-train that would take me to Columbus Circle. From there, I caught a taxi cab that drove me to 60th and Lexington. It took just about

MARIE FENTON GRIFFING

an hour and by the time I climbed out of the cab, I was perspiring. It was the high humidity. Never had I ever experienced such heat in my life—California heat is dry—not even in Europe did I sweat like in New York. My hair was wilted and my pink cotton dress was all wrinkled. Give me strength, I said to myself as I took the elevator up to the 22nd floor and into the offices of Petersen Publishing.

'Teen' Magazine was just one of many publications of Petersen Publishing—the others were all male oriented—Hot Rod, Power Boats and more. The only woman in the place was the office secretary. I saw a lot of young men walking in and out of office cubicles, acting very busy. A couple of them gave me "the once over." Angela, the secretary, greeted me in a friendly manner, said Mr. Gross was expecting me—he was the office manager for Petersen.

"Welcome to New York, Marie. Chuck said you'd be reporting today. Let's go see your office and you can get settled in. Then later we'll go to lunch and I'll introduce you to the advertising man for 'Teen' with whom you'll be working."

I spent the morning checking out everything. Angela showed me where I could get more stationery, etc., the coffee station, the ladies room and the business cards she had printed up for me. She was wearing a simple black knit skirt and beige sweater and looked fresh and cool. There I stood in my wrinkled pink shirtwaist dress and my hair flat as a pancake. I mentioned that the heat made me look like a wilted flower. She laughed, "Yeah, Mrs. Fenton, you'll have to get used to it—not like LA, eh?" I nodded, smiled and threw back my bangs with my fingers.

When I arrived home that night, I was totally exhausted and frustrated about the job. It was all so new to me. Bob had dinner ready—I had told him to make pork chops, boiled potatoes and frozen peas. He hugged me and said he hoped I'd be pleased with his cooking. I cried and laughed at the same time. What am I getting myself into, I thought as we sat down at the table. The kids started asking all kinds of questions about my first day at work. I tried to explain the whole thing in a humorous way which helped to lighten my worries about whether or not I could handle the job. After they were in bed, I gave Joanne a call and explained how I felt so much out of place what with my wilted dress and hair. She immediately came up with a plan. "I'll meet you after you get out of work and we'll go over to Bloomies to buy you some things that'll give you the Manhattan look. They have a great hair salon there too—maybe you can get a new cut that will hold up in this weather."

That was a fun shopping spree. After unpacking my purchases and showing them to Bob and the children, I cleaned out my closet of all the pastel cottons I'd brought from Tarzana, set up the new hair products in the bathroom. I went to sleep in Bob's arms not knowing what the next day would bring.

Soon my work attitude improved. In fact, I started to enjoy my days in the Big Apple. I learned how to wave down taxis, work with my new photographer, gab with the advertising guys in the office. My fears started to slip away and little by little I got the hang of being an editor among many other editors. The almost daily press luncheons and cocktail parties put me in touch with professionals. Beauty editors from such magazines as Vogue, Cosmopolitan, Harpers Bazaar, Glamour and more were very friendly toward me. It seemed they realized I was the new girl in town and went out of their way to make me feel very much at ease—some even gave me tips on the best modeling agents to use, expert stylists to help me set up my shoots and the best restaurants to choose when a public relations person asked me out to lunch.

I also was pleased that my children were quickly adapting to their new surroundings. Every weekend, Joanne would call and advise as to the most interesting places to visit in Manhattan and its environs. We were like tourists, taking in all the wonderful attractions, the plays, the little cities within this great city. When I came home from work, I'd ask Heidi to play something on the piano for me. She had progressed beautifully. One night she and Rick asked me to help them prepare humongous sandwiches for a contest being held in the park the next day. We rushed to the supermarket and picked out different meats, cheeses, etc. They won first and second prize. We ate them for four days.

Bob's work with his new Teen Syndicate was going well. I even wrote a beauty column for it. All seemed to be pretty calm until we got a phone call from Ruth, Bob's sister, that his mother had died. Neither one of us could go back West for the funeral because of our commitments. Bob was in a blue mood for days but thanks to his involvement with the children while I was away for the day, they took his mind off his sadness. They helped him with shopping for food, doing the wash, cleaning the house. But mostly outings with Joanne and Oscar subdued his grief. He and Oscar even went out fishing one day.

August was almost coming to a close and we suddenly realized that finding a permanent house was ahead of us. For the next couple of weekends, Joanne took care of the children while Bob and I scouted out newspaper ads. We visited houses in Long Island, Connecticut, New Jersey but saw nothing that we liked. I did go crazy about a villa-type house on the banks of the Hudson in Tarrytown, New York but the rent was $500 a month. "Too, much, Duff," Bob said to me. It was a grand place, like the one we had outside of Paris. I came to my senses and stopped thinking about it. Finally, one Friday Bob said he had found a great house only 30 minutes from Manhattan—a place called Snedens Landing. The house was over 100 years old, well kempt, with lots of rooms. Joanne told us this area was very secluded and was mentioned in a recent book "Exsurbanites." That Saturday morning we drove from New Jersey up the Palisades Parkway, crossed the border from New Jersey to New York state and found Palisades, NY but couldn't find a sign to direct us to Snedens. We inquired at the little post office in Palisades and they told us to go across 9W into Washington Spring Road. We finally found the house, not by number but by the Yates name on the mailbox. Mary Yates was waiting on the huge porch and waved us into the curved, gravel driveway lined with lilac bushes. I gasped. What a huge house with a lot of lawn all around and a charming gazebo in the back. I fell in love with it immediately.

It was sparsely furnished—some beds, a wonderful roll-top desk which grabbed Bob's attention and fireplaces in almost every room even the master bedroom.

Mary explained that she and her husband were moving to Washington—he was a news correspondent for one of the national TV networks. After showing us the house, she explained the uniqueness of Snedens—a private place for artists mostly—writers, actors, producers, architects, etc. When she learned we were both writers, she was so pleased that she reduced the rent from $350 to $300 a month. We accepted immediately.

Joanne was happy we had found the right house, looked into the schools for the kids and discovered the local little red brick schoolhouse had great accreditations—no need to send Heidi & Rick to private school. Now all we had to do was get all of our stuff out of storage and get settled in Snedens.

I hated living so far away from Joanne. She had helped me pack up the suitcases full of clothes we had brought with us—all our house furniture, etc. was to arrive on a big truck. It was a Labor Day weekend so I was free from work for a few days and could help get us settled in. One last important thing I did before going to bed was to phone Joanne and thank her for all her help and how much I would miss seeing her often.

Joanne laughed. "Marie, you'll only be an hour away. Of course we'll come visit and visa versa. Okay?" I nodded. She was right. We did keep our friendship alive and still do today. I feel I am blessed for having so many good women friends in my lifetime.

3. OLGA—THE "PERLE MESTA" OF SNEDENS LANDING

LABOR DAY WEEKEND, 1962, arrived sunny and warm when we moved to Snedens. The huge trailer with all our furniture, dishes, etc. from Tarzana pulled into our driveway Saturday morning shortly after our arrival at the house. It had rained the night before and the grass glistened, the air smelled sweet—there was a wonderful quietness all around. The children explored the property running in and out of gazebo. The house was hidden from the street but from the second story bedroom window I could see the hundred or so white houses which made up this exquisite community that curved around and dipped down to the banks of the Hudson River.

We had the moving men put all the boxes and crates in the dining room then directed them to put the furniture in the various rooms. I didn't realize we had brought so much—wondered if the weekend would be enough time to get the house in shape before I went back to work on Tuesday.

As I was un-taping a box, I heard the back door creak open. I went into the kitchen to see who came in. There stood this black woman, about 40 years old, dressed in a white uniform dress like nurses wear, holding a bouquet of flowers in her left hand and balancing a soup crock in the other. A large smile revealing bright white teeth stretched from ear to ear.

"Good afternoon, Mrs. Fenton. I'm Olga and I've come to welcome you to Snedens."

She handed me the bouquet and laid the soup bowl on the counter. "I made you some bean soup you can have for dinner and I'll bring you a salad later and some bread so you don't have to cook tonight." She said all this in a thick Spanish accent and kept smiling all the time. I was taken back by this sudden act of hospitality—it made me feel warm and I smiled back. I went over and shook her hand. I wondered who this woman was and how she came to know my name.

*   *   *

With the help of a sponsorship from a famous American architect and his wife, Mr. and Mrs. Gugler who lived in Snedens, Olga was able to come from Cuba to Snedens many years before with a small baby boy called Lenny. She worked for them and lived in one of their houses there, cooking, cleaning and taking care of their needs. It was a good arrangement for all. Olga was able to raise her son and the Guglers had a faithful helper.

Being the outward, gregarious person that she was, Olga made herself known to everyone. No one ever locked their doors in Snedens, so out of blue in would pop Olga always bringing something to eat, to show a baby animal that had just been born or to watch a child if needed and to see if all was right with the family. If anyone wanted to know what was going on in Snedens, you just had to ask Olga. She was a unique figure that seemed to be watching over the community like a guardian angel and when she laughed, it was contagious—all around her would laugh too.

She raised chickens, goats, cats, dogs—name it—the children loved to visit her house. If a child was missing, you just had to walk over to Olga's to find him. And she loved to entertain when not busy with her employers. When Olga invited you over for dinner, you knew it would be a very different type of evening, not knowing what to expect or who would be there.

*   *   *

It was Labor Day, the Monday before I had to go back to work and Bob and I were still working away trying to get the house in order. The kids were really getting into our hair, sliding down the long curved banister from the second to first floor—especially Todd, being only 4 years old was hanging onto my shirttails, demanding attention. There was a knock at the front door. A young woman in her late 20s or so was waiting. Tall with long blonde hair that almost reached to her waist, she smiled at me as I opened the door and stretched out her hand to shake mine.

"Olga said you had arrived. We've been waiting for you—Mary Yates told us all about you and I think it's great we have two new writers moving into Snedens, especially that you have children," Gail Hyde said.

To the side of her I saw a little girl and boy about the same ages as Heidi and Todd dressed in swim attire. I asked her to come in.

"No, not now, I know you're busy getting settled and I just thought if you wanted to get your children out of the way I would take them down with mine to the Waterfall for a swim. Do they swim?"

I told her they did but where was the Waterfall? She told me that it was like an old swimming hole, naturally made from a waterfall that came down from a stream above. It was about 5 minutes down the road, right on the Hudson River. What a magical place we had found, I thought.

I quickly called my three and introduced them to Gail and her kids, Philip and Annie, and told them if they wanted to go for a swim to quickly change into their swimsuits which they did without a moments notice. She said she'd bring them back in a couple of hours. I was a little anxious letting them go with a stranger but there was a trusting aura about Gail and told her it really would help us if the kids vanished for awhile.

An hour later another young woman, Frances, who said she lived next door stopped by to bring us a loaf of bread and a bottle of wine. Bob and I were pleased about this friendly introduction to Snedens. When the children ran in late that afternoon, they couldn't stop talking about the Waterfall and how much fun they had there—"It's like a secret place, Mommy," said Todd. "You have to go down a path in the woods. There's no one else around. Oh, but the water is so cold." He was shivering so I quickly grabbed a towel out of the closet wrapped it around him. Then I chased them all upstairs to a hot bath.

As I tucked the children in that night and before we all said our bedtime prayer, I asked them what they thought about their new home. There were smiles all around. "We love it—so much fun. Now can we get a dog again?" asked Heidi. "Honey, we'll see. Mommy and Daddy are really busy now. I'm going to work tomorrow and Daddy is going to take you to register at the school. Be good babies for me, eh? I'll be home for dinner but Daddy will be here if you need him and remember, play in your own yard, okay?" It was hard for me to leave them but knowing that Rick and Heidi would be in school all day eased my mind. I would have to find a nursery school for Todd, meanwhile he'd have to stay at home with Bob. I helped lay out their clothes for the next day, said their prayer with them, gave them a goodnight kiss and turned off the lights. I was glad they were pleased about living here and so hoped they would not ever have to be uprooted again.

I walked down the stairs to the living room where Bob had started a cozy fire in the fireplace and a bottle of wine and two glasses were sitting on the coffee table.

For the next two years, Bob and I were enveloped into the wonderful lifestyles of Manhattan and Snedens Landing. The environments and tempo of the two differed like night and day. Even the children were offered the best of both worlds. On weekends we'd drive to New York for a movie at Radio City Music Hall or visit a museum, walk through Central Park, go see West Side Story on 42nd St., watch the famous Macy's parade on Thanksgiving or the Easter Parade on Fifth Ave. One Thanksgiving when I was working at 'Teen' and too busy to prepare a dinner, we took the kids to the National Press Club of which I was a member. It was in an old historic building on 6th Avenue near the New York Library. The bar and dining room always stimulated me when I was there—poster-size front pages of the New York Times and other newspapers framed on the walls, heated discussions at the bar among well-known newspaper reporters and writers from around the world. Sometimes, I was invited to join in. There weren't many women members but the men accepted me. Occasionally, Bob would pick me up at 'Teen' and we'd have supper there. The ambiance was fabulous. We even took Olga one night. At first she refused saying "A black woman like me can't go to such a place." We told her that it would be okay—newspaper people are very liberal. She was most impressed.

'Teen' Magazine was progressing beautifully. I hired a fashion editor, Dee Grossman, to compliment my Beauty pages—the advertising manager, Ted, was picking up business like crazy. My Editor, Chuck Laufer, would fly in from LA once a month to see how we were doing and left pleased as punch. My features were going along smoothly. I was really getting the hang of being a New York Editor but one thing started to bother me. I was committed to attend all the press luncheons, cocktail parties, out-of-town junkets, etc. which meant time away from my family. It became very demanding but I knew I needed to do it if I wanted to be a professional. Olga was a big help during these busy years. She not only found a great nursery school for Todd only five minutes away in Palisades run by a mother and daughter in their own home but got a new piano teacher for Heidi and talked Rick into taking lessons too. She brought the neighbors children over to play with ours or took them all to her place to help her tend to her garden and animals. She and Bob were overseeing the care of the children, I was relieved but in a way envious that I couldn't participate.

I have to admit that I enjoyed and relished in the glamorous side of my business. Never in my life had I been pampered like I was by the public relations people of the beauty and fashion industry. I received beautiful gifts for the holidays and more cosmetics and perfume that I could ever use.

When I complained to Olga about my not spending enough time at home, she would laugh her famous laugh, "Marie, you have a wonderful work. Be happy, don't worry." Whenever I flew out of La Guardia to cover a beauty pageant or whatever, I'd cry at takeoff but by the time I arrived in a distant city, my tears dried and I looked forward to the adventure that lay before me.

Bob was working on 'Teen Features' but it was going downhill so it was necessary that I hold on to my job if we were to pay our bills. We were loosing bucks on this venture. He went back to his Tarzan novel and also started a musical play with a new-found friend, a musician, Manny Vardi. Olga helped to create interest in the play by talking it up with the various theatre producers who lived in Snedens. She even invited a few "angels" to her place for dinner to meet Bob and Manny. We were all excited about this project. I'd arrive home from New York and hear Manny playing show tunes on the piano—Bob wrote the lyrics. It was an exciting period.

4. OLGA—A PART OF THE FAMILY

OLGA TOOK THE Fenton family under her wing in earnest. When my mother came to visit from Los Angeles and Bob and I were both too busy to show her around our new territory, Olga took on the job. I didn't know how my mother would accept having a black woman escort her to the historical sites in nearby Nyack, Tappan and across the Hudson to Terrytown but Olga managed to win her over and they had a great time together—ironically, their birthdays were on the same day, September 30th and we celebrated with a big party at Olga's. It wasn't long before they became fast friends—they even went to Mass together on Sundays.

One Saturday the children came rushing into the house, all excited by a litter of puppies born to Sheba, Olga's black Labrador. "Mommy, can we have one. They're so cute," begged Todd. At first I thought no because raising a puppy took time and patience and I had neither of those at this point what with my work. But then I realized it had been almost a year since the family had had the pleasure of a furry animal around. "I'll discuss it with your father," I said looking down at these three anxious faces. Olga stopped by later with a beautiful bouquet of flowers from her garden and put in her plea on the kids behalf. "Maria, (she started calling me this after asking for my approval) I will help teach them how to train the little dog. It will bring them much happiness and give them a lesson in responsibility. Each one will feed him on different days. You will see. It will work." Bob and I agreed and after a few weeks when the puppy was weaned from its mother, "Little John" as we named him joined the Fenton household. He was a joy!

Our social life in Snedens was improving, especially on weekends and over the holidays. Olga had a lot to do with this. At the annual spring and fall plant sales, at the little local library, she made sure to introduce us to neighbors or at the traditional Christmas caroling at the Norman house, the Holloween costume parade at Palisades Elementary school the children attended. Little by little, we met some wonderful people who lived only doors away. The cocktail and dinner parties were great—interesting people, stimulating conversation—we were back in our element again. We even got into a Saturday night poker game with an exciting group—a doctor, harpist, architect, artist, musician. We often played until two or three in the morning at the different houses of the players. We became close friends. Sometimes Olga would stop in to bring a bowl of soup or leftovers from the dinner party she had prepared for her employers, the Guglers.

One day I complained to Olga that it seemed that I was the only working woman in Snedens. In the early 60s, professional women, like me, were not looked upon as a proper wifely role and it made it difficult for me to converse with a lot of the wives I met at parties. I felt isolated from the conversations which dealt with everything from the best diaper, PTA meetings to volunteer work at the library.

"Maria, It's not good you feel guilty about going to business. Yes, there are some women who go to work here. You just haven't met them. I will have you meet them." And she did. We became friends with Joan Konner who had just bought the Mike Wallace house on River Road—a magnificent place that overlooked the Hudson. At that time she was a newspaper woman for 'The Record' in New Jersey. There were a couple other women too. Unfortunately, we were all so busy being involved with our jobs and our family duties, we rarely had time to talk except socially at the local gatherings. But it did make me feel better—I wasn't the only working wife.

It was Bob's 40th birthday and I planned a lavish party for him. All our friends in Snedens were invited—Joanne & Oscar too from New Jersey, other people from Manhattan—50 guests in all. I cooked the entire weekend before the party—two huge soup tureens of Bouf Bourginon, dozens of potatoes, bowls of salad and a large decorated flat cake. Olga got the gardeners in the area to truck over the 20-foot long refractory table from Mr. Gugler's house, ordered a 15-long loaf of French bread from the Palisades bakery. It was one of the best parties we'd ever had in Snedens. All the children joined in to help hang up decorations, set the table. It was early September so the weather was perfect to serve drinks and hors d'ourves on the lawn and in the gazebo.

An hour before the party, in comes Olga with Lenny carrying this big 3-foot high birdcage with a huge black bird inside. "Olga, what is this?" I gasped as they placed the cage on the front porch. "Maria, this is Avi. He's a mynah bird and he brings good luck (Olga was kind of into voodoo which I took with a grain of salt). You can teach him to talk. He already knows a few words." With that she said "hello" into the cage—the yellow-beaked bird, answered "hello." I giggled then asked her who it was for. "It's my birthday present for Bob." When Bob saw it a few minutes later he was so pleased. Olga and he had become close friends. Of course all our guests were captivated by this bird. It wasn't long before he started imitating all our voices. He was an extraordinary bird.

A few weeks after the party Mary Yates, the owner of the house, told us she was putting up the house for sale. After her husband's death in Israel while he was working as a newsman there, she decided to live permanently in Washington D.C. She offered the house first to us before she would put it on the market. We just didn't have the money. The only income we had was my salary from 'Teen'. I've always regretted missing that opportunity. As usual, Olga, came to our behalf and found us another rental just a stone's throw away—a lovely 3-story house on the Sneden's Triangle where Washington Spring Road split into two smaller roads—Woods Road that led into a deep wooded area, and River Road which led down to the Hudson River. Another road, Lawrence Lane, led up to a famous oceanography lab. The rent was the same—$300 a month. Here again we had to move but I was grateful that it wasn't outside the community. We could still keep our friends and feel secure. Because it was so close, we were able to settle in over the long Easter holiday.

Olga helped me to set up the kitchen and brought over some of her plants for the small greenhouse attached to the living room. I fell in love with that immediately. Heidi liked her small angled-ceiling on the third floor and Rick and Todd easily settled into their huge bedroom on the second floor. Bob's and my bedroom was in the back of the house—an extension that had built on with a huge studio and kitchen—like our own private quarters. We were all delighted with his new set-up. There was a beautiful lawn with trees and flowering bushes all around. We did miss the gazebo but the greenhouse made up for that. There was an outside porch next to the library room which was perfect to keep the mynah bird. We turned the library into a TV room. To the children's delight, there was a dumb-waiter that worked between the kitchen and den. The first thing the children did was sit in it and be pulled up between the two floors—that is until I said it was a no-no—only to be used for food. We all had fun with this contraption—Heidi or Todd would open the door to the dumb-waiter and yell down—"Mom, send up some cokes and chips," while they were watching TV. It was a magical house!

MARIE FENTON GRIFFING

Our life in Snedens was absolutely fantastic. There were parties for the grown-ups, parties for the children. I was so happy to be in such an uplifting community. The dark side—little did I know of the drugs that were being passed around to teens at the schools and even in our small hamlet.

Bob was still working on his Tarzan book but suddenly became involved in a new business venture—RTF INC.,a company he and Bob Meisner (close friend of ours) and another man put together to do public relations for cosmetic companies, radio people and one exciting project—a woman who was scheduled to fly across the Atlantic from New York to England by herself. I thought all these ventures were crazy, but they kept signing more clients and eventually got enough so they were able to rent office space on 54th St. in Manhattan opposite the Dorset Hotel. I was thrilled that they were seeing some success. I had wished this for years for Bob. It had arrived.

Olga was excited too about this new happening. She engaged a daytime housekeeper to take charge of the house, feed the children when we couldn't be there for dinner and do all the things Bob and I couldn't do during the day. At night we were in the house to keep track of the kids, but it wasn't the same. They were into TV and Bob and I were too pooped to watch with them. Sometimes, Bob had to fly to Florida or wherever to promote his business and I had to go to a distant place to cover a story for 'Teen'. I was beginning to realize things were becoming too complicated. I was having too many hangovers from all the business luncheons, cocktail parties. Little did I realize I was developing a drinking problem. I did know things had to change. Let Bob work fulltime at his new business and it was my turn to stay home.

In June, 1965 I gave my resignation to 'Teen' Magazine. That created a fury. First, my editor, Chuck Laufer, objected and refused. I calmed him down. Then it was Bob who tried to talk me out of it. I found myself rethinking my decision until one day Bob and Heidi walked into my office. I had asked him to take Heidi to Gimbels to buy a new winter coat. She stood there with this huge wool coat on, at least two sizes too big for her—both had smiles on their faces. My heart sank. I couldn't let on that it looked outlandish on her but I knew then it was time for me to go home and tend to important matters like this. I was not only missing out on all the fun of being a mother but also not being involved in decisions now that the kids were growing up.

Out of the blue, a publisher called me to do a book for them. McFadden-Bartell, a big publishing house in New York contacted me to write their first book on teenage beauty. It only took me three months to write it—mostly working at night. It was titled "From Teen to Twenty" and sold thousands of copies. When I received the check from the publisher, I realized it would safeguard us financially after quitting 'Teen'.

The 'Teen' staff threw a great farewell for me—gave me a beautiful gold charm bracelet as a remembrance—the charms were a martini glass, a typewriter, a tube of lipstick and a cover of 'Teen' magazine. I really felt sad about leaving this glamorous scene but it was a must for me.

After a few weeks at home, everyday I realized how much more Olga knew about my kids' activities than Bob or I did. Todd was not keeping up with his schoolwork—he and some of his friends were causing disruption in the classroom. The principal called me in to discuss it. I had a long talk with him and said I'd work with him to get him back on course. Then I saw that Heidi was trying to keep up with the dinner portions of Rick and Bob—she was gaining weight. I tried to curb this but it seemed our dinners together got to be too frustrating for her—she often jumped up from the table when I'd say something like "enough potatoes, Heidi!" And when I noticed Rick was acting supercilious at times and other times, moody and depressed, I asked Olga "When did this all happen?" "Marie," she answered, "he's a teenager now and you know that's how they are sometimes. Maybe you give him too much sugar in his food." I thought about it but knew that wasn't the real answer. I was concerned about my children's behavior and was glad to have the time to help solve these problems.

Things started to come together for me after a year quitting 'Teen. Working mostly in the evenings, I finished my beauty book. It was published and selling well In the mornings when the kids were at school, I went to my desk and worked on a few articles I was doing freelance. In the afternoons I'd put on another "hat" and tend to the house, go to Brownie meetings with Heidi, help Todd with his homework. Rick was still a puzzle to me. His grades were good at school, he helped me with the dishes at night, but I sensed an uneasiness about him. When I questioned him, he'd say nothing's wrong, but I worried.

In late '66, Prentice Hall, a big publishing house in New Jersey, called me to do a beauty book as a co-author with the popular teen black singer, Leslie Uggams. They apparently had seen my "From Teen to Twenty Book," and were impressed with it. I signed a contract and the next year

I was involved with researching the data about young black females. I did about five interviews with Leslie. Her grandmother was always around. I could see was well chaperoned. She was wonderful and so pretty. It was a fun book to do and I knew then this was the type of work I wanted—write at home and still close to my family. Perfect!

I found it difficult to get skin and hair advice for black teens from the big cosmetic, skin and hair care companies around the country. Most of them didn't have the products or the research I needed. I had to dig—Max Factor and Revlon helped with cosmetic tips as they had some beauty products for dark-skinned women. I kept after Leslie to give me more info, but it was Olga who clued me into the different beauty problems that black girls have compared to white teens. She rounded up a dozen youngsters and I talked with them in the house and was amazed at the wonderful information they gave me for my book. But one thing bothered me: I was told by my editor not to use the words Negro or black when referring to the reader . . . rather use the word "colored" or girl of color. It seemed strange to me but I got around it alright by seldom using any of those words. Since Leslie Uggams picture was on the cover, it was self-evident that the book was about beauty tips for black girls. It wasn't too long after my book came out that the beauty companies started devloping makeup, hair care, and skincare lines for blacks.

During one of my meetings with my editor at Prentice-Hall, I mentioned the book that Bob was working on about Tarzan and creator, Edgar Rice Burroughs. She became immediately interested and within two weeks, Bob had signed a contract. We couldn't believe our good luck. The two of us would each have a hard cover book published in 1967. Our savings account was growing—everything seemed right in the world. We both worked furiously on the books—arranged the study next to our bedroom with two desks, bought another typewriter. I would write a few hours during the day—Bob in the evening when he came home from New York (he only had to put in the finishing touches to his book since he had written most of it years before). Olga got us a friend of hers who came in to fix dinner, clean the house, do the wash—all the things I couldn't manage. I was glad at least that I was there for the kids when they came home from school. We still kept up our social life in Snedens For that year's Holloween party, Bob and I dressed up as Tarzan and Jane. A friend sewed the leopard-skin fabric costumes. Bob wore his for a publicity photo for the book. He even posed with a chimp sitting on his lap. The local newspapers heard about our success, kept us busy with interviews. We and the kids had a lot of fun with all this excitement. Suddenly, we were celebrities. One of the headlines in the local paper read "Beauty and the Beast Team Up in Snedens". Sometimes I would stop what I was doing and reflect on how the difficult decision I made to quit 'Teen turned out for the better.

After both books, *The Big Swingers* & *The Leslie Uggams Beauty Book with Marie Fenton* were published, Bob got more seriously involved with his TV public relations office in New York and I took advantage of the quiet time to enjoy my new role of being a suburban housewife. I was able to get close to some of the women in the area and for the first time realized how creative they were. Most of them were fortunate enough to pursue their artistic ambitions for years at home because of their financial stability—unlike me in the past. There was Paula, a former ballerina before she got married—she taught her skills to children in the area; Helen constructed exquisite doll houses; Frannie played violin in local concerts; Jean painted wonderful abstracts. Another Paula was involved in so many creative arts projects I marveled at her versatile abilities. Their children were friends with mine but it wasn't until now that I had the time to know these wonderful women. In a way, I was envious that I had not been able to follow one of my dreams like they had done—write the novel of the year. Maybe now I could take time out and do that.

One of the foremost artists I met was an elderly lady, Carlotta, who lived up the road from us. Olga called me one day and said I should walk over to visit Carlotta and see her paintings. I was a little embarrassed to just pop in on her but Olga insisted—and I came to know that when Olga insisted, one better comply or else she may put a "voo-do" on you. So we went to her greenhouse which was behind her house. It was a huge glass-enclosed studio filled with 8 x 10 foot canvases of her classical Grecian-style oil paintings. I was astounded by the fantastic talent of this 70-year-old woman. She and Olga embraced and I could see they were old friends. Carlotta became my friend that day and her sweet, calm personality from then 'til today soothed me during many trying times ahead. She was formidable.

It was a late summer morning in Snedens. I was going to take the children shopping for their school clothes—something I hadn't done in a long time. I was fussing in the kitchen, getting the dinner ready because I knew I would be spending the afternoon out at the stores. Heidi and Olga popped in the door, both grinning like the cat that ate the bird. In Heidi's arms was a cat—I guess I would have to describe it as a typical-looking

Tabby cat. "Mom, the cat has been roaming around the church for the last few days. It doesn't have a home. Somebody has probably dropped it off. Can I keep it?"

I looked at the three of them. I knew Olga had put Heidi up to it. Heidi always wanted a kitten but because of Bob's allergy to cat hair, we had to refuse her. "Oh Gosh, Heidi, I would love to have a cat but you know how they affect your father. Honey, just put it back where you found it. I'm sure someone will take care of it."

Heidi broke into tears, pleaded, "Please, Please!" I threw up my hands. "Olga, what are you doing—you know Bob will get angry about this."

She came toward me looking very stern. "Maria, Heidi will take care of the cat herself. She told me so. She will keep it up in her bedroom on the third floor, feed it there and I will show her how to let it out of her window to climb down the tree to the garden. It will not be in house. Bob doesn't even have to know she has it."

I took a deep breath, looked at the tears on Heidi's cheeks and said "Okay, but you've got to promise, Heidi, that you keep the cat out of the house except for your room." She nodded, smiling bright. So MaMa Cat, as we named her, became a new member of our household. She was our first cat.

More and more, Olga became involved with our family. She not only helped me acclimate into the community, but became such a good friend I could depend on her for whatever came up, whether it be a cup of sugar or to call her in an emergency (like taking Todd to the dentist). It wasn't long before she declared me her "sister"—a title I liked because I'd never had a sister.

I was busy working with the library volunteer staff that was planning the October plant sale, when Bob came home early from work with blood all over his suit. I gasped as I looked at his coat. "Duff, I had a few bad nose bleeds at the office and came home to change. I'm okay—I feel all right—just this dumb nose doesn't want to quit bleeding."

I was frightened by this and said he should go see the doctor right away. He said, no, it would stop and kept applying ice compresses on his nose and it did stop. He left to go back to the city. I was concerned and called a doctor myself. He said Bob should come in to see him which he did the next day. "Duff, the doctor thinks it's just a blockage in my nose. He took X-rays and it seems it's just an obstruction which might mean some minor surgery if the bleeding doesn't stop." I was relieved but something didn't ring right so I kept a close eye on Bob during the weeks ahead.

Sure enough, a week later, Bob had another nose hemorrhage. He stuffed his nose with cotton and sped away in his car for New York. I immediately called Olga and told her about the situation and if she knew of another doctor who specialized in nose/ears problems. She said that Dr. Bob who lived in Snedens was a famous doctor who practiced at Presbyterian Hospital in New York. I didn't want to impose on him and I knew Bob would get upset that I butted into his problem but I was very concerned. I got lucky. There was the traditional annual library party being held. I made it a point to scout out the guests to find if Dr. Bob was there. He was. I went over and introduced myself. We chatted a bit, and then I brought up my husband's continuous nose bleeds. He looked worried but said it could just be a polop in his nose which would require simple surgery to remove. I then called Bob over to talk to the doctor. When I heard that Bob would go the next morning to the doctor's office, I was relieved. I think Bob was also glad to get a second opinion.

What turned out to be one appointment became two, then three. Even though Bob seemed unconcerned when he'd come home from Presbyterian Hospital, I felt he wasn't telling me everything. "It'll be okay, Duff. They've set up a time for me to be operated on the end of October. I'll check in the night before and probably be out the next afternoon."

I didn't like what I was hearing but because Bob's nose bleeds were becoming more frequent, I knew something had to be done. One day when Olga stopped in I told her about the problem. There was a gloomy look on her face. Knowing she had a bit of the "fortune teller" in het, gave me the creeps. But when she saw my distress, she smiled again—"Maria, it will all turn out okay—don't worry. Remember, you and I have to make the costumes for the children's Halloween night." Oh gosh, I thought, that's the night I have to drive Bob to the hospital. Well, I reflected—I'll just get Bob settled in early and get back in time to help the kids get started on their trick and treating tour. I didn't let on to them that I was worried about him—just a simple operation on his nose. Little did I know my worst fears would come true.

It was Halloween afternoon that Bob checked into the hospital. I went with him to make sure all went smoothly. He had a nice room. We were both nervous. "Duff, don't worry," he said as we kissed goodbye. He understood I had to get the kids together for Halloween and would be there the next morning when he came out of his surgery. I felt very unnerved about this situation. I hated to leave him but I knew I had to get back to Snedens. I was scared. The children's trick 'n treating went well. As they were counting all the candies they had collected, I told them I was going to the hospital early the next morning to stay with their father until he would come home. They weren't terribly concerned.

When I arrived on the floor of Harkness Pavillion, a prestigious building in the Presbyterian Hospital complex on the west side of New York City, the nurse told me that Bob was still in the operating room. I asked "Isn't he supposed to be out by now?" She shrugged and gave me no answer. I sat down in a small waiting room. I had brought a book which I wanted to finish, so I served myself a cup of brew, took a deep breath and tried to relax in one of their plush chairs.

After an hour of waiting, I went to the nurses desk and asked what was going on. The nurse said I'd have to talk to the doctor but he was still in the operating room. Two more hours passed. The nurse came over and suggested that I go down to the cafeteria to grab a little lunch. By this time I was really getting nervous and even though I did follow her instructions, I could barely eat anything. When I came back to the floor, the nurse still had no information for me. Two more hours followed and I was now terribly distressed. Finally, I saw Dr. Bob approach me—he wasn't smiling.

He sat down next to me and said, "Marie, I assisted the surgeon who performed Bob's operation. It wasn't a good outcome. We found more than just a little growth in his nose. If you go to Bob's room—the nurse will direct you—Dr. Jacobs will explain everything."

I was in a stupor. The nurse led me into the room. Bob wasn't there. I sat down at the dressing table. For about five minutes I just stared into the mirror and tried to figure out what was going on and why this was happening. My face looked drawn, my eyes dazed. I felt numb. I thought about how neither Bob nor I, even the kids had ever been seriously ill. The door opened and in walked Dr. Jacobs still in his greens. He shook my hand and said he was pleased to meet me. He was not smiling. I looked up at him, turned the chair around as he sat down on the bed. "Mrs. Fenton, your husband has gone through a long, serious operation but he's doing okay. He'll be out of the recovery room soon but I must forewarn you that what you will see is not going to be pleasant for you—his whole face is bandaged. We knew there were more growths in his sinus cavity but we didn't know if they were cancerous or not or how large. We had told him before the operation of the possibility of cancer. However, the procedure to cut out the growth turned out to be so dangerous and complicated that he doesn't even expect what we have done."

I clenched my hands together and couldn't speak. He continued, "His cancer is called Melanoma—a skin cancer—one of the most difficult to cure. We have taken it all out, unfortunately with some bone structure and the cleft of his mouth."

I couldn't believe my ears. "Melanoma? I never heard of it! Will he live? What is going to happen to us?" I suddenly realized this was all real and not a dream. I began to cry. The doctor patted my shoulder. "Your husband is going to need all the support you can give him now—it'll be a long healing process. He does have a 50/50 chance that the tumor will not return. Be brave. Now, I have to return to my duties. I'll talk to you again when you come to visit—he'll be here for a couple of weeks. I understand you have three children. You'd better prepare them for this."

As he closed the door, I threw my head down on the table and wept like I had never done in my life. "Not my Bob—my poor Bob," I kept saying over and over.

An hour later, Bob was wheeled into the room. I couldn't believe my eyes. Only his hair showed above the white bandages that covered his whole face. There were openings for his eyes, nose and mouth. He looked like something out of a horror movie or wearing a mask like one of the trick and treat kids wore who came to my house for Halloween the night before. I leaned over and called his name, "Bob, honey, it's me, Duff. Can you hear me. He nodded his head slowly but he couldn't talk. I squeezed his hand, kissed it and laid my head on his chest. His hand came up and he touched my hair. I must have laid there for five minutes, then sat down on the chair next to the bed. For the next hour I tried to get a response from him, but nothing. The nurse walked in and suggested I go home until the next morning. She said he was heavily sedated and would be better the next day.

While driving back to Snedens on the Palisades Highway, all sorts of thoughts ran through my mind. How would I explain it to the children? Who should I call back in California—I had no family close by. I'd have to notify his business partners in New York. I could only see our wonderful, perfect world crumbling around us. We had both worked so hard to come to this point. Everything was looking up for us. It just didn't seem possible that this was happening to us. The tears were streaming so fast down my face that I almost swerved off the road on a curve. That brought me back to reality—"nothing must happen to me, now. I have to stay healthy and strong—for Bob and the kids," I thought to myself. As I drove into the driveway of our house, the lights were all on. I'd forgotten how late in the day it was. I put a smile on my face as I opened the kitchen door. I smelled pork chops.

The next few weeks that Bob was in the hospital were bone tiring for me what with the driving twice a day in and out of the city, tending to the children, keeping the house in some order plus coming to terms with this tragedy that had suddenly popped into my life. With Olga's help, I was working my way through it. Even though the kids were urging me to visit their father in the hospital, I was afraid of the startling effect that his bandaged face would have on them but knew they'd have to be prepared for more disastrous things that had resulted from the operation. When they saw him, I knew they were feeling sad and probably unbelieving of his bandaged face, but they bravely kept up a light conversation with him.

Over dinner, I tried to dispel some of their fears by talking about plans for Thanksgiving when their father would come home from the hospital. I asked Heidi if she'd help me make pumpkin pies and cranberry sauce and if Rick and Todd would cut up some of the fallen trees in our woods for the fireplace because I was sure it would be cold that day. We discussed what kind of dressing to make and if we should have mashed potatoes or sweet potatoes. They all voted for mashed. It was a beginning but when I said goodnight to them, I could still see the anguish in their eyes—my heart bled for them. I whispered, "It's going to be okay. Daddy is going to get well and we'll help him."

A few days before Bob came home, I walked into his hospital room and his bandages had just been removed. I tried not to look shocked but his face looked completely different. The whole left side was sunken, his left eye dropped down due to the bones they removed underneath it. Somehow I got a smile going, came over and gave him a kiss on his good cheek. "Well, look at you. Now I can see my man, face to face. "He grabbed my hand, lowered his face. "Honey, I know how awful I look. You don't have to pretend. I'm so sorry."

No matter how uplifting I tried to be, inwardly we both knew that our world had changed and there would be tough days ahead. He hugged me so tight when I left that I couldn't catch my breath. I realized he would need me now like he'd never needed me before and that we would have to be strong to beat this horrible disease. I questioned myself—would I do right for him, for the children, for me? I needed someone to talk to.

A wonderful dinner was awaiting us when I brought Bob home. I had told the children about Bob's disfigured face and not to be startled by it. They were wonderful—giving him kisses and hugs and pulling him into the living room to tell him about their school work and happenings in Snedens while I set up the dinner that Olga had so lovingly prepared. Because Bob could not swallow regular foods due to the removal of the cleft in his mouth, I put some of the bean soup through the blender for him. He was smiling as he came to the table and I poured everyone's soup. When he tried to eat, some of the soup he couldn't get down his throat came spilling out of his nostrils—the children gasped. Bob quickly got up from the table, wrapping his napkin over his nose and walked slowly up the stairs to the bedroom. I went after him and sat with him on the bed.

"It's okay, Bob, it'll get better." I said as I patted him on the back. "The doctor says you have to practice eating to slide the food down your throat without it coming up through your nose until you can be fitted for a specially made cleft for your mouth. You must keep eating to gain back your strength."

"Yeah," he answered, "what a mess I am—like a baby, dribbling all over his chin." All I could do was tell him how much the children and I loved him that we needed him and things would get better. Lo and behold, little by little, they did.

CHAPTER FIVE

MY STRUGGLING YEARS
(1968-1972)

1. MY WOMEN FRIENDS RALLY AROUND

THANKSGIVING, THE CHRISTMAS of 1967 came and went. Bob's recuperation was going well. He finally got the prosthesis fitted for the cleft in his mouth, was eating well now, gaining back his lost weight and feeling his self again. Even though he had to go for periodic checkups at the doctor, he was back at work in New York with his company. I made it a point to drive him in and out of the city so the trip wouldn't tire him. I was still nervous about a recurrence of his illness; I'd check out the bathroom sink to see if any blood was around—in case he had another nosebleed. So far so good. I was still nervous. When Bob was working in the city, I'd get visits from my women friends in Snedens. This allowed me to sit over a cup of coffee or a glass of wine and release my fears. They listened, comforted me—I needed that.

Paula D. and Paula B., Margaret, Joan, Gail, Sally, Sue and a few others kept me on track. Margaret restarted our Saturday night poker game, others had us over for dinner every weekend. We were back in circulation again.

Out of the blue, Heidi's cat had six beautiful kittens—all different colors. She gave birth in Heidi's bedroom. We moved them over to the empty room across the hall. We were so excited; they were so darling. Even Bob said he would like to see them. So one day out in the fresh air on the patio where he would be free of any allergy attack, we brought out MaMa Cat and her brood. There's nothing cuter than seeing little kittens playing together—it gave much joy to Bob and to all of us too. When Heidi and I had weaned them, I knew I had to give them away—but how, to whom? Paula D. suggested we take them down to the supermarket, Grand Union, and capture an audience outside the doors. So one day, Heidi and I put four of them into a box and took them to the store (we kept one beautiful yellow/white striped one whom we called Calico and a teeny black and white one that looked like it would not survive plus I knew no one would take him—we called him Mite). I remember that Heidi was unhappy with all this. While I stood outside the store, holding the box of kittens, shouting out to the people passing in and out "Genuine thoroughbred kittens Free!" she went into the store to hide. Within a half hour I had given away all of them. Now we only had left, MaMa Cat, Calico and Mite. I told Heidi it was important she keep the kittens out of the lower floors of the house which she did. One day she called me up to her bedroom and pointed to the window. "Look, Mom, MaMa Cat has taught Calico and Mite how to climb out to the tree and down to the garden—isn't that fabulous?" I hugged her and said, "It's fantastic! We have an amazing family!"

I began to see a closeness develop between Bob and Rick. There were times in years past that I could see a disappointment on Bob's face when he was trying to teach Rick how to throw a baseball, a football or get him interested in any sports. Rick tried his best to please his father but I knew that his heart wasn't into it. Rick was a very sensitive boy with interests in poetry, books of all kinds, music. Now that Bob was doing commercials, working with actors, writing scripts, they had a common interest and Rick became involved discussing programs for Bob's business. They would spend hours on ideas. It pleased me no end to see their heads huddled together over the coffee table. At the same time, I could see Heidi trying to compete for her father's attention, especially at dinnertime when Bob and Rick would start talking about the media. Todd would grab Bob's attention about his Little League baseball games, the new bike he wanted for his birthday or ask his help on building a clubhouse in the woods for him and his friends. Many times, Heidi, would sulk over her food during these conversations. I noticed she was being left out and tried to make a plan to include her. So, with the suggestion of a friend Joanne who lived nearby, I talked her into joining the Girl Scouts. She liked that and became a Brownie. I went to club meetings—even bought a sewing machine so we could make simple skirts and did other things that she could be proud of and show her father. My kids were growing up and I could see they were demanding more attention from both Bob and me. We gave our all.

It was early summer of '68. We took a much-needed two-week vacation to Martha's Vineyard and had a great time. Bob's business was going well. Then suddenly one morning after we'd come back from the Cape, Bob's nose started to hemorrhage and I rushed him to the hospital in New York. His doctor told us the bad news—there was a recurrence of the tumor. The next two months are somewhat a blur to me. I recollect driving back and forth to Harkness Pavillion in New York for

Bob's various treatments and experiments with new drugs. He was going downhill fast. Finally, he was stabilized and back home in his own bed. Bob's sister, Ruth, and sister-in-law Bernice came for a week to visit us from the West. They were a big help—cooking dinners, sitting, talking with Bob, taking the children to movies. I unfolded an old army cot we had stored in the attic and made my bed in the office just outside our bedroom so that Bob would have our bed all to himself. That way I could be nearby if he needed me. He was in much pain.

One night after Ruth and Bernice left, I gathered the kids together in the living room and alerted them that their father was very, very sick and I believed we were going to lose him. They just sat there and looked at me. I held back my tears and then told them that maybe there would be a miracle and things would get better. They didn't.

In the middle of August 1968, I called my close friend, Paula D., for help. Bob was hemorrhaging and I needed someone to drive us to the hospital. She and her husband were at the house in five minutes. I sat in the back of the car, holding a towel over Bob's face to stop the bleeding. All I could do is check him back into the hospital and wait.

One morning, my friend, Joan, came over and we sat on the porch steps to talk. She handed me a $2000 check. "Marie, it's to help get you through this difficult time." At first, I refused . . . then thought of all the un-paid bills on my desk. I finally accepted the money and told her I'd pay her back as soon as I could (I did a year later). For the next week, I spent most of the days sitting next to Bob's bed. I kept worrying about the children but Olga and other women friends kept an eye on them, brought food over, went shopping for me, and would stop in unexpectedly, either at the hospital or at home, to give me a smile a hug, and words of support. I was in such a panic, trying to comfort my dying husband, trying to ease his pain (only the pills did that), worrying about the children, paying the on-going medical bills that were flowing in, that I barely had time to really think about what feelings my children were having. He was failing fast. One late afternoon I arrived at the hospital hours later than usual because I had so many things to tend to. The nurses were frantic when they saw me. "Mrs. Fenton, where have you been. Your husband is very bad." I walked into his room and I could see he was in a coma. I couldn't reach him no matter how loud I talked or how I touched him. Then came the long night: I sat on a chair near his bed, still knitting on the afghan I had started when he first came to the hospital. The hours passed. I would lift my eyes from my needlework and gaze soberly at this wonderful man I had shared my life with for 20 years—our 21st wedding anniversary would be Aug. 27—it was now Aug. 21. His breathing was shallow. His body had shrunk to a thin shell of the robust, strong young man that I had only a year before.

As I knitted and pearled along with my yarn, I was someway relieved that I had told Bob a few days before how much I loved him, what our life together meant to me and that I would never forget him. He never admitted to me that he was dying . . . like when he first got the cancer, he said he would beat it and wouldn't mention his "death sentence" to the children. I went along with him but did try in a delicate way, without going against his wishes, to forewarn the kids of impending doom for their father. He wouldn't allow the children to come visit him this time in the hospital. "I don't want them to see me in this state," he'd state firmly. I was the messenger between him and the kids. The phone conversations helped, especially the one from Heidi telling him about the new puppy she got from Olga . . . she named her Tanya. We took a photo of the dog for him to keep on his bed stand.

As I was reflecting on all of this, I went over to Bob and just stared at his quiet face. Then I went to the window, looked out at the bright lights of the city, gazed up at the star-studded sky and prayed, "God, please take him . . . don't let him suffer any more." I suddenly heard a loud gasp and ran to his bed. He was not breathing. I pressed the emergency button and the nurse arrived immediately. She nodded her head . . ."He has died." I grabbed his hand tightly, laid my head on his chest and sobbed. Twenty minutes later when the hospital attendants came for him, they directed me to the office where I was to sign for Bob's death. At 10:30 p.m. the corridors were quiet. I signed the necessary papers but was not asked for a check, nothing now. I was grateful for that. I had to run back upstairs because I had forgotten my knitting bag. As I approached the room, I saw two men wheeling a cart down the hall with a white covered body on it—Bob. I started to cry—I waved goodbye.

Somehow, I found my way to my car, drove over the George Washington Bridge and onto the Palisades highway. I tried to drive without going over the yellow lane. The tears were streaming down my cheeks and my vision was blinded by them, I kept thinking how I would break this tragic news to my children. Even though I had tried to forewarn them, I also realized they were not prepared to receive the bad news.

MARIE FENTON GRIFFING

As I drove in the driveway, I saw the kids still awake in the kitchen playing Monopoly. I took another deep breath as I opened the back door, gave them a hug. "How's Daddy doing?" they asked. Only Todd and Heidi were there. "Where's Rick?" I asked. He was on his way home from a rehearsal for a school play. I ushered Todd and Heidi into the living room to the couches. "I have some very sad news. I want you to be strong about this. Your Daddy died tonight, very peacefully, without any pain. We will always love him and miss him very much. I'm here for you now. It will be hard for all of us." I sat back on the couch and looked at them both for a minute. Their faces were blank for a moment; they did not accept the tragic words I said. My heart was aching for them. After a few seconds, I approached both of them, hugged them, rocked them as I had done when they were babes crying at night. We held each other for a few minutes. My tears were flowing. Todd started to cry, then Heidi. It was a very sad night.

2. OLGA—TO THE RESCUE—AGAIN!

O LGA WAS THE first adult I saw the next morning after Bob's death. We hugged and cried when I told her the sad news. She said the Presbyterian minister at our local church in Snedens would be coming to help me arrange all the details for Bob's cremation and burial; also if I wanted to have a memorial service.

"Marie, you should have a memorial service soon. Bob has many friends and it's important for the children to see his life acknowledged." advised Olga. I agreed. When the young minister came to the house, we sat down at the kitchen table and worked out a ceremony. It wasn't easy because Bob was Jewish and I didn't want anything Christian read even though he never practiced his religion. But I was concerned about his oldest brother and wife who were coming from Syracuse for the ceremony. No other relatives would attend. He quieted my qualms and said he would read from the Old Testament.

The phone was ringing constantly with calls. Rick was very supportive and answered most of them. When the local newspaper called, he gave them all the necessary info for the obituary column. He sat down with Olga and prepared an announcement of the memorial service and posted it in the Palisades library and post office. Through the grapevine we had reached most of the community.

Meanwhile, Olga put me in touch with the director of the Rockland cemetery and I picked out a plot to bury Bob's ashes and have a gravestone made. That occasion would take place a few days after the memorial service. I had not prepared or even given much thought to all this aftermath of Bob's dying. Without Olga, the minister and other women friends . . . . and my older son, Rick, I don't think I could have handled it alone.

The day of the memorial service arrived. I woke with a start and suddenly realized my husband was gone and I was going to say farewell to him. I rushed to the kids' bedrooms and told them to get up right away so we wouldn't be late to the church. Heidi turned over in her bed and said she wasn't going. I sat down on the side of her bed, stroked her hair and told her "Honey, I need you to come with me—it'll only be for an hour." She covered her head with the blanket and kept saying, "No, No." I left hoping she would come around. I then went to the kitchen and set up some boxes of cereal and milk on the table for their breakfast. I went upstairs to take a shower and get dressed, walking around in a daze.

Olga had arranged for Margaret, my dear friend and fellow poker-player, to play the harp for the ceremony along with one of her musician friends, Manny, who would accompany her on the viola. They were both well-known musicians. I knew whatever they chose to play would be beautiful. Olga also asked around for someone to donate bouquets of flowers for the church. Sue, my other friend in Snedens, immediately ordered a lovely array of white mums.

As I was trying to choose an appropriate dress to wear, Olga came into the bedroom, gave me a hug and said she'd help me pick out something. I didn't want to wear black. She suggested a soft blue-black-beige flowered sheath and black pumps. I knew that it would be warm in the church. "I've told the other children what to wear but Heidi is still in bed. I don't know what we're going to do about her." said Olga. Standing behind me as she zipped up my dress, she advised that Rick was calling the deli and ordering cold meats, drinks, etc. for a gathering following the service. My hands were shaking as I started to put on my makeup. My eyes were so swollen and red from crying that I couldn't apply my mascara. "Wear those pretty sunglasses you always wear," said Olga. "If Mrs. Kennedy can wear them to the President's funeral, so can you." I dug into my dresser drawer and slipped them on—that made me feel better.

When we went downstairs, Todd and Rick looked so nice in their sports jackets, white shirts and ties. I hugged them both and said we'd wait for someone to come over from the church when it was ready for us to arrive. I ran upstairs to Heidi's bedroom on the third floor. Her puppy, Tanya, was sleeping on the floor next to her. "Heidi, please, get up an dress or you'll be late for your Daddy's services." No response. I sighed and went back to the living and told Olga I couldn't raise Heidi. "Let me try again," she said. I don't know what she said to Heidi but 15 minutes later, Heidi walked into the room, all dressed. She wasn't smiling. I went over, gave her a hug and a kiss. "It'll be okay, Heidi," I said. "I know it's a sad day but I want us to go as a family. Thank you."

When the minister came over to take us to the church, he asked Rick and I to hold hands and Todd & Heidi to hold hands as we walked two by two down the isle to the front pew.

The service was quiet and meaningful. My friend, Dorothy, wrote a poem about Bob and read it at the service; Bob's friend, Bob Meisner, read another poem sent by Boyd Upchurch our friend in Los Angeles, who had been our best man at our wedding in Mexico, and another by Stan Noyes who had lived nearby us on the French Riviera . . . . all writers who dearly loved Bob.

Not Heidi, Rick or Todd shed a tear during the service and strangely, not I either. Seems we were all done in and cried out by this time. The gathering in the house was good for me and I think the kids too. Over 100 people came. There was a huge 10 foot poster of Bob in his Tarzan outfit still standing in the bar room. Friends at his office had it made while he was in the hospital and brought it to him, kind of a joke gift. He loved it so I brought it home and it had been propped up there for weeks. It almost seemed as if he were looking down on us, smiling and blessing us all.

This important day in late August, 1968 came to an end. While the children were sleeping in their beds, I stayed awake in my bedroom, listening to the radio and writing some poetry. Diane Warwick's new hit "One Less Egg to Fry" came on and hit home. I wept and wept; finally dozed off. My last thoughts: "Where do I go from here? Do we move back to California to be with my family? Do I dare uproot my children again when they have made good friends, and me, too? As the warm, balmy breezes swept through the open window and over my bed, I quietly said to myself . . . . "I'll think about it tomorrow." Then I laughed out loud, "My God, that sounds like Scarlet!"

3. LUCIE—LEADING ME THROUGH MY TRANSITION

A WEEK AFTER Bob's memorial service, the minister, Rick and I went to Rockland Cemetery to bury his ashes in the plot. I begged Heidi and Todd to come with us but they refused and I certainly couldn't drag them there. I was not only unhappy by their decision but worried about their mental state. I only hoped for the best.

The plot was in a choice spot . . . on the highest knoll of the rolling hills of the cemetery, overlooking the Hudson River. I had brought a bouquet of peonies I'd picked from the garden. The minister placed the canister in the grave, said a short prayer while Rick and I held hands. Then we both sprinkled some flower petals atop the canister. I still wore my dark glasses to hide my grief. We left in the bright sunlight and returned home.

One night soon after the burial, I talked with the children at the dinner table. School would be starting soon and I'd been thinking a "conference" about our future plans was in order. "Okay, let's discuss where we are going from here." I quietly said to them, hoping for a response. Nobody said anything, They're heads were bowed over their plates. They pretended to be eating vigorously. "Listen up," I spoke out more firmly. "This house we've been renting has been put up for sale and although I'd like to buy it, I do not have the finances. So, I've been thinking of picking up stakes and moving back to Los Angeles. We'll be close to grandma, my brother, Aunt Bernice and lots of my old friends. I think it would a good idea. What do you say?"

"No, No, No," they all chorused. I knew right then that I was going to be out voted. Suddenly they became aware of the importance of the situation.

"Okay, then, give me your thoughts on what we should do as a family?" They all started to talk at once.

"I can't leave Phil and my friends," voiced Todd.

"What will happen to my cats and Tanya?" Heidi shouted out.

"I'm going to graduate this coming year and want to go to college in New York. I'm making good grades!" said Rick.

My heart opened up to them. In years past when Bob and I moved from Europe to California, then from California to New York, they never had a voice in our decisions. This time I felt it important that they make their own decisions on what was best for them. I would support them.

So it was agreed that we'd stay put until the sale of the house came up. Meanwhile, we'd look for another place to rent in the area. I raised my can of coke at the table and we all toasted to the decision. "One for all—and all for One," I jokingly said. There were smiles all around but inside I was scared to handle all this by myself. As a last parting word, I told them that this meant that I had to go out and look for a job so I could support the household since my finances were in bad shape. I said that I couldn't be around as often as I had been and that they would have to be good children and get along on their own while I was working. I let them know that Bob had a small amount of life insurance but it wouldn't come through for another six months or so. None of that didn't seemed to bother them; they were just happy about staying in Snedens. Later that night I phoned my mother and the other relatives in California that we had decided to stay in New York. None was pleased but did offer help if I needed it. I was grateful for their support but realized that this time I would have to fend for myself.

Early the next morning I started to make calls to editorial offices in New York to let them know I was available as a beauty/health writer. Then I dusted off my faithful, old typewriter machine and began writing inquiries, my resume to the magazines and newspaper in Manhattan. It wasn't long before I received a couple of responses. For the next couple of weeks I spent going in and out of New York City being interviewed. Even though it had only been three years since I quit my job with 'Teen Magazine, it seemed that "Marie Fenton" had been forgotten. That's New York, out of sight, out of mind. I did get a few "bites" but not to my liking. Then I started figuring out the time involved just traveling back and forth to the city. With a 9 to 5 job, I wouldn't get home to 7 or 8 p.m. every day. It was not so much Heidi and Rick I was worried about—they always had after school activities, but it was Todd, who was only 9 years old and would be home early at 3 p.m. In the years past, Bob was at home for the kids when I worked for 'Teen. And a baby sitter wouldn't work. I had to change my plans from working in the city (even though I realized the salaries were better there) and look for something in the area.

One morning after the kids left for school, I dressed up in my best "woman's executive outfit" prepared my briefcase with my writings and resume and set off to The Rockland Journal News in Nyack, only 15 minutes away. The moment I opened the door to the Editorial offices, I heard the click-clack of typewriters, the noise of the AP-UP transmitter machines, the chatter and laughter, smell of printing ink mixed with cigarette smoke—all of which brought back memories of when I worked at the Los Angeles Times in the late 1940s.

I really don't know if it was sheer luck or God was watching over me but when I had completed my interview with the Editor, he asked me if I could start on Monday as Women's Editor because the editor they had was retiring. My mouth almost fell open. "But, of course," I said with delight. He then introduced me to Lucie, the Women's Editor who was leaving, and said we'd work together for a couple of days so I could get the "hang" of handling the job. Lucie was a pretty blonde-haired lady a few years older than I. I liked her right away.

"Marie, I've worked here for years and I need some time for myself, my husband and my daughter," Lucie said as she handed me a few issues of the newspaper. "Study these over the weekend . . . you have to do the layouts too and there are three reporters on the staff. Deadlines are quick. You have to be in at 7:30 to check over the mats for the paper which comes out at noon . . . then prepare your copy and layouts for the following day." She sounded so confident; I already felt I could handle her job. I relaxed, thanked her and said I'd see her Monday.

When I sat down to dinner with the children that night, I told them about my new job; they were thrilled. "That's great, Mom" said Todd. "Way to Go!" Rick exclaimed and Heidi gave me a hug. "You can do it, Mom!" I told them that my job begins at 7:30 so I could see Todd off on the bus to school and that I would be back at 3:30 p.m. My salary was about $5000 less than New York salaries but I would get low health insurance coverage. That was a relief for me because since Bob's death I couldn't get anything less than $3000 a year to protect ourselves.

I practiced page layout, headline writing, caption writing all weekend long. I was excited about this new job. My friends in Snedens were happy for me. I even won $20 at the Saturday night poker game—a good sign!

For the next two weeks I threw myself into work. Lucie guided me through all the office procedures, introduced me to my reporter staff, photographers who would work with me on assignments and the men upstairs in the printing room. I made a lot of mistakes but Lucie was there for me, even stayed an extra week. Little by little I got the hang of the daily routine. Meeting my daily deadline, editing the stories the reporters brought in, assigning new articles was a true learning experience for me.

Lucie was fantastic. She wanted me to succeed; never got upset with me for my mistakes; gave me insights to future story ideas. It was so different from my job as Assistant Society Editor of the Los Angeles Times. This time I was in charge. And there was no comparison to the magazine business I'd been in at 'Teen—there I had a monthly deadline . . . . here it was a daily deadline. But there was gratification in seeing my women's pages appear daily and people congratulating me on them. Even, Dick, my Editor-in-Chief of the paper, liked my work.

After Lucie cut "the cord" and left me to fend on my own, we still met for lunch once a week at a nearby pub and would discuss my progress and problems with my work over a Dry Rob Roy (a new Scotch drink for me). Without her help and support, I know I couldn't have made it. We became fast friends.

My landlady told me a month later that my house had been sold and gave me a month's notice to vacate. She was wonderful in that she held back selling the house until I got situated in my job and I appreciated that. I soon discovered her son, Bob Nichols, was the managing editor of the Rockland Journal News. He was a wonderful person, a good writer and aside from Lucie, offered me assistance when he saw I needed it. I often wondered if he, in any way, had something to do with my getting the job.

Out of the blue, a house in Snedens came up for sale. It was a low ranch structure, half the size of our big house on the triangle, but yet half the price. It had a large living room, dining area, small kitchen and two small bedrooms but it was on an acre of beautiful land on the edge of Snedens as you drove out to the highway, 9W. When I took the children over to peruse the property, I could see that the house was a "let-down" for them. "Mom, it's so small. How can we all live there with only two bedrooms," Rick questioned. I could see that Heidi and Todd were not pleased with my choice either but I knew I had to move in a month and there were no other places available. Plus I saw a challenge here. I was hoping Bob's life insurance check would come in shortly. Even though it only was for $25,000, it was enough for a down payment plus enlarging the house. With advice from Chappy, an architect friend of mine, I would be able to build another bedroom, a den, enlarge the kitchen for a low cost.

So, one night when all of us were at the dinner table, I told them I was planning to buy the house . . . . "It is going to be OUR house and we're going to make it really nice and comfortable for us. Remember, guys, you said you wanted to stay here in Snedens. You have your wish." The kids now seemed to understand and we talked excitingly about the changes to the house.

I had heard through the grapevine that many others had put in a bid for the Snow house but my friends had pressured the owner to accept mine. Now all I had to do was to receive my check from the life insurance company. A week later when I picked up my mail at the local post office, lo and behold was the check for $25,000. I kissed it, then started to cry. "This will get me through. I'm going to be okay now." I drove home quickly and that night the children and I started to make plans for our move.

It was over Easter break in 1969 when we moved all our stuff from the big house on the triangle to the little house in the woods. I had the place painted and all ready for us to live in. Rick, Heidi and Todd got a lot of their friends to help. The heavy furniture was transported by truck. Even though the little house was only a block away, the dish, pots, etc. cartons were too heavy for one person to cart over. Gail came by and suggested that all the kids make an assembly line from the big house to the small house and pass the boxes from one to another. I thought it was a good idea and the kids thought that too. So, she stayed in the big house and handed out the boxes to the kids who lined up along the road to the little house. I awaited the arrival of the boxes in the little house. It all was done with some help from friends.

Lucie, my friend, whose job I replaced at the Journal News, returned to take over my desk for a couple of days to help me out. My Editor, Dick, gave me the okay. We settled ourselves into the little house and I was ready to go back to work. Heidi wasn't too happy sharing her bedroom with me but I told her I had hired a contractor to immediately start construction of another bedroom, TV room and enlarging the kitchen.

Once a week, Lucie and I lunched. We talked about my work and progression but now I opened up to her regarding personal matters. I was worried about Rick. It seemed he was rushing into college too fast and

I noticed a more-than-usual hyperactivity in him. She reassured me that it was because he was trying to make me proud of him. He had been declared Valedictorian of the graduating class and had been accepted at the drama school at Northwestern University, the one he wanted. I was aware of his acting talent. As the lead in the high school play, Camelot, he was terrific.

"Marie, try to get him to go to NYU or one of the good schools in upstate NY. You know the first year in college can be tough for kids." advised Lucie. I brought that message home to Rick but he was so adamant about going to the "best" acting school in the states, I gave in and said okay. Little did I realize that was my downfall. Little did I know he was already into drugs.

There was another problem. Even if minor, I had to solve it. MaMa Cat would not leave the big house to come over to the little house. Her kittens adjusted well but she kept living in the big house. The new owners there were distressed and so was I. I didn't know what to do. Every time we captured her and shut her inside the little house, she would somehow escape and run back. Finally, she ended up living in the church across from the big house. The minister said it was okay. It finally worked out well. She lived in the church and the kids who waited every morning for their school bus would feed her pieces of their tuna sandwiches. I wondered if their mothers ever questioned why the same kind of sandwich each day. What a saga!

I had neglected to have our dog, Tanya, spayed. It was spring and so there we were with a pregnant dog. My friend, Lucie, came to my aid. She bought me a low wicker basket and told me to put it in a corner of the kitchen. "Marie, you'll know when she's going to give birth. She starts scratching, turning in circles on the blankets in the basket." One day her time came and she started doing what Lucie predicted. I had just come home from work and quickly called Lucie. "I'll be right over." she said.

We all watched as Tanya gave birth to five beautiful pups. They ranged in colors from one like her, two pure black, two brown/black/white. Within a few days all the puppies had been claimed, except we kept one pure black for us. Lucie, who had guided us all through the birthing process, advised not to give them away until they had been weaned. That meant we had to take shifts feeding them when their mother knew her milk had run dry. So, I took the morning shift . . . opened the sliding door of the kitchen where they hung out. The puppies came running to me, jumping and scratching my legs. After that, I slipped on my high-knee snow boots. What a fashion picture I made in my short silky nighty and black leather boots. Within a few weeks the puppies were weaned, given away accept for the black son of Tanya. Now we had two cats and two dogs and Avi, the minnah bird. Give me strength!

My work at the Journal News was very satisfying. I was handling it all my own, enjoying assigning stories to my reporters and doing the layouts. It had been almost a year since Bob's death and during our weekly lunches, Lucie said I should give myself time for social activities instead of just concentrating on my work and family.

"Lucie," I responded when we talked about this, "I'm so tired when I get home. There's Todd's Little Leaque baseball games I like to attend; Heidi and Rick have other demands. Plus after paying the bills, etc., not much left to party with. The only socializing I do is play poker every Saturday night in Snedens—thank God for that. I get a few laughs out of it, enjoy being with my friends, and usually come out a winner."

"Listen up, Marie," Lucie said one day at lunch. There's a big dinner that the Gannet newspaper chain (owner of the Rockland Journal News) is giving next Thursday. It will be a good chance for you to get out, have some fun and maybe meet a guy."

I thought about it. Dick Smith, my Editor and Bob Nichols, the Managing Editor invited me too. I accepted. Since I had not dressed up "fancy" for a long time, I didn't know what to wear. I chose a loose-fitting short white dress, black patent low-heeled shoes. I felt out of place in the large dining room with over 100 journalists but my friends across the table from me, set me at ease. A handsome man sat down on the chair next to mine. He was a little older than I with grey-peppery hair and a charming manner. His name was Jack and said he was an Editor at a Gannett newspaper across the Hudson in Tarrytown. After speeches and a delicious dinner, a band started to play dance music and he asked me to dance. I accepted and after we got on the floor, I realized the title of the song . . . one of my favorites by Tony Bennett . . . "Because of You." It put me in a romantic mood and when Jack held me tight to him, I felt I would melt. It had been such a long time that a man had held me close. Over an hour later, we had danced through five wonderful 1950s tunes. As the crowd started to disperse, Jack asked me back to his apartment across the river. I glanced at my co-workers on the other side of the table. They just smiled at me. I excused myself and went to the ladies room where I looked at myself in the mirror and thought to myself, "Am I ready for this?" I decided I was not. I returned to the table and politely told Jack that I couldn't because I had to get up early for work—which was not a lie.

The next morning when I was getting dressed, I stood for a few minutes in front of my full-length mirror and told myself, "Marie, you still look okay. Maybe, one day, you'll meet someone as wonderful as Bob." I knew then that I wasn't ready for a romantic escapade.

The next Friday when Lucie and I met for lunch, we giggled about the happening at the dinner. "Marie, you should have gone for it. I know Jack—he's a good catch." I replied, "I don't think I'm a good catch, Lucie—at least not at this time.

The fall of 1969 was settling in. With much trepidation, I drove Rick to LaGuardia airport and put him on a plane for Evanston, Illinois to start his freshman year at the Drama School at Northwestern University. I asked him to write often and that I'd send him a ticket to come home for Christmas. He was like a youngster waiting in line for an ice cream cone. As I drove home, crying at times because I knew I would miss him, I was worried how he would fare with so many new young people. This was his dream. He knew it and he wanted desperately to follow it through.

Meanwhile, Heidi was a senior at Tappan Zee High and I could see she felt a bit of relief now that her "famous" brother was out of the school. Their sibling rivalry was getting too much for me. Todd entered as a freshman. I hoped he would adjust. Heidi said she would keep an eye on him. Time would tell. I was hoping to put Todd in the private school where his friend, Philip, was enrolled, but finances would not allow me. I had already taken out a student loan for $5,000 for Rick's tuition; the credit cards were adding up.

My work at the newspaper was doing well but the salary didn't meet my needs. The additions to my little house cost me most of Bob's insurance money. I had to carry the monthly mortgage, plus pay for heating, electricity, clothes for all of us. The bills never stopped. I kept up with the holiday celebrations, birthday parties for Heidi and Todd. Also it became necessary to buy a new car. I began to lay awake at night worrying how I would get out of this terrible financial crisis.

One afternoon, when Lucie and I met for lunch, she suggested I look for a job in Manhattan at a newspaper, magazine or advertising office. "Marie, Heidi and Todd are busy in school until 5 p.m. with their social and athletic activities. They are able to fix their own dinner. Just lay it out for them." I thought about it but was nervous about leaving them alone. Also, I had made some good friendships at the newspaper and I really liked my job. However, I did write a few letters and sent them out together with my resume to various publications in New York. I doubted whether I would hear from them, but I tried anyway.

The late 60s were difficult years for young people with the Vietnam war, the coming of age of the flower children . . . the youth became a "me" generation. It was not only my children who reacted to this dramatic change of thought and feelings, but kids around the country were battling the society, questioning decisions being made by "old people." They wanted a voice of their own . . . they had been growing in numbers since the baby boom of the early 50s. I not only saw it coming in my own children but in their friends. I heard about marijuana parties in Snedens and what amazed me that even some of the parents were joining in. I felt absolutely helpless, confused about how I alone would handle this new drug happening in my territory. When Rick came home for the Christmas holidays, I noticed a dramatic change in his appearance and manner. He was extremely hyper, dressed in the hippie clothes of the kids I'd see on TV. I cautioned Heidi, Rick and Todd one night during Christmas Eve. "Please, guys, don't get hooked on drugs. You're too young. You'll regret it." No answer, just a nod of their heads.

"Yeah, Mom," Rick suddenly spoke up, "You and your friends drink booze. That's a drug, you know!" I didn't expect that rebuke, and it hurt me.

"Listen up, we do drink cocktails before dinner, wine at dinner, and cognac or whatever afterwards, but we don't get "stumble-down" drunk. We only party on weekends, have fun but it doesn't destroy our ability to cope with the responsibilities of our lives."

I realized their accusations were correct but what we were doing as adults was an accepted social act, one that had been going on for many years. I saw no wrong in that. Unfortunately, there were no forewarnings on TV or the radio or other media about kids and drugs or centers where you could go for help. In fact, I didn't know anything about drugs, their names or their dangers. I was naïve, and didn't know anything about this terrible problem that was growing. I just hoped my kids were not using.

I gave every spare hour I could to attend to the needs of Heidi and Todd who were both living at home. One morning, I rose early before going to work to prepare 50 crepe suzettes for a special school program Heidi was involved in—International Food Day. I had prepared the batter the night before, and woke Heidi up at 6 a.m. to help me fry the crepes;

roll them with different kinds of jams inside. She got "A" for her project. I could see that she was enjoying the art of cooking and shortly after that we prepared all sorts of dishes together and I took photos of each dish and made up a special cookbook for her. It was fun.

During this time, we lost Tanya's black pup, John. He just disappeared. Heidi and I drove all over Snedens trying to find him, but to no avail. Now we were down to one dog, two cats and one bird.

One day when I went to the post office I found a letter from my old friend Ben from USC. He said he had received my inquiry/resume and wanted to talk with me about a job opening as a copywriter at Good Housekeeping Magazine in New York City. He was a Managing Editor there at the time. I immediately called Lucie and told her about this new happening in my life.

"Go for it, Marie," she said without pause. "You'll not only be making more money but you'll be working in the most exciting city in the world." I told her I had worked in Manhattan with 'Teen' Magazine.

"Yes, I know, but this is a giant of a magazine. You'll need a new wardrobe. I'll go shopping with you."

I laughed, "Lucie, don't jump the gun. I haven't accepted yet."

I realized my family was getting to be an expense but I wanted them to have the best education. That was foremost for me. I knew nothing about copywriting. Lucie convinced me I could learn easily. "You write to count" she said, "just like you do the headlines at the paper. Believe me, you can do it!"

I made the move and gave notice to my editor. He tried to talk me out of it. I stayed on two weeks to train a new Women's Editor. I really hated to say goodbye to everyone. They all were glad to see me "step up" in the publishing business. I didn't know if I was "stepping up" or "stepping into treacherous territory." It was over five years since I worked at 'Teen in Manhattan and I knew things had changed there. I was scared but it was only my friend, Lucie to whom I could release my fears. My kids thought it was a good idea and said they'd be okay and not to worry about them, but of course, I did. The additions to the house were almost completed. Heidi now had her own bedroom; my new one was just perfect and the enlarging of the kitchen plus the new family room gave us a lot more space.

The hardest part of leaving the Journal News was that I would miss my weekly luncheons with Lucie and especially our intimate talks. I will never forget her bright, sparkly eyes looking across the table at me.

MARIE FENTON GRIFFING

"Marie, this is not goodbye—this is only farewell; in fact, why don't we meet on Saturdays when we can—same place, same time." I nodded, but I sensed I was again losing one of my most helpful and supporting friends. I wiped away my tears and sighed. "Okay," I said.

That whole weekend before I was to start my job on Monday, I practiced doing copywriting. I bought a Good Housekeeping Needlecraft Magazine, the publication on which I was to be Senior Copywriter. At least the subject matter was pleasing to me because I loved knitting, crocheting. The things I would be writing about were really beautiful. Thank goodness I didn't have to write instructions—only the flowery words under the pretty photos. It was early April of 1970 and the budding of the dogwood and azaleas around the house gave me a good feeling. "Okay," I said to myself as I went to bed Sunday night, "You're on, Marie. Let's do it." I looked over on my bed table at Bob's photo, smiled and said to myself, "Good lord, Bob, what a position you've put me in. Stick close to me."

4. SUPPORT FROM CO-WORKERS AT GH

I PASSED MY 45th birthday, April 11, 1970, two weeks after I had taken the job at Good Housekeeping Magazine in Manhattan. By then, I'd was used to the daily commute—up the Palisades Parkway to the George Washington Bridge, onto the West Side Highway and off on 57th St., park my car in a garage on 57th and 10th Avenue, walk two blocks to the Hearst Building on the corner of 57th and 8 Ave. I'd pick up a cup of coffee at Chuck'ful of Nuts, buy the daily New York Times at the little shop in the building, take the elevator to the editorial offices on the 5th floor. It took me about 45 minutes to do all this, weather and traffic permitting. Then, I'd sit down at my desk, have a cigarette, sip my coffee and read the newspaper until my associate, Charlotte, came in. My boss, Ben, (my friend from Journalism School—now Managing Editor of Special Publications at Hearst) liked the idea of us keeping up with the news, so there was no problem taking the first half-hour of our day to read the Times.

Charlotte, my assistant, was a pretty, blonde young woman almost 20 years younger than I, a graduate of Columbia University Journalism School. At first I felt intimidated by her expertise in copywriting but realized she had been in that position for two years prior to my appointment. The last Senior Copywriter had quit, so Ben put me in her place instead of upgrading Charlotte. The first few weeks were tense because I could see that she was disappointed not getting promoted. When I would ask her questions on the layouts the art director brought into us, she'd clam up and not offer advice. I struggled through but felt the bad vibrations.

As the days and weeks went by, she softened. Using a little sense of humor about the whole situation, I won her over. Thanks to a nice elderly lady who worked in the copy-editing department, my art director, Jim, and Charlotte's help, I soon became quite accomplished at writing the creative headlines and the four-to-five line captions to fit into the layouts.

Along with this editorial group, I also had to work with the women who did all the creative needlework. They had their own huge office across the hall from ours. I loved to go in their space, touch all the wools, admire the handmade garments. Helen, the Director of the Good Housekeeping Needlecraft Magazine department, was an elderly lady of about 70 years. She was an expert in the business and had worked for Hearst for over 40 years. I liked and respected her. She always checked out my copy before it went to press. She tactfully offered suggestions and corrections. We became good friends.

Helen's two assistants, Judy and Barbara, were young women in their late 30's and we too got along well. In fact we got to be "buddies" and would lunch together frequently. I was thrilled to have such a group of very creative people around me. The pressure of the job lessened. Every night when I came home from work, I usually found my children sitting in front of the TV. They really were not interested in my work. I still felt nervous of their being alone until I got home. I had little communication with them. Somehow, I knew I was losing it, trying to keep the family together. But we did all still have a roof over our heads, food to eat and a few bucks in the bank—that was important to me. I had this fear that my brother-in-law, Irv, could take custody of the kids if I was not able to provide for them. It was written in Bob's will. The last thing I wanted was to have them go live with Irv.

One of my co-workers, Judith, who was in our advertising department and with whom I worked closely regarding ads for the magazine, suggested at lunch one day that if I'm concerned about my brother-in-law taking the kids from me, I should write a Will and assign another person as guardian in case of my death. She introduced me to one of the Hearst lawyers. My new Will read that in case of death, my brother, Patrick Duffy, would be the guardian; I bequeath the house, etc. to the kids. After that, I felt relieved. I now had a good life insurance policy with Hearst plus medical insurance.

My job was going well. With permission from my boss, I was able to accept a free-lance job on the side—writing mini health/beauty books for Dell Publishing. Aside from my regular salary, I was now earning a few extra thousand from the books. The books took up most of my weekend time but I made sure to go to our Saturday night poker games in Snedens. That was about all I did socially and I enjoyed it.

Occasionally, one of my women friends in Snedens would invite me to dinner to meet an "available" man, but those "match-makings" never worked out. Bob was still in my mind and soul. My total concerns were on my family and work. It was getting close to Heidi's graduation from high school. Rick phoned me every Sunday and he sounded okay even though I could tell he was lonely. "I can't wait to come home in May," he would always say. I was looking forward to that, too. Rick had sent me clips from the college newspaper about his having the lead in a play on campus. I was so proud. Heidi seemed to be doing okay and Todd was busy with his sports interests. I was feeling pretty good about us all, yet I harbored regrets about not being able to be in closer contact with Heidi and Todd. I began to have premonitions that my little family was in danger.

On a weekend in the middle of May, 1970, just before I was getting dressed to go shopping at Grand Union, the telephone rang and it was a nurse at the hospital in Evanston, Illinois. She told me Rick had an emotional breakdown at the University and was in the psychiatric ward. She said to come immediately. I was terrified and tried to question her, but she said I'd find that out when I came. Heidi and Todd were still home at that early morning hour and I called them into my bedroom to tell the news. They both looked at me in amazement and I could only shake my head, "I don't know what happened but I have to leave immediately for Chicago. Can you please go shopping for me Heidi?" She nodded. Then I saw Todd plop on my bed and start crying. I held him in my arms, "It's going to be okay, Todd. I'll bring Rick home to get well. I'll be back Sunday night." I knew I had a lot of work to do at Good Housekeeping and since I had just started my job there, I didn't want to jeopardize that by taking time off. I quickly packed a small suitcase and drove to LaGuardia and arrived a couple hours later in Chicago. From there I took a cab to Evanston, just outside of Chicago and went directly to the hospital.

That weekend was one of the scariest of my life. I first met with the psychiatrist who asked me all sorts of questions about Rick, told me he had been taking heavy drugs for a long time and that his last dose of LSD and mescaline had put him into a psychotic state and I should be prepared to see a terribly disturbed young man. I started to shake and cry. The doctor did nothing to comfort me, just ushered me out of office as if I were to blame and handed me over to the nurse. She brought me a glass of water and I followed her to see Rick.

The hospital ward looked like a prison. All doors were locked; each had a small barred window at the top and one small barred window in the room. The atmosphere was very somber. Because I had just come straight to the hospital from the airport, I had brought my overnight case with me and left it in the little waiting room while I talked with the doctor. I noticed when I went to check on it before going to see Rick that one clasp was open. I immediately looked inside the bag and saw that my things had been ruffled through. I felt intimidated. I guess they thought I might be bringing in drugs for Rick or whatever.

As I entered Rick's room, I heard the nurse lock the door behind me. I looked toward the bed but Rick wasn't there. Then I spotted him sitting on the floor in a corner, rocking back and forth, playing with his toes. I went over and hugged him but he didn't respond. I sat on the edge of the bed and looked down at this pitiful person who was my son. I couldn't believe it. Tears started to flow. I kept trying to talk to him but could see he was in another world. After 15 minutes or so, I knocked on the door to be let out and caught the nurse's attention.

As soon as the door closed behind me, I started to cry openly. The nurse put her arm around me. "Mrs. Fenton, Rick will be okay in a week or so, but then he should go home and not back to school. He will need immediate therapy. We'll bring him out of this state but he is a very sick young man."

"How and why did he do this, take these drugs? I never knew anything. He seemed to be so happy and doing so well at Northwestern," I stammered through my sobs.

"I'm sorry," the nurse replied. "I don't know anything except a friend of his from the University brought him in yesterday; said he was suicidal. I can give you the student's name and phone number. Maybe you can get more information from him. By the way, Rick came in soiled clothes which we threw out and no shoes. Could you go out and buy him some? There are a few stores up the block." I nodded. As she gave me the name and phone number of the student, I asked about a hotel nearby. I knew I would be staying the weekend and had no idea where to go. She gave me the name of one a few blocks away.

It had been hours since I'd eaten anything. Even though I had no appetite, I realized I had to keep up my strength. I went downstairs to the cafeteria and ordered a strawberry malted milk; at least it was nutritious and would fortify me. From there I called John, the student who had brought Rick to the hospital. We agreed to meet for an early dinner at a diner near the school campus. Meanwhile, I rushed to get a room at the hotel; then went shopping for Rick. I was in a stupor as the salesmen of the men's store tried to help me pick out an outfit for Rick. I hadn't bought clothes for him in years. He always liked to buy his own. I described Rick's build to the man and little by little we selected a pair of beige kakis, a polo shirt, a cotton cardigan, underwear, socks and a pair of loafers. The nurse had said it would be best not to come back before morning.

I took the packages back to the hotel, booked a flight back to New York for Sunday night, called Heidi and caught her at home. I told her Rick was not hurt physically but he was not in good shape mentally and that he wouldn't come home for a week. I said she could expect me home late Sunday. She seemed very calm on the phone and said not to worry; she was handling everything. That made me feel better. I stretched out on the bed to relax a little, fell asleep and woke up in a dark room. I awakened with a start, not knowing where I was. Then I thought for a second, glanced at my watch and noticed that I had about 15 minutes to get to the diner to meet Rick's friend.

John beckoned me from a booth in the restaurant which thankfully was not crowded. He smiled and introduced himself. "I'm in charge of the floor in the dormitory where Rick lives. My job is to oversee the guys and make sure everything is okay. Well, Mrs. Fenton, Rick hasn't been himself for the last few months. He has been into heavy drugs like a lot of the students here who are in the Drama School. It seems they are trying the Timothy Leary belief that drugs open and elevate the mind to more creative experiences. I'm not in the drama group, but I can tell you that Rick is not the only one who has had a bad experience with these experiments. He has trashed his room before and attempted suicide but we all pulled him out of it. He had been working so hard performing in two plays on campus, taking uppers and downers but it was this last dose that wrecked him. I'm so sorry—he's a great guy. Everyone likes him."

I listened to him, leaning forward so I could catch every word and comprehend exactly what was going on here in this so-called "wonderful ivy-league school of learning," costing me thousands of dollars and to which I had sent a beautiful, intelligent son for an education, not a breakdown. I began to feel an anger build up within me.

"Tell me, John," my voice became suddenly strong. "Why in the hell didn't someone call me when Rick tried the first suicide? Don't you report such actions to the Dean so he can reach me? What went wrong?"

John hung his head and muttered something about the guys in the dorm trying to protect their buddies so they wouldn't get kicked out of

MARIE FENTON GRIFFING

school. I could only stare at him, completely numb. "You call what has happened to Rick, protecting?"

Because it was a weekend, I was unable to contact any of Rick's professors or even the dean or president of the school. I went home questioning myself as to what had happened. For the next week we anxiously awaited word about Rick's return.

Things seemed to go from bad to worse after Rick arrived back in Snedens. His behavior was scary for me, Heidi and Todd. We didn't know how to react to his depressions, then his sudden highs. My co-workers at GH suggested that I get him a therapist right away. It seemed they had been on drugs in college and had seen a lot of their friends hit bottom like Rick. At our daily lunches, they listened to my "horror stories." Without letting go of my feelings like I did with them, I might have gone "crazy" myself. They were a wonderful sounding board for me. No way could I tell my mother or brother in Los Angeles. They wouldn't understand. I didn't reveal what had happened to Rick to anyone except my friends at the magazine. I did tell Ben, my boss, because I would need a few days off to get Rick into Presbyterian Mental Health Institute. There was a new experimental program there that a doctor in Snedens said would be good for Rick. He would have to stay in it for six months. Rick agreed.

Those were a tough six months for the Fenton family. First thing we had to do after Rick checked in, was have a "conference" with the psychiatrists in charge of the program. Heidi, Todd and I and Rick, too, were to appear before the board at which time they would ask us all sorts of questions. I had to beg Heidi and Todd to come even though they didn't want to. It was very scary for us all.

There were about 30 doctors there. We were ushered to a stage-like platform on which were four chairs. One of the first questions asked was why we chose the particular seats we did. I sat between Rick and Heidi; Todd sat next to Heidi. To me it was a stupid question and none of us gave an answer. Then they asked a barrage of other questions about our lives, relationships with each other. Sometimes, I broke down in tears and I could see Heidi and Todd were terrified. Rick seemed calm and committed, almost seeming to enjoy the scene.

I tried not to lose my grasp at Good Housekeeping. I did my full day's work, but instead of having lunch with my friends, I'd rush to catch the A-train subway on my lunch hour and speed up-town to the hospital to visit with Rick. It was very tiring for me but as the months wore on, I could see he was getting better. He no longer thought I was

Elizabeth Taylor or that he was Jesus Christ. He had shaved his beard and was taking better care of his appearance and eating well. I would have meetings with his doctor who encouraged me. I was feeling a sense of optimism about the whole thing.

For the next couple of years, I felt I was on a roller coaster. Rick would seem back to his old self again, even went to a drama school in California near where his Aunt Bernice lived so she could watch over him. That didn't last but a few months because he again went back to drugs, crashed and tried suicide another time. His psychiatrist flew back from LA to NY with him. I paid for both tickets. Heidi and I picked them up at Kennedy Airport, dropped off the doctor on the East Side of Manhattan. He only said "Good Luck" and suggested I get Rick into Mount Sinai mental hospital. We were all so distraught. Thank goodness for my Hearst medical coverage—I got Rick into Mount Sinai. I did have to pay a lot of extra bills all through this time, but my insurance paid most.

Meanwhile, I felt Rick's illness was taking its toll not only on me but on Heidi and Todd. This was affecting their schoolwork and social relationships outside of school.

I pleaded with them to be considerate and understanding. I was so distressed but I couldn't let it affect my work if I was going to keep us together as a family. The two Judy's and Barbara at work reinforced my strength. They kept urging me to take time out to have a little fun for myself. It had been almost four years since Bob's death but it seemed to me that my whole life had been turned upside down. Heidi never went to her graduation. Todd was getting into trouble in Snedens and I knew he was going to marijuana parties. I could barely catch them for a talk when I got home. There were always excuses. Plus Rick was dismissed from Mount Sinai and living at home, going to an outside therapist and just hanging around the house all day which gave both Heidi and Todd bad vibes. I hadn't been able to pay for a vacation in several years. The last one we all took together was just after Bob's memorial service when people donated enough money for me to take my children to Puerto Rico. It was now time for a short vacation for Todd, so I scraped together some money and sent him off to visit with his Aunt Bernice in California for a month. That gave me more time for Heidi. She had decided to enter college in a small New Hampshire town but after a month there, she returned home. Then she said she was going to live in New York City and go to the School of Visual Arts.

When I told this to my friends at work and my old friend from the Journal News, Lucie, they all agreed I should let her go because she needed more air, less time around Rick. So, I supported her move to a small apartment on 76th street in Manhattan. At least, she would be close to home and I would be within reach if she needed me but I was worried.

Rick was coming along well with his therapist. I met with her many times and she said it would be only a matter of time before Rick would be able to go off on his own, get a job and take some acting classes on the side. I was relieved by that prognosis.

It was early 1972 now and I had been advanced in my work at as Editor-in-Chief of the Good Housekeeping Beauty Book, a special publication. Ben knew of my background at 'Teen' and felt I would be able to take on this new venture. I was most excited by this promotion. I had a bigger office and was in charge of creating the entire magazine's format. I had my own art director, copy editor and dictated my own wishes for model selections and photography shoots. I started to work with the best makeup artists and hairstylists in New York and was invited to glamorous press luncheons and cocktail parties. It was very uplifting plus my salary was raised.

I could see a rainbow coming from behind the clouds but I was still concerned about my family. Heidi was away from me now. Even though I kept in touch with her, I really didn't know who her new friends were or how she was really doing at school, except she said she liked it. Sometimes, she'd come home for the weekend, but she and Rick would always get on each other's nerves and she'd leave early. Todd was having a lot of fun with his buddies in Snedens, but still not getting good grades in high school. What with my new prestigious job, I just let it all flow and hoped for the best.

"Marie, you've come such a long way in such a short time here at Hearst," Judy said to me one day. "Who knows, maybe one day you'll be Editor of GH."

I laughed—"Are you kidding, they only have men as top executives. It's strange because the "mother" book (as we called Good Housekeeping) is for women, only, and all the top positions are held by men. I sure hope it changes." (And it did a couple of years later).

One night in late 1972 my friend, Gail, called me and asked if I would like to go to a book-signing party on McDougall Alley in lower Manhattan that was initiated by her husband's publisher. Gail's husband was a serious chef and just published his first cooking book "Love and Butter." She said she could pick me up in front of the Hearst Building at 6 p.m. and then drive downtown. At first I hesitated but she talked me into it. Little did I know that I would fall in love again on that eventful night.

CHAPTER SIX

MY AWAKENING YEARS . . . .
(1972 TO 1974)

1. GAIL LEADS ME TOWARD A NEW EXPERIENCE

A S GAIL AND I drove to the Village in lower Manhattan, I was nervous. I had alerted Todd I'd be home late and he should warm up some leftovers in the fridge for his dinner. "Relax, Marie," Gail said. "We'll only stay for an hour, then we'll drive straight back to Snedens. Let's have some fun, congratulate Joey on his new book and meet some interesting people. By the way I really like your new hairdo—it's a wig isn't it?" I held tight to my purse, and looked across at her. In the ten years that I'd known Gail, she had always been blunt when it came to personal things, so I took no offense and just smiled "Thanks. But it's not a wig really; it's a "fall" something new."

The small basement apartment was filled with wall-to-wall people all holding pretty wine-filled glasses and talking like magpies. I felt out of place and scared. After offering my congratulations to Joey, Gail's husband, author and guest of honor, I spied a space against a wall close to the hors-d'oeuvre table and with wine glass in hand, leaned my back against the cool bricks. I patted the skirt of my black A-line dress that had been wrinkled during our ride to the party. Casually, I touched the page-boy fall on my head. One of my hairstylists I use for "shoots" had given it to me. It was real hair with a black velvet band and when slipped on the back of my short black coif, gave me a completely different look. I liked it but it was the first time I'd ever worn it—seemed like I was going incognito.

I perused all the action going on in front of me. There were pretty models surrounded by distinguished older men—others in jeans and tie-dyed shirts which I surmised were artists. Then over in another corner was a circle of young, handsome men who I guessed might be gay. While munching on a piece of broccoli, I played this little game by myself, identifying everyone's role here. I began to feel more relaxed and accepted this new experience as an adventure.

I glanced to my left and noticed a man edging his way through the crowded room, coming in my direction, eyeing me. I looked down for a second, then up. In a moment he was beside me. I took a deep breath, wiped my lips with a napkin and turned sideways to face him.

"Hello, Marie." His voice was soft, deep and mellow. He almost sounded like Bob, my deceased husband—it was weird.

"Hi," I answered. "How do you know my name? Have we met before?"

"Don't you remember? I was at a dinner party in your home in Snedens some years back. A writer friend of mine and I rented Joey's house there on Woods Road. Your husband, Bob, used to stop by some afternoons and we'd discuss our writing projects. One day he invited us for dinner—that's when I met you. You are a terrific cook. You don't recall that night?"

"No, Sorry," I said with a smile. He had a handsome face, dark shaggy eyebrows framed his dark brown eyes. Wavy, ruffled dark brown hair dipped over his forehead. His whole look resembled that of Bob—except he wasn't as tall as Bob. He even smoked a pipe like Bob used to. That made it only more weird for me. "What is your name? I asked.

"Barry. I teach at the NYU, live here in the Village." he answered.

I nodded and said again, "Sorry. I guess I just don't remember—so many years ago." I set my wine glass on the table and nervously reached for a potato chip but this time no dip. We talked for a while. He kept asking me questions about my work at Good Housekeeping, said how sorry he was about Bob's death and how glad he was for Joey's success with the cookbook. Meanwhile, my shoulder-strap purse kept slipping down my arm and I kept lifting it back on my shoulder. I was unconsciously flipping my bangs back, pulling on my skirt, clasping my fingers together—all nervous clues that I'm sure he noticed. I felt like a 'klutz—more like a teenager waiting for a dance partner at a ballroom instead of a mature New York career woman.

"I have an idea," he suddenly said. "Why don't we get out of here and go to my apartment. It's only five minutes away. We can have a cup of coffee and talk quietly."

My heart was beating so fast, I felt sure he could see the palpitations through my dress. I looked down and smoothed my bodice.

"That's not possible," I gulped. "I'm going home with Gail, Oh look, there she comes now; probably wants to leave."

I waved to Gail approaching us. She smiled at Barry and planted a kiss on his cheek, then looked at me. "Marie, I see you've both met. Barry and I are old friends. I attended some of his classes at the University."

As Gail and Barry talked, I came to find out that he was a professor—an expert on Russian history, had an 8-year-old son, and often visited Gail and Joey in their Martha Vineyard's house.

I expected Gail to say she was ready to go home. Instead she accepted Barry's invitation to accompany me to his apartment for coffee. He called it his new "bachelor's pad" (his quick remark that he was recently divorced caught my attention).

Before I had a chance to say yes or no, Barry was guiding me toward the door. I turned my head back and saw Gail following us. She had a sheepish grin on her face and her smiling eyes gave me a quick wink.

"What in the heck am I getting myself into?" I asked myself. My palms were sweating and when his hand pressed more firmly on my arm as we climbed the stairs to the street, my legs quivered. I was experiencing all the same feelings that I had had the day I met Bob for the first time on the beach. "I've a crush on him!" I rejoiced to myself as we three walked down the street to Barry's building. What I didn't know was how this new heart throb would break my heart.

Later as Gail and I crossed the George Washington Bridge and drove up the Palisades Parkway toward Snedens, we giggled about the 'happening'. I had a feeling that Gail had somehow set this all up but when I asked, her face took on that same look she'd get at poker when someone would ask her, 'Are you bluffing?'—a blank!

"Gail, what should I do? He invited me to his country house in New Jersey on Sunday. I'm really attracted to him—could it be love at first sight?"

"Not likely—but I'd go if I were you. He's a really nice guy."

"Yeah," I said, "maybe I will but I don't want to go alone—will you come with me?"

"Can't," she answered. "Joey and I have another book party to go to—why don't you ask Sally?"

The next morning, I asked Sally and she said yes. I called Barry at his office at the school and said we'd be at his country house Sunday afternoon about 2 p.m. Just hearing his voice again revved me up. He gave me directions, and then I asked if I could bring dinner. He said fine. My first mistake.

Sally and I set out for Barry's house the next Sunday afternoon. I loaded the car with a pot of 'bouef bourguignon', a jug of wine and a huge loaf of French bread. Like Gail, my neighbor Sally was someone I could talk to about problems. She was always there to listen and support me since Bob's death but this time she got upset with me.

"Marie, for heaven's sake, why in the world did you make all this food?"

I spread my hands over my face, shook my head and started to laugh. "I don't know!"

She threw up her hands, then shook her finger at me and was just about to yell at me when she, too, broke out in laughter. We giggled for ten minutes.

The day was wonderful. Barry's house was beautiful and every time he stood near me or touched me, my knees weakened. I was a lovesick gal. Sally and I took a walk in the woods that surrounded the place with Barry's son, Steven, and picked pretty colored leaves and flowers. On the way home I asked Sally, "Isn't he the sweetest, softest man you ever met?"

"Uh Huh," she muttered. "Be careful of those men." And if anyone knows all about men, it's Sally. She's dated more than I can count on two hands. But I paid no attention to her warning. She would have the last laugh.

My head was in a whirl all the next week. My co-workers at Good Housekeeping noticed my euphoria and I told them all about it. They were happy for me but forewarned me to move slowly. Even my kids noticed a difference in my behavior.

I asked Gail to come over on the weekend and she helped me frame the pretty leaves and flowers which I wanted to give to Barry and his son as a remembrance of our day at his house. "Marie, you've just met the man—don't you think this is too much, too soon?" Gail asked me as we worked on the montage. Her words went over the top of my head. I was in love (that's what I thought).

In a few days I received a call from Barry while I was at work. "Marie, how about meeting me for breakfast tomorrow at the Algonquin Hotel before you go to work—say 8 a.m.?" I immediately said yes. My heart was going "pitter-pat."

That morning and many weeks after that we would meet for breakfast—sometimes for lunch. My infatuation with him grew deeper—I was walking around in a daze. I kept wearing my "fake fall" because I felt that was the way he first saw me and I wasn't ready for him to see me in short hair—not yet.

I began to do a lot of other silly things. I started to knit him and his son hats and scarves and would give them to him at our meetings. Then

I did a beautiful Irish sweater for him which I brought unexpectedly to his office at the New School. He loved it and gave me a kiss on the cheek—his first kiss. I was elated. Then I knitted him an afghan for his house in the country.

Meanwhile months went by and all we had ever done in our relationship was to have breakfast and lunch together. I was getting anxious. "Marie, you're going too fast. Barry is vulnerable; he's just been divorced. He doesn't even know who your kids are" said Gail one day in Snedens. It was true, I was rushing him so I decided to stop my "smothering pattern." But I still lay awake at night thinking about him in bed with me, making love. I began to realize I was caught up in an erotic obsessive situation and I didn't know how to get out of it and still save my relationship with this man who I thought was so great.

"Marie, there's a Snedens library party next week. Why don't you invite him. He can see your house and meet your children?" Gail advised. I took her advice and called him and he accepted. I was thrilled.

At 8:30 p.m., the night of the dance, I heard his car drive up. I had been dressed for two hours. Even though I had asked Heidi, Todd and Rick to be there to meet this man who was taking me to the dance, they split. So there I was alone, standing by the fireplace in a long, slinky black dress. I was not wearing my hair fall but coifed my short 'do in soft waves. Now, I thought, he'd see the real me. He knocked on the door and I ushered him into the house, planted a kiss on his cheek. He walked around the house and admired the paintings, the patio and some of my oak tables. He never mentioned my hair. We went off to the dance.

We sat with friends of mine from Snedens and I was so proud to introduce Barry to them. I was in "seventh heaven". Finally, a slow dance came up—music from the past. "Are the Stars Out Tonight—I Only Have Eyes for You." He asked me to dance and I melted when his arm held me close to him. We even touched heads. I was in paradise. An hour before the event was to finish, he suggested we go back to my house. I was in accord—hoping this would be the night. Instead of coming in, he gave me a kiss on the lips (our first) and said he had to get back to NY. There I was with all my hormones in high gear—he leaves. I was furious. As I crawled into bed, I vowed I'd never see him again.

The first thing I did when I awoke up the next morning was to wrap my hair fall in a bag to give to my housekeeper—she always admired it. No more pretenses, I said to myself—no more smothering. I vowed I'd get on with my life without Barry.

My work at the magazine was becoming more demanding. Heidi was doing well at the School of Visual Arts, Rick still had his ups and downs, changing therapists every few months it seemed; Todd was hard to keep up with, but all in all things weren't getting worse. I was enjoying the glamour of press luncheons and cocktail parties held in the most prestigious restaurants and hotels in New York City. I mingled with the best Beauty Editors around. We had a lot of fun and I often took weekend public relations junkets to exciting places around the country. My financial resources were getting better too from my moonlighting in mini books.

Then, one morning while I was opening my mail at the office, the phone rang and that mellow voice of Barry's was there. Immediately, my heart started to beat faster. He asked why I hadn't called, if I were okay. "I'm fine, Barry," I replied. "but I've been very busy. What's up?" He asked me to meet him for lunch. Of course, I weakened and we met at a Chinese restaurant on 57th and 8th Ave. It was a good encounter; I told him how I felt and he reiterated what my friends had told me "Marie, you are a special woman and I care for you but let's take it more slowly." I agreed and went happily back to my office. "All is not lost," I told Judy when I walked in. She gave me thumbs up.

I was back in the obsessive pattern again. When I got lonely at night, I'd pick up the phone and we'd talk for an hour. I loved to hear his voice. I began writing pieces of poetry about our meetings. I was sure that it wouldn't be long before he would confess his love for me. I was in a whirlwind of emotions.

MARIE FENTON GRIFFING

2. JOSETTE . . . . A WORD FROM MY WISE FRIEND

I T WAS THE spring of 1973, I was in love and the world seemed bright and welcoming. A book publishing editor in Chicago called me at the office one day and asked if I would do a how-to book for her house. I was flattered by the approach and asked what kind of book they wanted. "I'll leave it up to you," she replied. "I'm sure you know what the woman of the 70s needs." So, I gave the matter much thought and after conferring with my co-workers at Good Housekeeping, I came up with the title "Fitness for the Working Woman." I knew a lot of women were going back into the work force and looking for ways to look good, feel good on the job. The book was directed to women who needed extra money to make their households more secure. Inflation was terrible and most families required a second paycheck to meet the monthly bills.

The book proposal I sent the publisher was accepted and I got a good advance. Now that I had signed the contract, I had to make plans on how to pursue the book. First, I contacted a woman, Josette Paquet, who owned the Women's Health Club in New York City. I had worked with her on stories for my magazines. She was a physical therapist and ran a prestigious fitness spa on Madison Avenue. We met for lunch one day and she agreed to give me info on exercises, etc. and in return I would credit her in the book. We got along fine and within four or five meetings, we had become fast friends. Her expert information was a big help. Then I engaged the services of a young woman illustrator who said she'd love to do the exercise sketches for the book. I was on my way. The only thing now was to find the time to write the book. My boss, Ben, okayed the project but on time off from my job—which meant weekends. I agreed

Josette was an extraordinary woman—married three times. Her first husband was a Duke in Europe. She came from France and had a beautiful French accent. She was regal in stature, dressed in the most glamorous clothes and had such a gracious manner about her that I felt sometimes like I was in the presence of a queen. She was in her 60s but we came to know each other as if we were sisters only a few years apart.

When ordering at the restaurants, she introduced me to foods that I'd never tasted before. I was in adoration of her.

Aside from discussing the book, we'd talk about our personal lives. She had a husband older than she. Most of her time was spent in her fitness salon. She had a house in San Tropez on the French Riviera but was now living in a three-bedroom apartment on Riverside Drive. She became my mentor during this period.

When Josette heard about Barry and his manipulative ways with me, she began to give me advice. "Marie, this man is using you to serve himself, and it's putting you on a romantic roller coaster. Get off while you can before you fall down." I listened and thought about it but I couldn't stop my nightly calls to Barry. One day Josette advised that I take all the poems I'd written and give them to him, "tell him bye-bye."

I really tried to "wash that man right out of my hair," but was captivated by his charms. Another time when Josette and I met to talk about the book, she asked if I had cut off the relationship. "No, not yet," I said as I shook my head and twisted my fingers. "Marie, I've had many lovers in the past and I would say at least half of them were manipulative like your Barry. I suggest you consider other aspects as to why he hasn't committed himself to make love to you. I have a feeling that he is impotent and is afraid. I realize that talking about this subject to him would be embarrassing, but it could be the answer and if so, then you'd better rest the case. Get out before he breaks your heart. Give him air to work out his own personal problems."

That night I tossed and turned in my bed reflecting on Josette's advice. The next morning at the office I called Barry at his office and asked if I could meet him at the Chinese restaurant for lunch. He said okay. I had brought an envelope with over a dozen of poems I'd written for him. I even rehearsed the farewell speech I was going to make when we met.

When I saw him walk through the door of the restaurant and approach my table, I experienced a strange new feeling. He looked shorter than I remembered him, his clothes were wrinkled, his head was bent forward. His approaching me didn't make my heart thump. He sat down and smiled at me—that did melt my heart. As we were having our Won Ton soup, I reached over and grabbed his free hand. "Barry, I want this to be our last meeting. You see, I've had an infatuation with you that doesn't quit. Maybe I came on too strong for you and a relationship like we've been having doesn't work for me. I guess I need time too. I fell in love too fast."

He dropped his spoon into the bowl and covered my hand with his. "It's okay, Marie." He said it like a relief—as if a stone had been lifted off his head.

"You know Barry," I then replied. "there is a Japanese word—"deai" . . . it means encounter." He nodded his head. "Well, Barry, I discovered the real meaning of this word—a personal preparation and recognizing the opportunity must be in order for a good "deai" to take place. I feel that neither of us was ready for our encounter. We just met at the wrong place at the wrong time."

After a few minutes he got up to leave, planted a kiss on my cheek and smiled. I smiled back and handed him the envelope with the poems.

"Here, Barry, add these to your memories of me—all the scarves, hats, sweater." I giggled. "Now here's something else. Don't forget me. I'll never forget you. I still love you."

As I watched him go through the twirling door and onto the street, I felt sad but in another way, relieved and self-assured that I had done the right thing. The waiter appeared and asked, "Lady, you want another dry 'lob loy on the locks?'

"Good idea, Chan." I felt it was time I toasted to myself. I felt cleansed and free. Under my breath, I repeated a phrase I hadn't used since I was a teenager: "How could I be such a dope!"

When I told Josette about the scene at the restaurant, she congratulated me on my courage to make the "cut-off."

"Marie, it was a learning experience. The heart can play tricks on you and from now on you must watch out so you don't get trapped again in such an obsessive love. Take your time before entering a relationship. 'Mr. Right' will come along when you're ready."

I began to put my energies back into my work and my children. While Heidi was studying at the School of Visual Arts, a friend of mine who worked at the Museum of Modern Art, found her a position in their film division. Heidi was able to get a nicer apartment in the Village; Todd was doing well at high school—especially in sports. I worried about Rick. His problem was getting worse.

3. SALLY—MY COHORT IN THE SINGLES SCENE

THE FALL OF 1973 never looked so beautiful. The leaves were turning and the ride to and from Manhattan with all the trees in color was something to remember. The last four years had been tumultuous but I had weathered through them. In fact, all my experiences caused me to reflect that I'd been giving and giving and not really giving anything to myself. So, I started to ask for favors from other people. I inquired from neighbors who worked in the city if they minded if I rode in with them. They all said yes. Most of the time it was Jerry, but when he wasn't available, there was Andy, Jan or Marguerita. Some accepted payment for giving me the ride; others not. No longer did I have to drive in myself or take the bus and A-train. The latter was getting too dangerous with the crime scene growing. So I entered the new world of car-pooling. It was fun.

I was doing a lot of traveling covering beauty pageants around the country. These provided me with top stories for my Good Housekeeping Beauty Book which was selling well on the newsstands. I asked for a raise and I got it. I had just finished my book "Fitness for the Working Woman" and was expecting good royalties when it would be published. It always takes so long after you begin a book to actually see it in the bookstores.

The only aspect of my life that troubled me was my older son, Rick. He was 24 years old now and really not progressing with his life. He'd get a job, then be fired; he'd work with friends on a play and get so energized with it, that he'd crash and go into depression. I was terribly anxious about his mental health and when I talked to his many therapists, they'd just say let him be. He was on Lithium now but when he forgot to take his pills, he was impossible. That made me sad and scared and there were no support groups around.

One day his doctor called and said he should live outside of my house and said he could help Rick get a small room in a boarding house in Nyack, fifteen minutes from Snedens. In a way, I was relieved but still worried about him. I'd ask him to come to dinner on the weekends so he could still feel he was part of the family. With Heidi living in the city and now Rick away in Nyack, that left only Todd and me at home. Looking back at Bob's death, then a year later, Rick's breakdown, it seemed as though the years melted away. I felt that life was passing me by and I couldn't get the load I was carrying off my shoulders. But I knew I had to go forward and not break down myself.

Sally, who had gone through the "escapade" with my obsessive love, Barry, would come over to the house on the weekends and tell me all the fun and excitement she was having by going to the single scene bars in the area. "Marie, I met the cutest guy last night and we're going to dinner tonight. You've got to give this scene a try—it's really great and it would be good for you to meet new men."

"Come on, Sally," I replied. You're 10 years younger than I. Here I am 48 years old. The only man I ever slept with was Bob.—God, I don't think I even know how to make love anymore. Those men in the bars are too young for me. No way !"

"Marie, you're an attractive gal. You're good looking and have a good figure plus you're smart and personable. I'm sure there's a guy out there who would appreciate being with you. Forget that lousy Barry. He probably wasn't capable of getting it up anyway."

I laughed. "Sally, you're too much. Let me think about it. And anyway, what would my kids think about me, their mother, going to a singles bar?"

"Poo-poo! The kids probably wonder why there isn't a man in your life. You know at their age they only think of themselves I have three of my own, don't forget.

They're that way too. Come on, Marie. It's time for us now 'babe!' Give it a chance. The single bars are THE place to meet guys. You don't have to be a widow forever!"

I listened to Sally's comment. "Okay," I answered. "I'll give it a try next Friday and go with you to a singles bar—where?"

The place I go to is up the Parkway—Tom Swifts it's called. It's only 15 minutes from here. We'll take two cars so if you don't like it you can go home or we can go to another place nearby, The Bicycle Club. The action doesn't start until about 9 o'clock, so I'll come over and you can follow me. Believe me, you're going to have fun."

"Wait a minute, Sal," I replied. "What do I wear?"

Sally laughed, "Dress from the waist up because you sit at the bar so no one really notices your shoes or anything. Wear a pretty blouse and whatever—nice earrings too."

When I told my co-workers at Good Housekeeping about my new venture, they expressed their support. "Go for it, Marie. It's the new craze. It'll be an experience."

That Friday night when I came home for work, I had dinner with Todd. He was going out to a basketball game at his school. I told him I was going out with Sally and probably would be home late. He didn't ask where I was going. We did the dishes and he waved goodbye—"have fun, Mom," he called out as he left.

I was a wreck. I didn't know what to wear. Finally, I chose a silk leaf-patterned autumn colored long-sleeve shirt and my bell-bottom jeans I'd just bought, a pair of plain gold earrings. I applied delicate colored makeup and brushed my dark brown hair into a soft pageboy. (I was glad I went back to my natural color.) I looked in the mirror at myself. "What am I doing?" I asked myself. "Is this crazy?"

I sat in the living room on the couch awaiting Sally to toot her horn in the driveway and started to take deep breaths to relieve my stress. My thoughts wandered back to my youth. I recalled the advice of Aunt Toni and Aunt Marie who always moved me forward with my goals and gave me positive suggestions. Then I thought if they were around tonight, I bet they would say "Go for it, Marie." But they were not. I realized I had lost a lot of self-confidence and self-esteem even though I had been able to carry out my financial and family responsibilities. Tonight, I knew it would mean putting myself on the line as an attractive woman.

Suddenly, I heard Sally's car drive up. I grabbed my bag, turned off the lights except the outside light, jumped into my car, waved to Sal to go ahead. I followed her down 9W to Tom Swifts and parked just behind her on the street.

People were filing into the place; we followed. Disco music was blaring from the juke box. I walked behind Sally almost wanting to clutch her arm, but I didn't. The bar area was set in a circular pattern. Sally walked to the right, then turned to the left. I was close behind. There seemed like a hundred people milling around—some were seated, some were just standing, others were strolling with glass in hand. Sally found two seats at the bar, next to a large wooden column. I chose the seat next to the column so I could lean and hide next to it. Everybody was chatting, the music was pulsating—I felt like I was in another world. Not that I'd never been in a bar before, but the ones Bob and I would go to were quiet places with piano music and people sitting at tables. This was another world—the "single scene", they called it. So, here I was—God help me!

We ordered a scotch and soda. The bartender was real nice, gave a sweet smile and welcomed us. "Marie," Sally whispered, "Sip very slowly on your drink; we don't want to get high. Usually a guy will buy you a drink, but don't accept more than one, Okay?" I nodded, laid my purse on the counter, sat back on my high swivel chair and took a deep breath. Sally was right—sitting at the bar, no one could see below your waist.

All of a sudden, a voice behind said "Hi !" I turned around and there was a good looking young man. I smiled and said, "Hi" He started the conversation and his charming manner caused me to respond. We talked about our different jobs (he was a salesman, recently divorced). He introduced himself as Brad. I told him my name was Marie, then a little about myself but not too much. I introduced him to Sally but he kept his gaze and conversation directed to me. Sally said she was going to the ladies room. My friend sat down in her chair. Then another man appeared behind, apparently a friend of Brad's. The three of us started to discuss all sorts of things. Brad told some funny jokes. I realized that I was having a good time with these two younger-than-I men but they were so nice, intelligent and friendly, I felt very comfortable. Ever so often they would throw in a compliment on the style of my hair, my pretty smile.

When Sally returned, I introduced her to Brad's friend and the four of us were having a grand time. They bought us each a drink. I remembered Sally's warning—no more than one. We even danced a bit and I learned a few new steps. I realized that it had been years since I'd personally enjoyed having such a good time.

I looked at my watch; it was already 11:30 p.m. I got a little panicky thinking of Todd home alone and told Sally I was leaving. She said she'd follow me in her car. We bid farewell to our new-found single-scene buddies. It seemed they weren't too happy and were hoping to get more out of our meeting.

When I got home I peaked into Todd's room and he was sleeping. I was so stirred up by the evening's happenings that it took me a long time to get to sleep. I think I had a smile on my face as I dozed off. It turned out to be a good experience. In fact I slept until ten a.m. the next morning. Usually on Saturdays I'd do my weekly grocery shopping at nine.

I felt energized all weekend long—even at the Saturday night poker game, I didn't get sleepy and won $40. On Sunday I called Sally and asked her if she was going again to the singles club the following Friday. "Sure, Marie," she replied. "See, I told you it was going to be fun. You really made a hit with those guys. I'll pick you up next Friday at nine. No sense taking two cars. If one of us wants to stay on and the other one wants to go home, we'll work it out—taxis are easily available. Okay?" I thought that was a reasonable solution.

I couldn't wait until Friday night. Todd was going over to a friend's to watch a ball game. After we had dinner and washed the dishes, he left and I ran to my bedroom closet to see what I would wear. The weather was getting cool now that it was almost winter but the bar scene had a lot of body heat in it. I chose a light cotton sweater that had a V-neck and showed a little of my cleavage, a pretty pair of pearl earrings—and of course the usual bell-bottom jeans. I don't know if it was my hormones acting up or all in my head but after my shower, I stood in front of my full-length mirror and looked at my body. I turned sideways, around and perused my back and buttocks. "Yeah, I still look good. I touched my 36-C breasts and grimaced . . . "Oh, well, a bra will pick them up a bit."

A half hour later, Sally and I were spinning up 9W in her little Toyota. "Tonight, Marie," she said, "we're going to start at the Bicycle Club. It's only a couple of blocks before Tom Swifts. I want you to see the action here—it's wild."

Her description of this single's place was accurate. The bar was bigger, the crowd looked younger; the place was a madhouse when we walked in. There wasn't a seat available at the bar. "What do we do?" I asked Sally. "Just follow me. We'll circle the place and find the best looking two guys sitting down and stand behind them. Keep chatting with me as if we don't notice them. Got it?" I was amazed at the different strategies that Sally employed.

We did connect with three book editors from a nearby publishing house. For over two hours I talked seriously with two of them about my work at Good Housekeeping and the books I had published. It was great. At the 11:30, the witching hour for me, I asked Sal to come with me to the ladies room so we could synchronize our plans for the night.

I couldn't believe this "behind-the-singles scene" in the ladies room. Crammed in front of the mirrors with the toilets flushing in the background were at least 20 young women applying their makeup, brushing their hair, arranging their outfits and talking like magpies. I stood there in amazement and listened to the conversations while Sally went to the bathroom. Expressions like: "Did you see that cute blond guy over on the curve of the bar. I'm going after him!" "Gloria, we've got to drop those two losers we've been with. Let's take off to Tom Swifts." "Judy, why do you want to do sleep with your guy? I can't stand mine. Meet me back here in an hour." "Grace, I knew I should have worn the sequined blouse; this one does nothing for me." "Let's cut out of here; I'm starving and none of these guys are going to foot the bill for a dinner." I wished I had a tape recorder with me.

Sally stood behind me as I was trying to brush my hair in the middle of all this chaos. She said she really liked the guy she'd met and asked if I minded grabbing a cab home. Because I had now become her "buddy" in the singles scene and we had made prearranged plans for situations like this, I replied, "No problem, Sally. I'll be okay. Have fun."

The next Friday Sally suggested we go back to Tom Swift's. I was all in agreement. I was having so much fun partying. Unlike Sally I was not on the "hunt", as she called it. She felt that since her divorce, she would soon meet her 'Mr. Right', whereas I was only going out to have a good time. Strangely, however, it had perked up my sensual feelings—that made me feel uneasy. Would I be able to control my sexual emotions if they got away from me?

All my co-workers at the office said I was looking terrific. I was feeling good about myself and beginning to realize that I wasn't too old at 48 to enjoy companionship with the other sex, even though I was a widow with three kids. Little by little I was starting to gain back some self-esteem. I bought myself a few new clothes, had my hair restyled and added highlights to my dark brown hair. I even began to use some of the free skin-care products I received as a beauty editor. It was more than four years since Bob's death and I was a bit skeptical about approaching a relationship.

The children and my work at the magazine were most important to me. I kept telling myself that I didn't want to continue on with this single scene and yet, I did. I was in a quandary about what I should do. I had told Rick and Heidi a little about my evenings out with Sally, but of course, not everything. I'm sure Todd suspected but never let on. I felt it was time to have a talk about this.

The Christmas holiday season, 1973, was upon us. I always loved this time of year but since Bob's death, I could feel the tension among us all as we opened our presents. I sensed my children were overextending themselves to please me. Nevertheless, we always had fun decorating the tree. I'd tell them when they went out to buy the tree to get a short one, like five feet tall and inevitably, they'd arrive with one nine feet tall. I laughed—it was kind of a joke among us.

That Christmas, Heidi had come home from her apartment in the city to spend a couple of days, Rick came on Xmas Eve from his half-way house in Nyack. Everyone slept late except Todd. When I heard him up, I began preparing a big breakfast for us all. I gazed at the presents under the tree which brought back memories when Bob and I would pile them underneath on Christmas Eve and it was the children who woke us up. Tears came to my eyes but I brushed them away quickly. I wanted to make this time special for me and my kids.

With holiday music in the background, we began to open our presents. As usual, Heidi played "Santa Claus" and handed out the gifts. When it came to opening Heidi's present for me, I couldn't quite figure it out. She gave me four gifts, each of them individually wrapped. When I opened the first one, it was a pretty pair of glittery earrings. The second one was a small paperback book on the singles clubs in New York. The third was a pretty sequined wool sweater and the last was a diary—and with all this a fantastic message. "Mom, we approve. Go out and have a good time with Sally in the singles scene . . . but write down all your experiences."

I started to cry. Then I walked over to my children, grabbed them all around me and started to laugh. "I guess I don't have to tell you guys about what I've been doing. Yeah, it's fun and different. Thanks for your support. I love you all."

CHAPTER SEVEN

MY REBIRTH YEARS
(1974 TO 1976)

1. FEEDBACK FROM THE TWO JUDY'S

AFTER THREE MONTHS of being prepped by Sally on how to work the singles scene, I had come to learn the ins and outs of flirting, dating, discovering my femininity again. It was a quick painless experience. Sally was a good teacher. I now felt indoctrinated and confident I could carry the ball on my own.

The interactions I had with men were all good. My self-esteem was in place again. Also my career wasn't suffering from my new lifestyle. In fact, it, too, seemed to gain momentum as I gained self-assurance in these personal relationships.

I began to wear bright colored clothes—gave away the dark browns and grays. My co-workers at Good Housekeeping even noticed a change in my appearance. I even went so far as to have all my teeth capped. It did cost a lot but I wrote another book in order to pay for the procedure. At a press conference for a famous dermatologist, I learned about a new skin treatment (silicone injections) to diminish facial wrinkles. I wanted it yet felt reluctant about it. Thinking about a needle being stuck into my face was scary to me. Plus, I questioned myself whether I was being too narcissistic. I decided to ask my two co-workers (Judy P. & Judy G) at Good Housekeeping with whom I had become very friendly. We lunched together at least twice a week when I wasn't going to some in-house luncheon meeting or a public relations fancy affair. From then on, my relationships with men turned me around. I was keeping my career going, my family together as best as I could. I don't know if it was my hormones kicking in (My doctor did start me on estrogen)—whatever, I seemed to be exercising my female powers, becoming a total woman again.

The episodes I had with the men I met were varied. John, the head of construction work being done on the building next to the Hearst Building where I worked (We met at Polly's Cage; a bar/grill where my friends and I went for lunch.) He was much older than I was, that didn't matter to me. He treated me like a "queen." He took me to the races, brought me gifts, flowers. Then there was Abavi—a young Lebanese man I met at

Tom Swifts bar in New Jersey when I went there with Sally. He would invite me up to his apartment a block away from the bar and serve me great cappuccino coffee. We'd make love and then he'd drive me home. When I told the two Judy's about my adventures, they flipped out. "Make them use condoms," they cautioned. I smiled and nodded my head. "I'm on birth control," I replied. They were the only ones who knew about my escapades.

One lunchtime with the two Judy's, one remarked, "Marie, take it easy. Don't go too fast." I nodded. I didn't know then what would happen that night.

I had a 6 p.m. press cocktail party hosted by Chanel. I'd advised Todd that morning I wouldn't be home until late and gave him instructions for dinner. The party was great but by the time I went to catch the late bus back to Palisades at Port Authority, it had just left. I went to the bar to relax after the subway ride and decided to call a taxi. There were three well-dressed men at the bar. The jukebox was playing romantic music. I sat to one side while the bartender called me a cab. As one of my favorite songs, "Love Theme" came on, one of the men asked me to dance. He introduced himself as Peter. As he held me in his arms, I felt another escapade coming as the words of my girlfriends "Marie, take it easy," came to mind. I just enjoyed the moment.

Five dances later, the bartender told me a cab would be coming. Peter told him to cancel it and then said he'd like to take me home. I said okay and we had one more dance to the Bee Jays singing, "How Deep Is My Love." I was feeling very sexy. This good-looking guy made me feel alive. It was like something our of Erica Jung's latest book. As we left the bar, he asked if I'd spend the night with him and for some crazy reason, I said "Yes" but I had to call my son back to tell him I was staying with a friend. Todd was half-asleep but I got through to him. At the time, I was too euphoric to feel guilty about not being home.

It was the first time I had ever gone to a motel with a man. When he got out of the car to go in to register, I followed him in. He turned around and said to me "Go back to the car, please!" I saw this as amusing. Who was I to know that this was done so privately. It was the first time since Bob died that I'd spent a whole night with a man. After our lovemaking and he had fallen asleep, I stayed in bed, feeling his warmth and experiencing for the first time in years how wonderful it was to have a man next to me all night long. Finally, I fell asleep with the thought, "Jeez, I'll have to wear the same outfit to work tomorrow!"

When Peter drove me to work the next morning, we didn't speak much. As I got out of the car on the corner of 57th and 8th Ave., he gave me a kiss and said he'd call me soon. I had heard that "goodbye" other times and it never happened, but somehow when Peter said it, I believed him. I then stopped off at a little dress shop and picked up some clean underwear and a new blouse.

When I told the two Judy's at lunch they shook their heads. "Marie, you're getting into dangerous territory with Peter. You say he told you he was an FBI agent? They're the worst kind. Is he married?" I shook my head, "No, I don't think so."

What troubled me most was that I was not really in love. Since my obsession with Barry a few years back, I was not able to recapture that feeling no matter how many encounters I'd have. It was as if I knew this was not the time for a serious relationship. I just counted myself lucky to be able to feel warmth toward the men I'd met. I figured after the deep love I had for Bob, I could never have another experience like that. He and I were so compatible; we could almost read each others' minds. I never thought once of cheating on him and I even hated being separated from him for just a few days when I had to go on junkets for 'Teen' Magazine in the 60s. I guess you could say I was 'crazy in love' with him.

After five years of being a widow and pursuing one avenue which was work and security for my family, I was relishing this sexual freedom. I figured it would run out one day as I wasn't growing any younger, but for the time being I was enjoying it

One Saturday, I was just getting out of the shower when I heard a knock on the door. I slipped into my long white terry robe and wrapped a towel around my wet head and walked toward the door wondering who it could be. I peaked through the stained glass side window and couldn't believe my eyes—it was my dentist from New York—the nice older man who had capped my teeth. I opened the door, stared at him and quietly asked, "Leonard, what in the world are you doing here?"

"Hi, Marie. I happened to be driving by and thought I'd like to see you. Can I come in?"

I tightened the belt on my robe, smiled at him and said, "Of course, Len, come in." He entered and gave me a kiss on the cheek.

Then I ushered him into the living room where he sat on the couch and I sat on the edge of a lounge chair nearby.

"You're looking good," I said, really not knowing what to say. "Would you like a cup of coffee or tea?" I had smelled Scotch on his breath and wondered what that all meant. He said okay. I ran to the kitchen and warmed up a cup of coffee in the microwave and brought it to him.

"You look beautiful," he said. I laughed nervously and excused myself saying I was going to blow-dry my hair quickly and would be back in a few minutes.

As I was blow-drying my hair, I was puzzled This lovely man who had helped me through all my teeth problems with such gentleness and caring, like an older brother or whatever, is suddenly here in my house and I feel like he's hitting on me. Why? I asked myself.

As I came out of the bathroom into the bedroom, he was standing at the door, swaying a bit with a big smile on his face. I approached him and he grabbed me and planted a big kiss on my lips, then hugged me.

"Marie, I love you. I need you."

I stood up straight, pushed him away and told him that I thought it would be a good idea if he left. I didn't want it go any further but I kept my calm.

"Len, I like you, but not this way. You're a dear friend and have been a big help to me. Let's not ruin that."

He backed off, held his head high and I could see that the coffee was working. He said okay and walked to the door and left.

It took me time to get over this experience. I was completely unaware. Anyway, Len and I remained good friends. I knew he was married and one of the most prestigious dentists in New York and that he would be feeling pretty bad when he sobered up.

One Friday night, Sally called and said she had heard of a great singles bar/ restaurant in New York City on West End Ave, Michael's and it was a fabulous jazz place. I told her I wasn't into going to single bars much any more but she begged, so I said okay.

We drove to the city and entered into an environment that reminded me of places in Harlem during the prohibition years of the 30s I had seen in the movies. I was a little nervous but we found two chairs at the bar and perused the place. Black and white people were mingling. I was feeling uncomfortable. I nudged Sally. "Sal, let's go—this spot is not quite my cup of tea."

"Come on, Marie," Sal whispered. This is the 'new wave' listen to that jazz music. Isn't it wonderful?"

I nodded; took a deep breath. The trio was playing a new song "You Make Me Feel Like a Natural Woman" being sung by a striking black female. She almost looked like Aretha Franklin who had just recorded it. I sat back, relaxed in my chair, listened and sipped my wine.

One of the most gorgeous looking black men I'd ever seen approached us and announced that he was the owner of the place and would like our first drinks be on the house. We thanked him and then began to engage in conversation with him. He was very charming and his attention to us made me feel safe.

After an hour listening to the great music, I told Sally I had to go to the ladies room which I discovered was down some stairs to the basement. As I came out of the room, there in the narrow corridor below the stairs was the owner, Michael. He grabbed my right arm gently and pulled me through a door just opposite the restroom. Then he started to kiss me and grabbed me tightly to him. I could hardly catch my breath. I pushed him away and looked around to see where I was—it was a storage room for food.

"Michael, come on. This is not a place to make love," I tried to say in a soft, calm voice but inside my heart was beating a mile a minute (I asked myself if this was going to be rape). "Just look around—huge cans of Campbell tomato juice and these pickle bottles. No, Michael—not here." Don't ask me why but I started to giggle and he looked at me for a minute, then turned his gaze to the cans on the shelves and started to laugh too.

"Okay, Marie, I'll see you later," and he let go of my arm.

I ran up the stairs to the bar, grabbed Sally and said, "Let's get out of here—now!" She looked stunned but took our purses from the bar counter and off we ran to the car. We quickly drove back to Palisades laughing all the way about an incident that could have been right out of the book "Looking for Mr. Goodbar." We never went back to that place again. I was lucky.

I could go on and on with other amusing and not so amusing experiences I had during this short period in my life. My two Judy friends were a part of them, too. Some of our lunches out were short stories in themselves. For example, Judy who was in the advertising department took me to lunch at one of the most popular places in Manhattan. We met a picturesque elderly man there who was a well-known artist. He treated us to lunch, drew my caricature on the tablecloth and as we were leaving asked me if I would like to go to his apartment to see his Koala Bear. Judy and I fumbled our way out of that invitation and of course never went back to the restaurant. However, the owner of the restaurant was nice enough to fold up the tablecloth and gave it to me as we left.

I think my life slowed down about then and it all started to come together when I had an almost fatal accident in Snedens.

2. GIRLFRIENDS GIVE ME STRENGTH!

T HE MONTH OF January in 1974 was a cruel month, weather-wise and otherwise. One night I was driving home from New York to Snedens in Jerry's car along with another neighbor. The snow was blinding when we got on the West Side Drive heading for the George Washington Bridge. We switched over to Riverside Drive but that too was impossible. Traffic was backed up, so we pulled into a parking place, got out of the car and went into a nearby restaurant to wait out the congestion on the highways. We had a light dinner and passed the time with small talk and cursing the bad weather we had been having. Commuting back and forth from the suburbs to the city takes a toll on working people, but that's the price we have to pay if we want the best of both worlds.

After an hour in the restaurant, I suggested we try it again because I knew Todd would be worried plus Rick said he was stopping by. I did try to call them, but as usual the phone was busy.

The traffic had cleared out a bit, so we made our way slowly across the bridge and onto the Palisades Parkway. It took us almost an hour with the blinding snow still hitting our windshield. Finally we found the Exit #4, turned off and took 9W down to Washington Spring road, our path into Snedens.

I breathed a sigh of relief that we had finally arrived safe and sound. Jerry stopped the car opposite my little house in the woods. I had a couple of shopping bags filled with papers I wanted to work on for the weekend plus some gifts I received from the cosmetic companies. I was dressed in a heavy coat, hat, gloves, scarf so it was hard for me to maneuver myself out of the car. My boots sunk into a foot of snow. I wiped the snowflakes off my eyelashes, held tight to my shoulder bag and the two shopping bags I was carrying. Jerry's car drove off and as I started to walk across the road, suddenly I saw lights to my right and they were coming right toward me. I couldn't lift my feet out of the snow. Within a split second two bright headlights were almost in my face—I dropped my bags, put my arms out front, palms up and when the car hit me, I turned to the side, placed my hands on the hood and yelled out "NO, NO!"

I must have slid about 20 feet on the snow in front of the car until it came to a stop. I remember seeing three anxious faces peering at me from behind the windshield of the car. Then I fell backward into the snow, looked up and saw a tire just a few inches away from my head. I think I blacked out for a second or two. When I opened my eyes, people were staring down at me.

"Oh, Marie, it's you. Are you hurt? We're so sorry. We didn't see you. What can we do?" one of them said.

I looked up and recognized them as friends of my kids. "I think I'm okay, but I can't feel anything in my right leg."

The three of them were in tears. One ran to my house to get Todd and Rick, the other ran to another house to get blankets and call 911.

Within five minutes there were loads of people taking care of me—covering my head with an umbrella to keep the snow off, throwing blankets on top of me. Rick came over and gave me a kiss and said that the ambulance would be there soon and not to worry.

Three ambulances showed up and off I went to Nyack hospital emergency room. The three young men and women who had hit me, followed the ambulance. I asked that Todd stay at home and that Rick come with me in the ambulance.

After they looked me over and finally wheeled me up for a leg X-ray it was amazing how alert I still was. I came back to emergency room to see the group of young people terribly distraught. I sat up and tried to comfort them.

"It's just a bad bruise, I'm sure," I said to quiet their anxieties.

But the nurse knew better. "You'd better take this pill, Mrs. Fenton, because you will be in a lot of pain later when the shock wears off. You were lucky that you were wearing all that heavy clothing when you were hit, and the snow cushioned your head when you fell to the ground." I took the pill.

Well, to make a long story short, the Xrays showed I had no broken hip. I was lucky. It was a deep Hematoma—like I predicted, a bad bruise, only a little worse. The doctor suggested I stay the night at the hospital but I insisted I go home.

I felt like a queen as they all tucked me into my bed. I bid them goodnight and told them not to worry that I'd be okay. Rick and Todd said they'd come in to check on me. I waved them all out and fell asleep immediately. All through the night, I kept seeing headlights, it was so weird. Finally, I fell into a deep sleep and didn't awake until the morning sun came shining through my drapes. The worst had passed.

I tried to get out of bed but my right thigh pained me so much, I couldn't do it. I rang the bell that Rick had put aside my bed. The clock showed it was 9 a.m. I couldn't believe I slept so late. It was Saturday, my shopping day to go for our weekly food supply.

"Oh dear," I said as Rick and Todd came rushing into the room after they heard me ring the bell. "What now—I can't even walk to the bathroom. How can I go shopping today?"

"Don't worry, Mom," said Rick. "Todd and I will do that. I called Heidi and she's coming this morning. Meanwhile, let me help you out of bed to go to the bathroom. And Johnny is coming over with his crutches he used when he broke his ankle."

Everything seemed under control and after I showered and put on a gown, I got back into bed and fell asleep again.

My daughter, Heidi, appeared around noon with a tray of soup and crackers. I was so glad to see her. She said she would spend the weekend and not to worry but that she'd have to leave Monday a.m. to get back to her job at the Museum of Modern Art. I said that was okay and thanked her for coming.

I was starting to feel better by early afternoon. The crutches had arrived. I hobbled around the house trying to get used to them. My upper right thigh was swollen but I thanked my lucky stars that I didn't have a broken hip.

Flowers arrived from the three young people who had been in the car that hit me. Other people stopped by to say hello. By late afternoon I was tired and took another nap while my kids took charge of the house.

It must have been about 5 p.m. when I awakened and heard voices in the living room. I rang the bell and Todd came in to tell me that Margaret and Sally were here to see me. I was feeling blue thinking about the stupid accident. I told Todd to let them in as I propped myself up in bed.

"Hey, Marie," my friend, Margaret, greeted me. "So, what's going on with the poker game tonight? We only have five so we need you."

"Margaret, give me a break," I answered with a laugh. "I can't possibly sit up in a chair."

"No problem," she replied. "We'll bring the game to you and you can stay in bed. You have the low round oak table here and we'll all sit around it and you can play from your bed. How does that sound?"

Sally then voiced "Yeah, Marie, go for it." "Hey, Marie, you can't let the poker group down!"

We all started to laugh. I shook my finger at them. "You're bad. You just want my money."

We agreed for an eight p.m. poker party. My kids were a bit aghast that I was going along with this. I felt revived after dinner which Heidi served up first class and I kept practicing on the crutches. My leg still hurt but a few painkillers solved that.

That poker night will always remain in my mind. Jerry, Margaret, Sally, Andy, Sy and Bob Meisner crowded around this low round oak table with me propped up with pillows. Whenever I had to lean over the table to place I bet, I'd yell "ouch." By one a.m. I had had it and called a close to the game. I won $10—so not all was lost. Without my girlfriends urging me on and taking my mind off my injury, I probably would have slept the night away waking depressed. But their laughter and a lot of Scotch and wine, I smiled myself to sleep.

Sunday morning arrived and I was able to think more clearly about what had happened and how I was going to cope going back to work on Monday. Over dinner I expressed my appreciation to my kids for their help and assured them that I would be okay. It scared me since Bob's death that if I wouldn't be around to care for them, what would happen to them all. I was not prepared to die now. I made up my mind not ever to leave them in distress.

All day Sunday I limped around the house without my crutches to test my leg and I was doing okay. I would be able to go back to work on Monday. The skin on my thigh had turned three colors already. I said to myself, "Well, there goes my sex life." During the late afternoon while in bed I reflected on the whole episode.

"Was this a message from "above" that I cool down my singles scene and go back to the sedentary life I had led before—all work and no play?" I questioned the whole past six months and couldn't come up with an answer.

Just as I was going to sleep, the phone rang and it was Peter. "Can I come over?" he asked. "Peter, I've been in an accident. I think you'd better wait a few weeks."

Within the half hour, Peter was at the door and Todd let him in. Peter sat on the other side of the round table next to my bed and I told him the whole story. He was so concerned and asked if he could just cuddle me. I agreed and we held each other in my bed until I told him he must leave because I had to go to work in the morning. That little bit of snuggling was comforting. Peter was a nice guy; I couldn't let him go.

At 7:30 a.m. on Monday, I hobbled out of the driveway, got into Jerry's car and we drove to New York. My co-workers questioned my limping. "I got hit by a car but I'm okay." They all gasped. My boss said I should have stayed home for a few days.

"Ben," I replied, "I've got to finish this issue and we're on deadline. Don't worry I'll be okay." I got my job done and felt good when I arrived home that night.

Day by day, I improved. I was now able to walk without a limp but my thigh injury still pained me. All colors of the rainbow showed up on my skin. My doctor said it would go way but he said the dent in my leg caused by the deep hematoma would remain and that unfortunately plastic surgery couldn't fix it. That distressed me no end. I had always prided myself on shapely long legs. Other women pride themselves on their narrow waist, long lashes, whatever—my best feature was my legs. I never sued for damages. I didn't want the kid who drove the car to be encumbered by a lawsuit. After all, it was an accident—no one was to blame.

A couple of weeks passed and I was back to my old self again, going to work, coming home to fix dinner for Todd and sometimes Rick, playing my Saturday night poker sessions. I became bored. I did see Peter once in a while but I began to realize that our relationship was going downhill because he was so unpredictable due to his FBI work. John was still attentive when I dropped into Polly's Cage with my girlfriends. The two Judy's advised me to cut out from that relationship.

"Marie, he's too old for you," said Judy P. one day. "Look for a younger, more supportive man."

"I guess you're right," I replied. "But he is sweet and has told me he loves me."

"Pooh, pooh," interjected Judy G. "You make him feel good and that's nice but there's no future with him. Give it up. And as for Abavi, he's only 26, Marie, let him off the hook—all he wants is your body. Sure, he's a great lover but he doesn't suit your lifestyle. Remember, you are a well-known woman in the magazine field. Find someone else your age; someone who'll fit in with your lifestyle."

I debated about taking my friends' advice. I thought I'd just let it flow. I knew I was not in love with them; I liked and cared for them but there was no "chemistry" between us. I preferred it that way. Maybe I was leery of falling in love again. Since Bob's death and Rick's illness, I had put my emotions into the closet. I was fearful of opening the door and letting all the pain out. This way I felt secure—I had admirers.

Near the end of February, 1974, I accepted an invite from Abavi to go out to dinner. We would meet at Tom Swifts—our old "hang-out." It had been months since I'd been to the single scene in New Jersey. It was a Friday night and I was alone. Todd was out to a movie. I dressed in a pretty silky blouse and my usual bellbottom jeans, slipped in my diaphragm (no way did I want to get pregnant). I drove to Tom Swifts and went to the bar to have a drink while I waited for Abavi to appear.

Tom Swifts had not changed much. The music was blaring "Did You See That Beautiful Woman Walk Out on Me?" My thigh still hurt when I sat on a hard chair so I tilted on my left hip. I ordered a Scotch and water, looked around to see if he had come early, but I couldn't see him. I relaxed and observed people around me. One young guy was trying to catch my eye but I disregarded him. I wasn't in the mood for that.

Suddenly, I saw a tall grey/blond-haired handsome older guy walk in the place, dressed in a dark blue top coat. I gasped to myself. "What a hunk!" I watched him as he sat on a stool on the opposite side of the bar. He looked like a banker, a lawyer, I surmised. I was definitely attracted to his aura.

I have always been attracted to tall men. The ones I went with were only 5'8 or so—this man looked over 6 foot tall. As he sat at the bar I kept an eye on him but did not stare. I saw him looking around and his gaze traveled toward me. It was then I looked straight back at him, smiled. He smiled back. It was a nice smile. Then the waiter came over and said, "The gentleman would like to buy you a drink." I thanked him and said no that I have one. After a few smiles across the bar, the tall man came around to my side.

"Hi," I said. "I've never seen you here before. Where are you from?"

"No, you've never seen me before," he replied. "This is my first time in a singles bar. I feel a little strange. Are you sure you wouldn't like another drink?"

"Thanks, no," I answered. "I'm waiting for a friend and we're going out to dinner. But, listen, I think I can clue you into how to handle the situations that go on in a singles bar if you want me to." He laughed. "No, I'm okay."

We then chatted a bit. I liked his face and his manner. I thought to myself, what is a nice guy doing in a place like this? So I questioned him.

"I'm just in the middle of a divorce," he replied. "My son urged me to get out and mingle with other people. I was feeling down."

"Nice son," I responded." What kind of business are you in?"

When he said he was in the funeral business, I almost choked on my Scotch. I took a deep breath and the only thing I could say was, "How interesting."

Nevertheless, I felt a deep attraction to this person. Suddenly I saw my date waving to me from the door. I jumped off the bar stool and excused myself.

"Hey, wait," said the man. "What's your name, mine is Bill? Where do you live? How can I get in touch with you?" I gave him a wave as I walked away and shouted out my response.

"I'm in the book, Marie Fenton in Snedens Landing." Then I walked away feeling sorry I was leaving this charming man though I knew a lot of the guys one meets in a singles bar ask for your phone number and never call. Why would this be different? C'est la vie.

I did not think about meeting Bill for the rest of the week. Suddenly, one night my phone rang at night just before I was going to bed. He mentioned his name and it took me a minute to recognize him.

"Oh, Yes, Bill, I remember now." I said. "I never expected to hear from you again."

"It wasn't easy," he replied. "Finally the operator found Snedens Landing and your listing. So here I am. Listen, I have to go out of town for a week but I'll be back and maybe we can get together for dinner. Would that be okay?"

"Sure, Bill." I answered. I hung up the phone and contemplated the conversation. It seemed he was interested in me but then again I questioned the reality of him actually calling me back in a week. I forgot about the whole conversation.

Meanwhile, I was very busy with my work at Good Housekeeping and was preparing for a photography shoot in Mexico. Rick was having a hard time with his mental illness. We met often with his therapist. It was very painful for both of us. Sometimes, he seemed so angry with me, other times nervous and withdrawn. He seemed to be coming more effeminate as the years went by. Ever since he was a little boy and wanted to put on my lipstick and dance around in my scarves, I wondered if he were homosexual. His lack of interest in normal male things, especially any kind of sports, made my suspicions grow. His interest in acting, dance and creative outlets entered into my thoughts, too. One mysterious thing

I learned recently was that pregnant women who had a special kind of estrogen shot back in the 50s to keep them from aborting might likely have a child with gender problems. I don't think this was ever proved, but I did have those shots in Paris when I was pregnant with Rick. I wanted to mention it to Bob many times but was afraid to bring up the subject. Bob never gave me any clue that he suspected anything different about Rick and died before I could get any opinion from him. Now, with his frequent feminine manners and female stride, I knew that others must be drawing the same conclusions and nobody was talking, nobody was giving me any confirmation that I was right. I would just have to wait and see if he would "come out of the closet,"—as they now called it.

At this point I didn't care if Rick were gay, black, yellow, whatever. I just wanted him to get well and live a normal life. I loved him so much. He was so smart and talented and creative, I knew if he could overcome his mental illness, he would be a success in show business. I was trying everything to help him reach his full potential but I was failing. I stopped crying at night. It only wrecked my sleep and left me wasted in the morning. I decided to put all my worries on the back burner for the time being, concentrate on my job and cut off dating men.

3. JOANNE—SHE GETS ME BACK ON THE RIGHT TRACK

AFTER A WEEK of concentrating on my work, my family interests plus trying to find a man to fix my roof which was leaking water into my house every time it rained, it seemed to me that I was sinking into a bit of depression myself.

My two friends, the Judy's, tried to perk me up at our weekly luncheon at Polly's Cage, My bills were piling up what with Rick's illness and suddenly Heidi was asking me if I could help her out. Of course, I couldn't refuse either of them but I wondered where the money would come from. I was making a good salary. It was just that even when I wrote an extra mini-book or an article out-of-house, those monies were gone to pay bills even before I could use them to buy myself a new outfit for work.

My boyfriends, John, Peter and Abavi kept calling. I stalled them off.

One night in late February, 1974, I was reading a book by Anis Nin, a writer who was enlightening me with every word she had written back in the 30s, 40s. The phone rang.

"Hi, Marie," Bill said, "I'm back from St. Louis. Are you free for dinner?"

I put my head back on the pillow, took a deep breath and waited a few seconds before answering. I hadn't thought about this man I'd met at Tom Swifts for weeks, yet he kept his word saying he would call me when he got back after his business trip. Why not? I asked myself. I think I need a night out.

"Okay, Bill," I responded. "Do you like Chinese?" He said yes. I told him to pick me up on Friday and we'd go to China Chalet in Northvale, nearby. I then gave him directions on how to get to my house. But I was still skeptical that he'd come.

When I opened the door to welcome Bill, I was smitten by this tall handsome man, just as I had been when I first saw him at the bar. He was dressed in a beautiful blue suit with a tie, his gray/blonde hair softly done and a bright smile on his face. I took a deep breath and told him I'd be right out as soon as I got my jacket. I didn't ask him in because I had pots all over the house catching the drips from the roof.

He asked as I closed the door, "Don't you lock your door?"

"Oh, no," I answered,. "Not here in Snedens. Everyone leaves their doors open. Anyway, I don't have a key." He smiled but said nothing as we walked to his car, a big yellow Plymouth station wagon.

On the way to the restaurant which was just a few miles away, we chatted about the weather and he mentioned that he'd had a good business meeting in St. Louis. I then remembered he was in the funeral business . . . I kept my cool and uttered something goofy like, "Well, I guess that's a business that'll never die."

The restaurant was crowded and I hadn't thought to make reservations, so we went into the bar area and found a booth in a quiet corner.

I ordered my favorite, a Dry Rob Roy on the Rocks and Bill asked for a Manhattan. We started dipping the Chinese noodles into the sweet dip. I slipped off my coat, smoothed back my hair and leaned back. Suddenly, in this man's presence, I felt safe and comfortable like I hadn't felt for a long time. I wondered why.

We started to talk. He asked me about my work. He discussed his first marriage which ended when his wife died of cancer. Then I told him my husband had died of cancer, too. We kept munching on the Chinese noodles, talking, talking.

By the time our dinner arrived, we had revealed a lot of our past histories to each other. Bill was easy to talk to—and he listened, which I liked. He had three children, two boys in their twenties and living on their own by his first wife who had died and a nine year-old girl by his second wife whom he was now divorcing. I told him I had the same genders of kids—two boys and a girl. We laughed about the coincidence.

I felt confident telling him about Rick's mental illness and all the trouble I was having with him. He tried to comfort my fears by saying that eventually Rick would be able to cope with his illness. That made me feel good.

After dinner, we drove back to my house and I saw a little bar on the side of the road which I knew was a nice quiet place to hang out and suggested we stop. We had a drink, put on the juke box and he asked if I'd like to dance. It was a Beattles' song "In My Life." The lyrics were very relevant to what I was feeling right then. Then one of my favorites came up "Dream a Little Dream of Me," by Mama Cass. We only had a small dance floor but he guided me carefully. I was beginning to feel infatuated with this new man I'd met.

When we pulled into my driveway, I started to open the door to go in. I didn't want to invite him in because I had my period and felt it wasn't a good night for sex. So, I bid him goodnight and he gave me a strong kiss which set my hormones on fire. We kept necking. "Call me soon, Bill," I said jumping out of the car and into the house. When I went to sleep that night I had the funny feeling that he would.

Bill did call back during the week and we made a date to go out again. This time I invited him into the house. The pots and pans were still standing around in the living room and kitchen. We were in a non-stop rainy period. Everyday before I left for work, Todd and I emptied the pots. I knew I would have to have the roof fixed but I didn't know who to go to nor did I have the time to pursue it at this time. Spring was coming soon.

"What's going on here?" Bill asked as he walked through the house. I told him what was going on. He laughed and without hesitation said, "I'll help you fix your roof."

Todd came out of his bedroom and I introduced him to Bill. Todd was getting used to meeting all my new boyfriends, so he was polite and probably figured that this guy would be in and out of his life in no time.

Then Bill asked Todd if he would be around to help him and some other workers fix the roof the following weekend. It seemed that Todd liked the idea, especially since he had three pots sitting in his bedroom. Bill advised him to stay home the following Saturday and they'd work on the roof. Todd said okay.

Bill and I went out to dinner at the Tappan Pub, a small cozy restaurant. We talked a lot the whole evening and I enjoyed his company. I thanked him for his interest in repairing my roof but told him I would have to pay for it over a period of time since my financial funds were low this month. He said okay and that he'd work it out. Our waitress, Jeanie, was very attentive to us that night, even brought Bill an extra salad at no cost. After that, she was our exclusive waitress whenever we came to the Pub.

By the time we got back to my house, it was almost midnight. Todd had planned to sleep over at a friend's house, so I invited Bill in for a nightcap.

As I sipped my cognac, Bill preferred coffee, we sat on the small couch in the living room. I turned on the hi-fi and heard an oldie but a goody come on: "When I Fall in Love, It'll Be Forever." I found it easy to feel romantic.

I knew after this third encounter with Bill there was good chemistry between us. He slipped his arm around me and we cuddled quietly on the sofa. Then he kissed me and I kissed him back and before I could count to ten, he picked me up bodily and carried me into my bedroom where we made passionate love. Occasionally, I would shout out, "careful of my hematoma, I was in "seventh heaven." He was very gentle. I experienced my first orgasm since Bob had died.

It must have been about 2 a.m. when he left. I awoke the next morning with the sun shining through the blinds. "Wow," I said out loud, "That was a fabulous night." I quickly got up, showered and rushed to the supermarket to pick up groceries and extras for the weekly poker game that was to be held at my house that night.

On Monday, I was feeling so great that I invited the two Judy's to meet me at Polly's Cage for lunch. I told them I had exciting news. When they heard about Bill and his attention to me, they were thrilled.

"Marie," said Judy P. "I think you struck gold—stick with his man, forget the others. I think you've got him hooked."

"Yes, I know what you're telling me," I replied, "but it's scary to get heavily involved with one guy. I don't want my heart broken again. Look what happened when I was obsessed with Barry. These other boyfriends I've had are just that—boyfriends. I feel that now is not the time to concentrate on Bill. He could just cut out. How do I know?"

They agreed and we let the subject drop. However, I did think about all this that night as I was getting ready for bed.

On Wednesday a.m., Judy G. came rushing into my office and said that a marvelous woman writer was giving an interview and lecture at the New School during lunch hour and asked if I'd like to go with her to attend the meeting. "Wow, yes, Judy," I answered with enthusiasm. "I'll meet you at the elevator at noon."

Anais Nin, now in her early 70s, had become my mentor because of her personal diaries which I'd read over and over. Her other books about relationships with famous artists like Henry Miller and, a famous psychiatrist in the '20s and '30s in Paris, Otto Rank fascinated me. I not only loved her style of writing but her openness in revealing her sexual and sensual feelings. It was comforting to me to learn the sexual feelings I was having were not new and strange. The feminist movement had

MARIE FENTON GRIFFING

opened my eyes and ears to exciting new things. Anais' encounters and feelings regarding men sometimes were so poignant I recognized them easily. Her self-expression had stimulated me to write about my escapades in the diary Heidi had given me for Christmas.

When I came back to the office at 2 p.m., I was so invigorated by having listened to this lovely, intelligent woman who had so much insight into the female id and ego that I knew I was going in the right direction with my own feelings. And, it made me focus more strongly on Bill's and my relationship.

The following Saturday Bill pulled up in the driveway, his station wagon filled with huge cans of tar. A small truck drove in behind him. I was just getting out of the shower and heard Todd in the kitchen. "Bill's here to do the roof, Todd." "Yeah, I see him. I'm ready."

I was pleased that Todd was putting importance on this situation. I had felt for sometime now he needed a man around, a father figure to help guide him during these young years of his life. Even though Rick was now in his twenties, I still thought a serious, common sense man like Bill could bring him out of his fantasy world but maybe it was too late. I was also hoping that when Heidi got to know him she, too, would feel more secure—if not for herself, then for me. But I was only a mother, who was I to know.

This generous action that Bill took—to fix my roof—was the first of many to come. It not only showed his caring for me and my family but it brought stability in my home that had been missing since Bob died. For the first time in many years, I thought of my father and I felt protected again.

Bill and I started seeing each other more often, sometimes three times a week. Over Memorial weekend in May, he asked me to spend a weekend in his trailer which was in a park next to a New Jersey lake about two hours away. I thought it would be a wonderful escape and plus I'd never been inside a trailer or seen a lake around our area.

"I'd like to bring my daughter, Tracey, if it's okay with you. I get custody of her every weekend."

"Sure," I replied but I felt a little nervous, wondering how this nine year old would take to me—her father's girlfriend. His divorce wouldn't be final for awhile. I had read "divorce" articles recently about the delicate situation that can occur when a child encounters the "other woman" in her father's life. But I felt it was the time to meet the girl and handle it the best I could. I still had not met Bill's two sons. I did have second thoughts, like why am I getting in so deep?—Can we really pull this relationship off? I could see there were a lot of differences between Bill and me: he was conservative. I was liberal minded. He offered me strength. I gave him a new outlook on life. I guess in some way, we complimented each other. I decided to let it flow for the time being and just enjoy his attention and loving nature, something I knew would be good for me and my kids.

My first adventure in the trailer on the lake was wonderful. Tracey was friendly to me but I could feel a barrier between us. I took that as a normal reaction to her meeting me. I tried to please her in little ways. I liked the way Bill gave equal attention to both of us. We went swimming and sailed on his little sunfish boat. It was the first time I had ever been on a sailboat. We picked wildflowers which I flushed a few down the new toilet Bill installed in the trailer. I called it a "christening." We all laughed. We even fried up a small fish that Tracey caught in the lake—one bite for everyone.

The following Tuesday, I called my good friend Joanne whom I'd met in Tarzana and had helped me when I first came to New York. We had lost track of each other. She had divorced her husband and moved from New Jersey into Manhattan. Luckily, she had a wonderful job at the Museum of Modern Art and custody of her two girls, Andrea and Pauline. Both of us had been through troubled times and when we talked on the phone we agreed it was time that we touch base. Each of us was singly trying to keep afloat financially as well as handling our families as single mothers. When she told me she had met a marvelous man, Richard Koch, head of the Museum and would get married soon, I was so happy for her.

Joanne and I met for lunch at my favorite Chinese restaurant on 57th street. I was looking forward to the meeting. I had so many things to tell her and I knew she would have a lot of news for me.

I arrived early at the Yang Zee River restaurant and was sitting sipping my Dry Rob Roy when I saw Joanne walk toward me. She looked so regal with her brown hair pulled back into a tight bun revealing the wonderful bone structure on her face. She was dressed elegantly in a Channel-like navy suit. She smiled when she saw my wave. Her eyes shone. We both kissed and she ordered a glass of wine.

"Marie, I can't believe we're meeting once more. How are you? What's going on? I hope you have good news to tell me because I've good news to tell you." she said.

"Yes, Joanne, I've good news. But tell me yours first."

"Dick and I got married," she replied. "It was a spur-of-the-moment ceremony. Andrea and Pauline were there and Dick's kids too."

"Wow," I responded. "That's wonderful. I wish I could have been there."

"You'll probably receive an announcement in the mail any day now. It all happened so quickly. But now, enough of my good news—let's hear yours."

Meanwhile, we ordered our lunch and I proceed to tell her about Bill and my past encounters with the other men I'd met the last six months. We laughed a lot and she couldn't believe some of the episodes I recounted to her.

"Marie," she said, "I'm so afraid your past sexual experiences could become dangerous. From what you tell me, Bill sounds like a stable guy and one you should hold on to. It took me a long time to get serious about a new man, but I did and I've never been happier. Why don't you bring Bill over to our house one night for dinner and then I can give you a more true opinion of him?"

Later, we discussed our kids. I told her how appreciative I was that she helped Heidi get the film job at the Museum of Modern Art. She had known about Rick's problems. I could only tell her he was still having his ups and downs.

"Marie," Joanne said. "I'm sorry to hear about Rick but I'm sure in time he will find himself again. He's young and with good medical advice, he'll be okay."

I sighed. "I hope so, Joanne," I replied. "It scares me because of his previous suicide attempts. I love him so much. He's such a smart, talented young man but it just seems he has lost the will to live. It's like a burden for him to carry. He just can't focus on what he wants to do or what he is. It's those damn drugs he's been into for years. They really fucked up his head and I'm furious at our government, people selling this crud to youngsters but I can't do anything about it."

Before we knew it, our lunch meeting was over and both of us had to get back to our offices. I told Joanne we'd come for dinner at seven p.m. the following Friday. I helped get her a cab and then slowly walked back to the Hearst Building.

As I sipped on a cup of coffee back in my office, I reflected on what Joanne had said. It made me feel good what she said about Bill. I was glad we had talked.

Bill and I went to dinner at Joanne and Dick's apartment in the Village. Dick was gracious, charming and handsome. I remarked to Joanne while we were in the kitchen alone. "He's wonderful. You're so lucky!" When we finished our after-dinner-coffee and liquor, Bill and I said our goodbye's. As Joanne helped me slip on my fur coat, she whispered in my ear, "Marie, I think you have a winner here—don't let him go." I smiled at her and whispered back, "Okay, we'll see."

That summer of 1974 was a mixture of euphoria, stress and sometimes "burning the candle" at both ends. My assignments at work were growing. I was now doing shoots out of town, covering beauty pageants around the country, sometimes being a judge; interviews with young TV and movie stars plus trying to keep up the growing sales of the Good Housekeeping Beauty Book. My boss was very pleased how the magazine was developing. I was now invited to the monthly luncheons for top editors and given a larger office with two assistants. With so many press parties I had to attend, I was only able to lunch with the two Judy's once a week. I enjoyed those meetings the best because we laughed a lot and I could open up and talk about my personal life. They tried to cheer me up whenever I mentioned the problems I was having with Rick. I just didn't know how I could resolve the situation. I always was on pins and needles whenever my phone rang.

Bill and I usually ate dinner out at the Pub or China Chalet when we were dating. Finally, I asked him to come one Saturday for dinner at my place. I cooked a simple meal of lamb chops, boiled potato, salad and apple pie for desert. Afterward, we planned to catch an eight p.m. movie in Nyack, a town nearby.

While sipping our coffee, Bill started to complain of abdominal pains. I gave him some stomach pills but the pains got worse, so bad that he called his doctor. Meanwhile, I tried to reassure him that the pains would go and we could make the movie. The pains kept coming and he called his doctor again who told him to immediately go to Pascack Valley hospital in New Jersey, about a half hour away.

"Marie, you'll have to drive, he cried out as he struggled to get up. "Let's go!"

I jumped into the driver's seat of Bill's huge stationwagon. I had never driven such a big car. Bill stretched out in the back seat, groaning like a sick calf.

"Bill, tell me where in the hell do I go to get to the hospital?" were my distress words as I drove 9W to Route 4 which I knew would take me to

New Jersey. He only kept moaning. I must have been driving 70 miles an hour when I heard a police siren behind me. Trying to keep the "yellow monster" on the road was more than I could handle . . . I was swerving and weaving at a fast pace. I could have gone off the road and killed us both. I pulled over and the cop came and asked for my identification and registration. As I reached into my purse for my license I said in a panic-stricken voice, "Officer, I have a very sick man here and I have to rush him to Pascack Valley Hospital. Please tell me where to go!"

He pointed his flashlight into the backseat of the car and saw Bill wrenching with pain. "Okay, lady, just drive till you get to Route 4, then you'll see a sign marked "Pascack Valley Hospital"—just follow that road."

I breathed a sigh of relief as I pulled back onto 9W and drove more cautiously until I finally found the emergency entrance to the Hospital. I helped Bill out of the car and with the aid of a nurse gave him into the care of the emergency doctors on duty.

While I paced in the waiting room, all sorts of thoughts fled through my head—"What if this man dies, who do I notify? Did my lamb chops poison him?

After about a half hour, a nurse came into the room and asked for Mrs. Griffing. I said I'm a friend, not his wife. She said that the cause of his pain had not as yet been diagnosed and he would have to stay in the hospital over night for diagnosis and that I should go home. I said okay but then thought of Bill's son, Mark, who would be worrying about him if he didn't come back to the trailer. I had Bill's phone number in my purse but no change for a phone call. A couple people in the waiting room donated a nickel and some dimes. I am sure they thought me weird.

I finally reached Mark. He said he would come to the hospital and I should go home in the car. I slowly drove back to Snedens. It was already midnight, Todd was in bed and I took a quick shower and fell fast asleep still quivering from the experience. And I whispered a silent prayer to God, "Please don't let him die!"

The next morning, I told Todd over breakfast about the happening. He suggested I call the hospital. I was shaking as I dialed the number and asked about Bill. The nurse at the station told me "Mr. Griffing had a kidney stone and passed it during the night. He will have to stay in the hospital for a day or two for further tests."

Thank God, he didn't die. I went to visit him that afternoon carrying a little potted violet (one of my favorite flowers) for him. He was happy to see me. As I recapped the whole incident for him, we both started laughing at the whole episode. I left him with a kiss and a hug. I was glad to have my man back and realized how important he was to me at that time. However, I reflected on what might have been if he had a more serious illness, like cancer. Could I go through another sickness with Bill as I had done with Bob. I thought not. No way am I going to think of marriage now. It was a long time before I cooked Bill another meal.

Summer '74 was coming to an end. Bill and I spent Labor Day weekend alone at his trailer on the lake. It was perfect weather. I was getting acclimated to trailer living and enjoyed it. We'd go sailing on his little boat. I liked the hominess of mingling with the other people who had trailers around us. They were unsophisticated families who spent their spare time barbecuing, swimming, and just sitting around on their beach chairs in front of their trailers. I got to know some of them and learned a lot about "trailer" people I'd never knew before. Before we left on Monday, Bill went sailing and I took a sunbath on the grass next to the trailer.

I slipped on my short-short cut-off jeans, the bra top from my bathing suit, sunglasses, slathered suntan lotion on my body, and poured myself a drink of half Scotch, half orange juice. I grabbed a blanket from the bunk bed and set up my spot on a small plot of grass next to the trailer.

It was a perfect day, about 75 degrees, lots of puffy clouds floating in the sky, the breeze crisp and cool and the sun shining brightly. There were no noises or voices emanating from the surrounding trailers. Most people had gone down earlier to fish, boat or swim on this, their last vacation day in this lovely place.

I stretched out on my back and gazed toward the sky. I felt wonderful today, all seemed calm in the world around me. The wonderful lovemaking that Bill and I had had the night before still stirred my loins. Busy Manhattan, my worries about Rick, my office commitments for the week ahead seemed to be on hold. I breathed in the fresh air and closed my eyes for a while. Then I began to think about this experience I was having and remembered that I had written hardly any verses since Barry and my relationship ended. I decided I'd record the feelings I was having right then. I jumped up from the blanket and walked back into the trailer where I found a pad of paper and pencil; returned to the blanket, laid down on my tummy and started to write.

"A NATURE SUNBATH"

What warmth, what a delicious way to take a sunbath,
smack dab in the middle of a country field.
My sunbaths have always been on the hot sand
with people running by, kicking the granules onto my oily skin.
Or in my back yard on a hard chaise, the telephone ringing
just as I get settled down.
Or on a high terrace with air conditioners buzzing in my ears,
voices screeching out in the afternoon heat.
But today it's different, and good.
As I lay flat in the tall grass, I look around.
The weeds are tossing and twisting in the wind, so tall around me.
The black-eyed Susans are nodding approvingly
and the clovers have an iridescent glow about them.
The mini grasshoppers jump off and on my bare feet as if to say "Welcome,"
The honey bees that I'm always so fearful of, keep their distance.
I only hear their low hum.
When I look upward, I see a blueness that like the sea, cools, refreshes.
And the sun's so strong I feel it's focusing all its strength just on me.
As I turn my head to the right, I see trees moving in rhythm to the breeze.
When the wind stops, so do the trees.
Then like a conductor, the wind song begins again.
There's an encore and the trees vibrate once more.
The field grass is blown to one side ordered so by the gusts.
They're so green and shiny I want to get up and do a roll in them.
But I feel too calm, too warm—maybe later.
I wish you were here with me to feel this wonder of being a part,
just a small part of nature in its true form: simple yet beautiful,
with its summertime lushness, its richness of color,
and its hypnotic ways that captivate the human being into its world.
Now it's time to roll in the grass.

When I showed this piece to Judy G., she liked it so much she asked
if she could submit it to a friend of hers who published "Letters" a
poetry pamphlet regularly put out by a small book press company. I said
okay—and was pleased she thought it worthwhile to have published. And
it was in their next issue.

"Marie," Judy encouraged "Do more of this type of writing. You're good at it; forget the magazine business."

"Yeah," I laughed. "Who's going to pay the mortgage and put food on the table?" She hugged me.

4. OLGA . . . "MY SISTER" GUIDES ME ON

THE FALL OF 1974 passed quickly. The trees around my house turned into more colorful hues than I had ever seen before. Bill called them "Marie's trees." I liked that because for the first time I felt I had something very special surrounding me. I wondered if it also included Bill. I felt it did.

Through a series of painful but amicable breakups with Abavi, Peter and John, I was now settling into a relationship with one man, Bill. He had made changes in my life, and all for the better. However, I wasn't ready for any life-long commitment—I did not want to consider the prospect of marriage.

Although I was busy with my magazine work, Bill and I kept dating more often. One time he asked me to fly with him to Las Vegas to attend a funeral supply business convention. Because it was over a short weekend and he said he'd pay for the flight, etc., I agreed. I wanted to fly from Vegas straight on to Los Angeles to visit my mother and brother first while he was doing his business on Friday and then fly back to Vegas to be with him. He said fine.

Thursday afternoon when I got back home, I received a call from Rockland Hospital that my son, Todd, had been in an accident and was in the emergency room. He used my car that morning to go to school and had a collision with another car. I ran across the street and Gus lent me his car to drive to the hospital. Apparently, Todd had two friends in the car with him driving back from school and collided with a car driven by another 16-year-old. It seemed it was no one's fault, no one was hurt, so no one was charged, thank goodness.

Todd was emotionally devastated when I arrived in the emergency room. All the other kids involved were okay except one who had a slight gash on her face. Poor Todd was so upset. I tried to quiet him down and told him that accidents do occur and most times it's no one's fault. I then talked with the mother of the injured girl and things were quieting down.

I told Todd I would cancel my trip to Vegas to stay with him. He insisted I go and that he'd be okay. I smiled at him, gave him a hug and said okay.

I learned my favorite little Toyota had been totaled. I didn't want to think about all the aftermath of insurance calls, etc. I'd have to do. I then called Rick to stay with Todd while I'd be away. I strongly felt I needed this time away with Bill. I also wanted Todd to know that his urging me on to go to Vegas was a mature decision. And for me it would give me an opportunity to see my family in Los Angeles whom I hadn't seen in many years.

Olga, my friend in Snedens, walked into the house as I was packing for the trip.

"Marie, I heard about the accident. But the kids are all okay. You go and have a good time with your boyfriend. You deserve some fun. Don't let this worry you, I will keep an eye on everything."

I gave Olga a kiss and thanked her. She was an amazing woman—always there for me when things got tough. I never knew how to repay her for her caring and kindness. I guess she would get her reward in heaven (as my mother used to say).

There we were on the plane flying over the Grand Canyon and with my little Kodak camera I caught beautiful photos of the wondrous colors of the canyons, the clouds and blue sky. For awhile I felt guilty about leaving Todd alone in his misery of ruining my car but Bill quieted my qualms. "We'll handle all that when we get back home. Let's enjoy the now."

I laid my head back on the chair and dozed through the next couple of hours.

We kissed goodbye as Bill got off in Vegas. I said I'd be back at the airport the next morning to be with him over the weekend. I was looking forward but a little nervous about seeing my mother who was in her 80s plus other family members I'd hadn't seen in years.

It was good to see the Duffy clan again. It pained me to see my mother old and fragile but being in her 80s, I knew this was part of life. She was happy when I told her I had a boyfriend and thought Bill was very handsome when I showed her a photo of him. One of the first things she asked was if were Catholic. "No, Mother, he's Presbyterian." She shook her head than said, "Well, it's important your children have a man around." I smiled and gave her a hug. And that was the last time I saw her. She died in a nursing home a few years later. I went back to LA for the funeral. I never did tell her about Rick's problems—it would be hard for her to understand, plus I had the feeling if she knew, she'd blame it on my not raising the kids in the Catholic religion. I was still carrying a lot of leftover grief from Bob's death and Rick's break-down. I didn't need to be burdened with more guilt feelings.

When I got off the plane from LA in Las Vegas, Bill was there to greet me with a bouquet of flowers. I was so happy to see him. Spotting his smiling face in the crowd of people, caused a queasy feeling in my tummy. Somehow, I knew then that I was in love with this wonderful man.

I did not know his parents would be there too. I had never met them and I was very nervous because Bill and I were sharing a room. I suspected they were conservative people. I didn't want them to think I was a "floosie." But to the contrary they were warm and receptive to me. We had cocktails together and attended the exotic shows in the casino. Harriett, Bill's mom, was a gracious lady and Ken, Bill's father, had a wonderful sense of humor. He said I looked a lot like one of his aunts. To my delight, we all seemed to get along very well. It was a memorable vacation.

When we returned to Snedens, all seemed to be going okay and I returned to my job at Good Housekeeping. The only problem was that I no longer had a car—so back to the bus.

A couple of evenings later, I heard a car pull up in the driveway. I ran to the door and saw Bill get out. He stretched out his arms. "It's all yours," he shouted. I laughed and walked slowly over to him, gave him a kiss and looked at the car. It was a Buick burgundy-colored station wagon. I didn't know the year, but didn't care. It looked good to me. I would be receiving money from the insurance company soon.

"It's not new," he said, "but I checked it out and it won't cost you much." I was pleased to think that he took the time out from his busy job to go look for a car for me.

My friend, Olga, would stop in on the weekends when she knew Bill would be there. He would always be working on some repair job in the house. She and Bill became good friends, always kidding each other. Her English wasn't the greatest and it was hard for Bill to understand her sometimes but somehow that didn't matter.

"Mr. Bill," she'd say time after time, "You take care of 'my sister'. If you don't, I will put the voodoo on you." Then she'd laugh. Bill would raise his right hand and answer, "I promise."

When I was alone in the house, Olga would pop in with a bowl of soup or a loaf of Cuban bread and we'd talk while I was fussing around in the kitchen.

"Marie, you know I loved your Bob," she'd say. "But he's gone for five years now—stay with Bill, marry him. I like him very much and he's good for you and the children. I know because the spirits tell me."

She always scared me when she'd bring her unique spiritual advice into my world. But I loved her all the same. To me she was a part of the family and we did have a "sister" relationship even though she was more than ten years older than I was.

With the Christmas holidays approaching, I didn't know quite what to buy Bill for a present. We had been growing closer and closer. Our dog and cats were used to him being around—Heidi, Rick and Todd too. He was spending five out of seven nights with me now. I really missed those two nights he wasn't with me and wondered about asking him to move in with me.

One night while I was preparing supper, Olga walked in unexpectedly as she always did. She looked at the newly painted walls that Bill with the help of the kids had done. "So, when are you going to get married," she asked.

I laughed. "Olga, give me time. I'm thinking of inviting him to live with me but what would the kids and neighbors say?"

She started to giggle, stretched her arms and said, "Marie.—you are living in Sneden's Landing. Laurence Olivier and Vivien Leigh lived "in sin" here—and I can name dozens more through the years. You may not know, but others are living together right here now. This is a 'free spirit' neighborhood where no one cares what a neighbor does as long as they don't hurt or violate another's territory. If he or she wants to live with someone even though they're not married, we don't care. We're not gossipers. This is a spiritual community." It was food for thought, but I was still dubious.

I mentioned our conversation to Bill on the phone and he thought it was a great idea for us to live together. The next evening when Todd and I were about to sit down to dinner, Bill's yellow station wagon drove up the driveway with a huge queen-size mattress and spring on the roof. I started to giggle as did Todd. As the two men lowered the mattress from the roof and brought it into my small bedroom, I stood stunned at the door. When they had replaced the twin-bed mattress Bill and I had been sleeping on for months with the big new one, the only thing I could say was, "Now, I have to go out and buy sheets!" We all laughed and I knew then I had accepted Bill into my life.

Christmas Eve, 1974, came and I felt I had a complete family around. Rick, Todd and Heidi went on their annual hunt for the perfect Xmas tree which I told them emphatically should not be more than 8 feet tall. Meanwhile, Bill and I started a roaring fire in the fireplace and I prepared a buffet-type dinner. Lo and behold, in come the kids dragging this gorgeous pine almost 10 feet tall. I admonished them but their giggles won over. Bill and Todd cut off 2 feet so it would fit to the ceiling, and I used the remaining branches to decorate the house—all was not lost. I think they liked to play this little game with me, and I got a kick out of that. One of the things I love about my kids—they always find the right times to make me laugh.

We decorated the tree, ate up a storm and had a really good time. Then the carolers from around Snedens came to serenade us about 10 p.m. It was a lovely evening and the best holiday I had in a long time.

The following morning, we all gathered together for breakfast. Bill made his fabulous pancakes and we began opening presents with Heidi being "Santa Claus." Bill and I both received great sweat outfits from the kids. I gave them clothing of one sort or other—telling them they could exchange if they wanted to; I had the receipts. Then I presented my gift to Bill for everyone to see. They all had to come into my bedroom—I pulled out two of the four drawers in the bureau and displayed a dozen T-shirt, a dozen pair of underwear, a dozen socks, some handkerchiefs and a couple of dress shirts and ties.

"Welcome to my house, William," I said laughingly. The kids applauded and I think Bill was a little befuddled by all this attention but he clapped too and gave me a hug.

Then we went back to the living room where now Bill called for attention. "Come hither, Marie, I have a surprise for you." I could see the gleam in my kids' eyes. He ushered me to the kitchen and lo and behold—a washing machine and dryer appeared from behind the door that led to the den. He and the kids had hidden it there all night. I was absolutely flabbergasted. "See, Mom," said Todd jumping up and down, "Now we don't have to go to the Laundromat any more!"

I think this was the most thoughtful gift I'd ever received in my life. After Bill, Rick and Todd plugged in the machines, we gleefully put through a machine full of wash. Similar to what I did when Bill installed his new toilet in the trailer and I flushed wild flowers down, I grabbed a couple of fresh bay leaves I had growing in my kitchen and dropped them in with the clothes. Everyone looked at me strangely, but they did dissolve and left a nice scent.

And so it went. For the next four months, Bill and I were enjoying our new lifestyle—The funeral business was getting bad. He felt one day he wanted to start his own cabinetry business. He was so talented with making furniture and creative with his hands that I urged him to do so. He helped keep my house in shape, fixing broken cabinets or doors, repairing my sunken sofa—so many wonderful changes he made. I was so grateful for having such help in my life.

Olga came over one day during the weekend when Bill was away and said she was worried about Rick. I told her I was too. Since Xmas, he had been having ups and downs. She looked tired and a little depressed. I gave her a hug and thanked her for her concern and told her to take care of herself.

It wasn't more than a week later in early 1975 that Rick rushed into the house on a Saturday afternoon when I was preparing dinner. He was crying and jumping up and down. "What, Rick? What has happened?" "Olga is dead," he said.

I was stunned. I hugged Rick and we cried together.

"Mom, she had a stroke and died yesterday. A neighbor found her on the floor; the dog and bird were going wild because they were hungry. People said it was awful. Oh, Mom, what are we going to do without Olga?"

I tried to quiet Rick down. He like all the other kids in Snedens had grown up with Olga; she was their "safety net" when they were in need. I tried to stay calm, gave Rick a bowl of soup that I was cooking. I puttered around the house to stay sane myself. Like Rick, I thought, what am I going to do without Olga?

About an hour later, other friends in Snedens brought me this huge bird cage with Apollo in it. I had given Apollo to Olga years back because she loved my first mynah bird. They said I would know how to care for it. I had to take it. Apollo was distraught, flying around the cage. He slowly settled down and started to cry out, "Lenny, Lenny," which was Olga's son's name. We all were flabbergasted; grabbed one another because the voice was just like Olga's. Then we started to laugh. It was just too incredible to believe. Then Apolla started to yell again, sounding exactly like Olga, "Who's there; Who's there?" It was rather spooky, but somehow I felt that Olga's spirit was still around us. Even though Rick was still distraught, the presence of the bird and hearing Olga's voice, quieted him down.

Olga's son, Lenny, had been living in California. He came back to Snedens the next day and I asked him about the bird. He said he'd be grateful if I kept it. What else could I do but say yes. From that time on until Apollo died five years later, Olga's voice would echo through the house. I'll never forget Olga.

5. MY OTHER "SISTERS" HELP ME
THROUGH MY WORST TRAGEDY

EVERYONE IN SNEDENS grieved Olga's passing, especially Rick. He went into depression again. I called his analyst and he said Rick would probably come out of it and he would talk with him. I didn't like the tiny room he was living in at a halfway house in Nyack. I suspected drugs were still easily available in that area. I called him almost every night to see how he was doing.

Meanwhile, I was very busy with my magazine work. Bill and I had become closer. I had his parents along with his son, Mark, and girlfriend, Debbie, his daughter, Tracey and my kids, Heidi, Todd and Rick over for Easter dinner. It really felt like "family" again with so many people gathered at my table. Bill was a big help in carving the lamb and doing cleanup afterwards. Heidi and Debbie carried dishes in and out. We all got to know each other better and I could sense that my kids liked being included in this unique setting. For years they had missed the intimacy of family get-togethers. I hoped it would heal a lot of wounds.

The early summer of 1975 was a mixture of out-of-town business projects for me, spending weekends with Bill and his daughter, Tracey, at the trailer by the lake, celebrating Rick and Todd's birthdays in June. I couldn't believe that Rick had turned 24 and Todd was 17 and would soon graduate from high school. The only graduation I attended so far was that of Rick back in 1969. I couldn't have been more proud of him at that time—valedictorian of his class, star of the play, "Man of La Mancha," and accepted at Northwestern University. But my dreams for him vanished when he crashed because of drug use—and the rest is history. I felt so bad for him. I wished I could wave a magic wand and we could go backward in time. There were times I hurt so deeply.

The 4th of July weekend, 1975 was approaching, which meant Heidi's 21st birthday on July 5th called for a birthday party. I invited her to come back to Snedens from her NY apartment and join us for dinner on July

4th. After that Bill and I would spend Sunday and Monday in his trailer on the lake for another get-away.

Rick and Heidi arrived early Saturday afternoon and helped me decorate the table. I planned to eat outside in the garden. The cake was bought and everything was ready to go by the time Bill arrived. We all had bought Heidi a little something and she seemed pleased. Yet, I sensed a lot of tension around the table but couldn't put my finger on it, even when Heidi went to our piano and started to play. Rick joined her and sang "Send in the Clowns," a marvelous song and he sung it with so much heart that it brought tears to my eyes. I felt sad but knew this was not the time to show my emotions.

The kids began to appear edgy. I could tell they wanted to take off. Todd said he was joining his buddies to watch the fireworks; Heidi said she had to get back to the city. Even Bill and I were anxious to hit the road to the lake. It was Rick that didn't seem to have any place to go and that bothered me. When I questioned what he was doing for the evening, he shrugged and said, "Don't worry, Mom, I'll figure something out." I gave him a kiss and a hug and the same to Heidi and Todd.

The weather was getting terrible as Bill and I bid farewell to the kids on our way to the lake. All night long as we slept in the trailer the thunder storms kept going and coming. I clutched Bill in the small bed and had a terrible fearful feeling. He calmed me down with hugs and comforting words.

When I arrived home on Monday night, I called to see how Rick and Heidi were doing. Todd was at home and I fixed him dinner. Heidi said she was okay but I couldn't get a response from Rick. The lady in charge of the half-way house said she hadn't seen him since July 4th. I became worried and called some of his friends, but they too said they had not seen him.

Then, when I was walking past the fireplace on Tuesday evening after coming back from work, I saw an airmail letter tilted behind a vase. I grabbed it. When I opened it up, I was aghast. It apparently was to be mailed to Rick's friend, Peter. It was dated July 4, 1975. It read: "Dear Peter: This is a suicide note. I'm going to jump off the George Washington Bridge tonight.

No hope left.

Everything's changed

Can't speak serene for me

Please take care of yourself and Sandy and break the news as gently as possible to my mother (I regret her feelings after this all. For that I'm sorry.)

If you find my remains, please have them cremate me.

We've been friends for so long now. I really am so sick of the life I've been leading that I must end it. It's just too much.

I hope God will forgive me.

Remember me with good feelings. love, Rick"

For ten minutes I sat on my bed and read and re-read the letter. I got a horrible sinking feeling in my stomach. I immediately phoned Bill at his shop and asked him to come home quickly. Then I called Heidi in NY but she wasn't home. Todd was over at a friend's house but I forgot which one.

When Bill arrived he could see I was very distraught. "Bill, we've got to find Rick. Maybe he's alive in some hospital. He just can't be dead. Please help me."

Bill immediately called the police. After that, my memory doesn't serve me right. It's like a blur—answering all their questions; Bill calling the morgues in NY and NJ, the Washington Bridge authorities, Todd's friends, his psychiatrist, all of whom had not seen Rick in the last few days.

His psychiatrist gave me hope. "Rick told me that he was considering checking himself into a mental hospital again." We called all the institutions around but got nowhere.

By morning I was a wreck and called into my office saying I was sick and would be out for a few days. I didn't tell them what happened.

The next few days were sheer terror. I couldn't sleep. I finally reached Heidi and she came home and said that Rick seemed fine on the night of her birthday party. He had given her a letter to mail and she forgot about it so it lay partially hidden on the mantel until I found it a couple of days letter—it was the suicide note that was supposed to go to Rick's friend, Peter. We couldn't reach him.

We kept checking back with all the police agencies but they said nothing had come up. The bridge police said the Hudson waters were so rough on July 4 and 5th because of the weather storms, there was a good chance that Rick's body was washed out to sea—if he indeed jumped off the bridge.

My women friends in Snedens came over to comfort me. The terrible news had spread. I thanked them for their consideration but I was still in turmoil. Heidi and Todd both seemed stunned by it all and I started to worry about them. My friend, Sally, gave me the name of a family therapist she felt would help us all through this trauma. I approached my kids just as I had done when their father had died, but unfortunately, they would not cooperate and go for therapy sessions with me.

I tried to keep myself together because I knew my livelihood depended on my job. So on Monday I went back to work. Everyone was concerned about me.

"How are you feeling, Marie? What was wrong? Are you better now?"—were questions asked by my fellow workers. I just couldn't hide the story, so first I told my male boss and he comforted me and said maybe I should take more time off. I refused. "I think it is best if I get my head back into work for now."

At lunch hour I discussed my feeling with the two Judys. They just listened. I told them everything about Rick. They couldn't believe how I had coped all these years. I not only told them he was into drugs and now had schizophrenia but how guilty I felt about it all. I explained how the last time I went with him to his therapist he suddenly turned on me with such anger and yelled out "I'm a homosexual!" And that he got so upset the therapist asked me to leave the room. And that was only a few weeks ago and now he is gone—where to, I don't know.

We all cried for a while, hugged each other, held hands. Letting out my emotions to them was a big help. They urged me not to give up hope and maybe Rick changed his mind and did go incognito into an institution for help. For days they consoled me.

The following week, Bill and I were on the phone continuously. We went over to the halfway house, collected Rick's things. His bankbook was intact and nothing drawn from the small balance. Everything except his wallet and watch were there. I clutched his diary as we left, hoping that within I'd find answers and where he had gone.

Rick was not only a brilliant student and potential actor, which is the work he wanted to pursue, but he was a poet, a gentle kind young man who had strong sensitive feelings that sometimes he revealed in jovial ways, but I knew he hid most of his saddest ones especially since his father's death—and he hid those feelings under the cover of drug use which at that time I had no control over.

According to all the therapy sessions I attended with Rick for the past five years, the prognosis was that because of excessive drug use years before, he had entered a schizophrenic mental state and only Lithium or other drugs would help. He did try them but had bad reactions. I urged him to continue. He did have very clear periods and functioned well in society—then, he'd go "goofy" again. He did try suicide once that I know of with an overdose of Lithium, but Bill and I came home just in time and took him to the hospital where he had his stomach pumped. Then, he was okay again. That was about two months before this last suicide attempt.

Anger was building up in me over the failure of the police or anybody in charge to find my son. One of Rick's closest friend who had just become a minister, caught me at the Palisades Post Office and said he'd like to hold a memorial service for Rick. I was astonished and immediately said "NO"—not without Rick's body found. How could I declare him dead. I still had to work to find him. Even Peter, his friend to whom he had addressed his suicide note, could offer no explanation or information.

I kept up my job at Hearst; Bill was a great strength to me. The two Judys at Hearst were trying their best to help me through this period. My dear friend, Paula D. in Snedens would stop by to see how I was doing. Her younger brother had committed suicide so she knew my suffering. "Marie, let it go. Rick needed to do what he did, not only to protect himself but to protect you and the family. Believe me, there was a reason for his madness," she said.

"Yes, Paula," I replied, "but there is such an ache, a hurt inside me that I knew I can never cure. It hurts so bad. He was a delicious child and young man with such a desire to live and succeed." I immediately had a terrible hate for our government that never stopped this drug scene and those people who enticed our young people into it. I'll never forget the torture of losing my son and causing such pain to my entire family.

Not enough was done to help me. America, because of ignorance and lack of concern during the terrible late '60s & '70s, so many lost their young to drugs.

For the next couple of months, my life seemed to be on hold. Sometimes on the streets in New York I'd see a young man who looked like Rick and run over but in embarrassment, excuse myself for touching his shoulder—it was not Rick. At a mall one Saturday when Bill and I were shopping, we both saw a boy who resembled Rick and chased him but lost him in the crowd. I sometimes felt like I was going crazy. I would sit in my bedroom and read his poems—so beautifully written but in such despondent tones I realized that he was truly sick and tired of his life and needed to do what he did even though I didn't want it. It was getting to be the time for me to release him. The worst thing about it all was no recovery of body or possessions. How could I put him to rest? I wrote a letter to be opened on my death. It reads "when I die, Rick dies too and to put a grave marker with his name on it next to his father's in Rockland Cemetery." Somehow, that seemed to put a partial closure on what had happened. However, I still suffer about losing my firstborn, and know I will until I die

Bill gave me an unexpected diamond engagement ring in November. I accepted it but told him I wasn't ready for marriage. The year ended on a sad note for Heidi, Todd and me. Without my women friends supporting me, Bill being with me, I don't know how I could have gone on. My verse writing helped me through.

New Year's Day, 1976 arrived and Sally Savage, my dear friend from the singles scene, was having her annual "Bloody Mary Party". She insisted we come even though I wasn't in the mood. "Pooh, pooh! Marie. You better bloody well come. Now that you've got your engagement ring from Bill, we've got to set the date!"

CHAPTER EIGHT

MY TRANSITION YEARS . . . .
(1976 to 1986)

1. MY BUDDY SALLY . . . SHE PERKS ME UP!

THE CHRISTMAS HOLIDAYS were hard to get through. I so missed Rick not being with us. We all did our best to make it festive. I just couldn't believe he was out of my life forever. Many nights I would awake crying and Bill would soothe me with a touch or just hugging me. He was becoming more important to me every day.

My work at Hearst was going well. I was appointed Editor-in-Chief not only of the Good Housekeeping Beauty Book but of the new Cosmopolitan Beauty Guide and Cosmopolitan Exercise Guide. That meant I was in charge of three bi-annual magazines (6 magazines a year). My staff was small: two assistants, two copyeditors, two art directors. I was under a lot of pressure but thinking back, maybe this helped me get through my grief.

Unfortunately, I had to give up my job with Good Housekeeping Needlecraft Magazine that my dear friends, the two Judy's, were associated with but we still kept in touch. Thelma, the editor of this magazine was a 70 year-old-lady who knew her P's and Q's when it came to needlework and crafts. When I told her I couldn't write for her because of my other commitments, she graciously thanked me for all my work and gave me a present, a beautiful blue and white handmade quilt from a famous festival in Massachusetts. I kept it for years, then gave it to my daughter as a treasure.

My friend, Sally's invitation arrived inviting us to her New Year's Day 1976 "Bloody Mary" party. I really wasn't in the mood but Bill said he'd like to go.

Sally's house in Piermont, NY sits on a hill overlooking the Hudson River. It is an old structure but she kept it in good condition. Her wide, spreading porch is the highlight of the house. Many nights I spent talking out there with Sally with just candlelight illuminating our faces. Her New Year Day's "Bloody Mary" party was always looked forward to by her many friends. When she didn't have one for a serious reason, we always felt something was missing in greeting the New Year. It was a day to see friends you'd hadn't seen for over a year—or maybe saw just last week. Whatever, the chemistry of the occasion and Sally being such a gracious hostess, put everyone into a festive, joyful mood. Her food and Bloody Mary's were great. Sometimes there were 100 or more people passing through. I often wondered if the porch could hold us.

After much urging by Bill, I got myself dressed to go to Sally's New Year's Day party 1976. Trying to find a place to park on her winding narrow road that led to her house was always a challenge. We brought a bottle of vodka to help replenish her stash for the occasion. It was a wonderful sunny day even though the temperature was 32 degrees. With the fireplace aflame in the living room and the many bodies huddling around the dining room table, the house felt like a summer cottage.

When we walked in, hung up our coats in the entry, I felt exhilarated by the wonderful smells from Sally's kitchen and the music mixed with people's chatter. I told myself I'm going to have a good time even though Rick was still in my head. Sally squeezed me with a hard hug. "I'm glad you came, Marie." she said. "Come and greet the New Year with your friends. This is good medicine for you."

I did feel better after awhile. Maybe it was the Bloody Mary I sipped or the warmth of laughing people but suddenly I felt relaxed and enjoyed talking with old friends and seeing familiar faces from my poker games.

Because we arrived late, we stayed past the 2-5 p.m. time on the invitation. There were only a dozen of us left as the embers in the fireplace were burning out. We settled down on the couch and chairs in the living room while Sally and a couple of the women were cleaning up in the dining room and kitchen.

Sy Isenberg shouted out "Well, Marie and Bill, when is the wedding?" I hung my head and said, "We haven't set a date."

"Why not?" replied Manny Vardi, my other friend from the poker group.

"It's up to Marie," said Bill.

"Well, Marie, let's help you make up your mind" voiced Sy's wife, Anita.

"It's too soon." I answered.

"Nonsense," shouted Sally from the dining room. "It's now or never!"

We all laughed and sat around sipping our coffee, nibbling on the last of the sweets.

"I'll open my house for your wedding," offered Paula Silverman who had a lovely large home on Woods Road in Snedens where she lived with her husband, Jerome Silverman. a fellow poker player and old friend of mine.

"I'll write a song for your wedding," said Sy. "Manny you write the music, okay?"

"Okay, I'll do it and get a professional singer for the wedding." replied Manny.

"Well, while everyone is offering their professional service, I'll play my harp if Manny plays his viola with me," said Margaret Diederich, another poker player and well-known harpist. Manny gave thumbs up.

Sally's voice echoed from the kitchen. She had been listening to the whole scene. "I'll take the wedding photos."

After all this constant chatter, Bill and I looked at each other and started to laugh.

"What are these people trying to do to us?" I asked

"I think they want to have another party!" replied Bill. We all laughed again.

Things quieted down for a while and we sipped our coffee. I could feel everyone's eyes on me. I don't know how it happened or why but I stood up and said, "Okay, you've talked me into this and you are responsible for your commitments. I accept all your generous offers. If Bill agrees I will marry him on Valentine's Day, Feb. 14th."

Bill raised himself from his chair, put his arm around me and gave me a kiss. "Okay, our friends, you're on. We will arrange for a caterer so that nobody has to cook."

The dozen of us stood up, raised our coffee cups, toasted and agreed that Feb. 14, 1976 would be the big day. Chatting and laughing, we dispersed to our cars and left for home.

I was nervous driving back to Snedens. I burst out, "Bill, I don't think I'm ready. Can't we get ourselves out of this arrangement. I think I spoke too soon. It was just crazy how we were all caught up in this frenzy of a wedding."

"Come on, Marie," Bill replied softly, "We've been living together for a year and a half, I gave you an engagement ring. We could elope and get married at some time, but let's think about our kids. Let's set it straight for them."

As I crawled into bed that night and cuddled next to Bill, I thought about what he had said. I agreed to myself that, yes, the kids needed responsible direction as to our values and responsible commitments. I knew within my heart that Bill was the only man I wanted to live with for the rest of my life. I woke Bill up at 2 a.m. in the morning. "Okay, honey," Feb. 14th, Valentine's Day, will be our wedding day. He nodded. February 14—that only left a month and a half for Bill and me to get our wedding day ready. We interviewed caterers and settled on one. I went shopping for a special dress. I chose to go to Bendel's in the city even though it was an expensive store and one I seldom went to. But I wanted something special, and I found it right away. The moment I walked out of the elevator on the 3rd floor and spotted a dress on a mannequin I knew it was perfect for the occasion. It was a burgundy suede wrap-around with violets painted on the collar and little embossed hearts around the tie-waist. I bought it immediately. On the same day, I found a pair of burgundy spike-heeled sandals at the same store. To complete the look, I would carry a small bouquet of one of my favorite flowers, violets.

Our kids were a little stunned by our decision but they supported us. Todd agreed to be one of our witnesses as did Heidi, Tracey and Mark. Bill's other son, Bill, was in Las Vegas and couldn't make the trip North. I couldn't help reflect on Rick and wonder what he would have thought of my decision. I quickly blocked it out.

At the Saturday night poker games. there were lots of discussion about how the plans were going. It seemed everyone was on top of his or her commitment as planned at the New Year's Day party. Sy was not only writing the lyrics to "Marie's Song" the title of the song Manny composed, but he printed it out on sheet music. And to top it off, he printed out amusing invitations for us to send out. Everyone was wonderful.

We all agreed it was going to be a funky happening but done in a classy Sneden's style. Todd got some of his friends to help tend the bar. Suddenly, everyone in Snedens and Palisades was caught up in this special event. I invited my New York co-workers and friends, Bill invited his family and friends. Over 100 people accepted. We had to advise the caterer to make sure to bring enough food and drink and especially, a heart-shaped cake!

Meanwhile as the day grew closer, I was twisting my engagement ring around and around like a nervous Nelly. Bill ordered the wedding bands from Jerome Silverman, our friend and well-known diamond merchant in New York, and whose house would host the wedding ceremony.

As for someone to perform a non-denominational ceremony, we chose the local Palisades minister, a young woman who said she'd do any type of wedding vows we wanted. I thought about it seriously and one night wrote them down with Bill's approval. I called the local florist and ordered a small bouquet of violets for myself and one for Bill's lapel, plus other small violet "pin-ons" for our children standing up for us. I also ordered special jewelry gifts for them. It seemed that everything was set up—except our honeymoon. Bill and I discussed it. We were both pressured with our work so we decided to take the three days following the wedding day and spend it at the Plaza Hotel in New York. We knew it would be expensive but I'd always wanted to stay there. We made the reservations. Now it was time to get the show on the road.

Before Bill and I went to sleep that night, we set the alarm for 7 a.m. Bill woke up first. While he showered and got dressed, I straightened up the house and made the bed. The makeup artist and hairstylist were coming later in the morning. Meanwhile, we hugged and kissed, not believing this was the big day. I tried to make a joke, "Bill, you can't see me in my wedding dress until the ceremony," Then seriously, I said, "I hope this day passes quickly. I'm so nervous. I hope it all comes off okay."

"No worry, honey," Bill replied. "All is under control. Just come and we'll be husband and wife once and for all." I threw him a kiss from the door as he drove toward Woods Road only a minute away. He was headed for the Silverman's to offer any help they needed.

I showered quickly, washed my hair and put on my new undergarments and a terry robe. I thought it so amusing that the hostess, Paula Silverman and even the minister wanted to have makeup and hairdo, too—Heidi, also.

Sally arrived at 9 a.m. and was set to go with her photo shoot. She saw me with wet hair, in a robe. "Marie, what's going on here?" I told her to calm down and explained what was going on. "Great," she answered. "I'll begin my shoot with all of you being made beautiful." I breathed in deeply as she started by taking lighting exposures on her meter, standing on the bed to get angles, etc. etc.

The bedroom "beauty salon" was in progress. The makeup artist finished with me. I ran to the closet, grabbed my dress, hose and shoes and went into the bathroom. I waved to the others out in my bedroom being coiffed and made up. It was the funniest scene I'd ever seen. Sally was standing atop of the bed, the dresser, wherever to capture all the pictures.

A million thoughts went through my head—I thought of Bob, Rick, my parents, my friends in Los Angeles, my aunts. All of their images flashed before me.

We all arrived at the Silverman's house right on time. When I saw all the parked cars on the road I got the jitters and took a deep breath.

The house was filled with loads of people milling around, holding drinks in their hands. Bill and I insisted we open the bar early even though it was against the tradition which as to wait until after the wedding. Everyone seemed in a festive mood and applauded when I walked in. Someone took my coat; others came up to greet me. Bill approached and said how lovely I looked. I was embarrassed and nervous. "Let's begin soon!" I whispered to the minister. Meanwhile, I walked around and said my greetings, thanked people for coming. The caterer came with a glass of Scotch and water for me which I almost gulped down in one swig.

Manny and Margaret started playing the harp and viola prior to the service. The sun was beaming into the large living room and in moments the minister called the wedding to begin. It took no more than five minutes. Our children were dressed to the tee and I was so proud to have them standing up for us. Sally kept clicking away with her camera. I gave her a hug and thanked her for all her hard work. She said, "You're my Yankee friend. I'm having a ball on this job." Sally has always been there for me.

Seconds after the service, the real festivities began with food and more drink being offered. Congratulations were in order. I don't know if it was the Scotch I'd had or just knowing it was over, but suddenly I relaxed and really began to enjoy my new transition of being Mrs. Marie Fenton Griffing.

Instead of a signature book at the entry, we had a huge brand new mailbox on a pedestal that Gail Hyde had given us for a present. With a magic marker, everyone signed the box and gifts were piled atop and around it.

Our garbage man, Bob, who we knew played in a band as a hobby, was up on the balcony overlooking the living room with his group and they started playing wonderful Frank Sinatra style music. It was wonderful. Bill and I took the first dance on the beautiful parquet floor; others joined in.

Before we cut the heart-shaped cake (Valentine's day, remember?) Manny announced from the balcony the playing and singing of "Marie's Song" the composition that he and Sy wrote especially for us. It truly was a work of love. Manny introduced the young professional singer who had come all the way to Snedens from New York. She stepped forward against the rail and belted it out. We all stood around in the living room, looking up as she began to sing—"What Did He Mean By That?"

I gave him the finger
He gave me a ring
Did he mean it to bring
some thought to linger like a string
round my finger?

I gave him the eye
We had us a ball.
Did he mean me to fall
down like a quick rye
with the chaser, my own guy?

Never will I turn a cold shoulder
Never give him the back of my hand
He have the shirt off my back
I'll strip but I won't ever let him give me the slip

I gave him my hand
He gave me a lift
Did he mean me to shift
Stand-in to stand-out
Did he have it all planned out
Like a wedding
Is he stretching my rib?
Bending my ear?
Pulling my leg?
Meeting me here?

Please get me off the trapeze,
I'm no acrobat
Do you think he meant
what I think he meant by that?
What did he mean by that?
         THE END

Everyone laughed and applauded this wonderful personal song meant just for me. I was just astounded. Nothing had ever been done like that for me. I was overcome. They kept playing the song over and over while people danced around.

After everyone had left, Sally packed up her camera equipment, I said, "I think you've taken enough pictures to fill five albums. Stop now. You must be tired. Thanks so much."

"Okay, Marie, but open that little box on the bottom of all those presents. It's from me."

I gently undid the pretty bow and gave it to one of the girls who was folding up the wrappings ever so gently. I laughed when I pulled a coffee cup out of the box, bright red with white lettering on it—MS! "Touche, my friend!" I said and raised the cup to her. "Yes, my name from now on is Ms. Marie Fenton Griffing." Sally and I smiled at each other and I knew she would be my friend forever. I would never forget the fun we had during our "singles bar" escapades.

I didn't throw my bouquet of violets. I wanted to keep them and enjoy them. They suddenly brought back memories of my youth when my dear friend, Chuppie, and I would make paper corsages of violets and sell them from door to door in the 30s. I clutched them as Bill and I left to go home to pick up our bags and drive to the Plaza Hotel in New York City for our three-day honeymoon.

2. MY NEW BUSINESS ASSOCIATES . . .
FUN, STIMULATING WOMEN

THE HONEYMOON WAS over—short but sweet and most memorable. Bill and I were energized now to get down to serious work. He had cabinetry jobs to get started on and I had the 1976 spring issues of my magazines to put to bed. At 7:30 each morning, Bill drove to his shop, 15 minutes away in Garnerville, New York and I drove to Manhattan.

When I arrived at my office after my honeymoon, I found a huge bouquet of flowers from my associates. Also, I was pleased to discover almost every detail connected with getting our magazines out to the printers had been done. I called a meeting of my new art director, Irene, my three new editorial assistants, Jacquie, Helen and Susan and my copyeditor, June and thanked them for their responsible work. They all wanted to know about the wedding and honeymoon. We chatted and laughed for awhile and when they left, I stretched back on my chair, looked out of my window at all the skyscrapers surrounding me and said a prayer of thanks for all this—a fulfilling career, a wonderful new husband, a beautiful home, great kids and loyal co-workers. Except having lost Bob and Rick, I considered myself a very lucky woman.

Somehow, my own being told me that I had crossed a bridge into new territory, that I shouldn't be afraid anymore of what's to come but to enjoy the pleasures that go with success and a second chance to find happiness.

From then on for the next couple of years, I was hitting the big time in New York. My job as Editor of the Hearst Special Publications was not only productive, but the amenities that went with the position were plentiful. My women associates with their youthful enthusiasm (they were all in their late 20s or early 30s) offered me, a woman who had just turned 50, a new outlook on life. We were, as they say, "an admiration society." We respected each other; we helped each other in creative ways;

nobody wanted to be "top gun." We worked together in unison and for the betterment of the publications.

The best part of it was that our working together was filled with laughter and love. I knew I was lucky to be surrounded by such highly talented, sensitive, creative and intelligent young women. I loosened my reigns when I sensed they knew better than I what type of stories appealed to young women (our readers ranged from 18 to 34) but I guided them with themes I knew would be appealing. At the same time I was stretching my creative abilities and my top editors of Good Housekeeping and Cosmopolitan (John Mack Carter and Helen Gurley Brown) recognized that too and gave me the green light on whatever projects I wanted to pursue, especially since all the magazines were selling well.

Whenever we did photo "shoots", my associates and assistants were right on target with the right locals, wardrobe, makeup artist, hairstylist, stylists, name it. I simply had to approve or make changes as I saw fit. Out page layouts were the greatest. We all worked in rhythm with each other. Even the models and cameramen said we were the best group to work for in the city.

I did have to do a lot of ground work for each edition of a magazine—designate themes, do mock-ups of an issue, write opening copy, titles, cover blurbs, okay written copy before being sent to the copyeditor, interview new photographers, models, stylists, and update my top editors with frequent memos.

I didn't realize it at the time, but I was growing and becoming a better professional. Having my "gals" around was a joy. Whenever I felt that the "sky was falling" they'd come through to lift my mood and set us all straight on line.

"My girls" (as I called them) and I would lunch together at least once a week, like I used to do with the two Judy's years before. They urged me to take risks—like proposing to my top editors that we go to Mexico to do a shoot. I knew that would incur a lot of cost, but because my girls arranged with airlines, hotels, etc. to exchange their services for a credit in our magazine there was little cost to us. The trip to Club Med in Mexico was approved. My assistant, Jacquie, chose the type of fashions we needed and put them on assignment for the shoot; Helen arranged for a makeup artist and stylist in Mexico; Susan picked out jewelry and other accessories to take with us. Irene, my art director, selected the models. Before I knew it, the free airline tickets, hotel reservations, etc. were set for early spring and the plan was set.

I got clearance for Bill to meet me in Mexico City after the shoot for a few days and we had a wonderful time. We did succumb, however, to Montezuma's Revenge, but we still managed to see all the tourist sites.

The momentum of attending social affairs, press luncheons, publicity evening parties, doing out-of-town "shoots", kept me so busy I had little time for myself and what was worse, I had to give up my poker games. The "moonlighting" I was doing with how-to books on weekends kept progressing. I was receiving invitations to more events than I could handle personally. I asked my girls to help me out. My luncheons with PR people took me into all the expensive restaurants in New York City—the 21, The Twin Towers, The Four Seasons, The Tavern on the Green, Sardis's—just to mention a few. Bill and I attended evening parties at the Plaza, the Metropolitan Museum of Art, disco dancing at Regine's and other famous clubs.

The public relations scene in New York was at its height. Beauty and fashion editors were treated like royalty in the hope that we would mention their product in our magazines. I now entered the prestigious group of New York editors in the field. I was wined and dined, received expensive gifts during the holidays and bags filled with all sorts of new products from hundreds of companies. At Slate's bar and restaurant where I used to meet Jerry Silverman to get a ride back home some nights, my CBS-TV friends would call me the "bag lady" because I always walked in carrying shopping bags full of "goodies".

My associates were enjoying all this attention, too, but I knew we had to keep our heads on straight through the glamour and excitement of this new phase in our careers. At special meetings with them, I emphasized the importance of putting out a good magazine and not let these other distractions take us off course. They agreed and so everything kept going smoothly along. In fact, things got better and we were given the okay to pursue another fantastic "shoot"—this time to Rio (Brazil)!

The trip to Rio is unforgettable, for reasons good and bad. We had an entourage of eight: my art director, my photographer, two models, my assistant, Jacquie, and her husband, Bill and me. Jacquie took care of all the fashions and accessories; I took care of the plane tickets, hotel reservations at an ocean front hotel in Rio de Janeiro; Dick, the photographer, brought steel cases of all his camera stuff; the models just brought themselves.

The weather in Rio was glorious. We all went crazy about the exotic locals where we could do shoots. The hotel had arranged for a Brazilian hair stylist and makeup artist. It was a wild week. We photographed on Ipanima beach a few miles away from Rio; at waterfalls in the nearby mountains, in their Regine's night club, at the fresh fruit market places, on the balconies of our apartments overlooking the sea. It was exhausting work but we loved it. The bad part of this shoot was that my diamond engagement ring was stolen along with my credit cards. Disaster! I fretted and cried a lot over the loss. Bill felt sad about the loss but he tried to make me feel better by saying we have insurance and we'll buy me another one just like it. (Unfortunately, our insurance didn't cover the loss and I did without for awhile.) Meanwhile, we shopped at local stores in Rio and I bought a beautiful aquamarine ring. Their jewelry is beautiful and inexpensive.

We got some fantastic photos. I knew the expenses we had incurred on this trip would come to the attention of our top editors. However, when I showed them how many photo articles we could reap from this shoot for other editions, they did not give me much flack. My girls and I began to put our heads together to make all the photos stretch through four new editions of our magazines. We came out "smelling like roses!"

3. HARRIETT, MY MOTHER-IN-LAW, SHOWS ME ENDURANCE

BILL AND I together with other beauty editors flew to St. Croix for a weekend junket as guests of a well-known skin-care company. We attended a fabulous party aboard the Chanel yacht; we flew to Miami to cover the Homecoming Queen contest and went aboard a gorgeous yacht, hosted by the publisher of the Miami Herald and were a part of the annual boat parade on the inter-coastal. We both went to cover the Miss America pageant in Atlantic City; Bill did my photography. We now were living in the "fast lane."

During the late 70s, there were personal tragedies that entered our lives. One in particular was when Bill's father, Kenneth, died of a stroke but thank God it was not a prolonged passing. Kenneth and Harriett always came over to our house for Sunday dinner. They were married for over 50 years. Now it was only Harriett who came to spend an occasional weekend with us. We didn't want her to feel alone although she was quite content living in her home in New Jersey and being well taken care of by a housekeeper. Then she became diagnosed with Parkinson's disease, so that caused us some worry, but she always insisted she could do well on her own. She was self-sufficient and self-confident. I admired her so much.

Harriett was a lovely woman in her 70s. To me she was the ideal mother-in-law. She never complained; she always was cheery, accepted my free style of living. She seemed to enjoy coming to visit even with all the kids coming in and out. She always kept her cool. I never had to make special foods for her; she ate whatever we had on the table and appeared especially interested if she had never before tasted the dish.

She always was impeccably dressed and gracious to whoever walked into my house. I guess I can only describe her as a "great lady."

My extended family became closer and closer together. Now with Debbie and Mark married, Billy (Bill's other son) and his partner, Lorraine, moving back North and buying a house in Rhode Island,

Tracey living with us for six months because of health difficulties with her mother, Heidi coming for weekend visits and Todd still in the house, our little home on weekends was always spilling over with relatives coming and going.

I really liked it but found it difficult to give special attention to each and every person plus birthdays parties, mother's day, father's day. With such a large family I inherited, I began to feel overcome.

When I learned from my brother in California that my mother had died, I was devastated. I just had talked with her a week before in the nursing home and she sounded okay. Suddenly, she was dead. Bill and I flew to Los Angeles for the funeral. I took a week's personal leave; my assistants would keep the magazines going. Harriett gave me a kiss and expressed her condolences to me and not to worry because Mark would look in on her at her home in New Jersey.

I was now a "motherless mom" it was very painful. On the plane to LA, I kept thinking of my mother, her strength, her fortitude, her exuberance, especially in the last days of her life. I called her quite often on the phone to the nursing home where she was diagnosed as having Alzheimer's, but whenever we spoke, she seemed so down to earth. I ended each phone conversation with "I love you Mother," and she answered back, "I love you, too."

Bill was my strength during the funeral services. I released a lot of guilt, anger but tried to concentrate on loving feelings. The plane trip back to New York gave me five hours to reflect on my loss. I then began to think of my own mortality—I was scared. Bill held my hand until the plane touched down in Newark.

Bill and I were still as much in love through all these transitions. His work wasn't going as well as we thought it would but I kept urging him to keep trying, that it would come around and that financially, my monies were enough to carry us through. My job was going along beautifully but I could feel myself getting "burned out" with all the social activities associated with it. It was like I was burning the candle at both ends. I expended so much energy in New York. I found it hard to keep my personal scene together; I wondered if I could handle it all, but I kept going.

Bill built a lovely little greenhouse onto our back bedroom and with Todd living with his girlfriend, Pat, we took over the master bedroom. The greenhouse was a real pick-up for me. I redecorated the bedroom and fixed up the greenhouse with new furniture and plants; it was a

MARIE FENTON GRIFFING

wonderful extension to our bedroom. We only had to open the French doors and walk out to a glassed-in area and see the wonders of nature in our back yard. I bought a live parakeet in a cage and hung it up from the greenhouse rafters. It loved to stretch its neck and nibble on the hanging flowering baskets. I called it Ms. Green. My cats kept their eyes on the bird (I could see them lick their chops), but thank goodness they couldn't reach it.

Every weekend when Harriett came, she loved to sit out in the greenhouse and read or do a little water-coloring painting (she was a marvelous artist). Sometimes, she and I would sit together, shelling peas or cutting beans for Sunday dinner and just talk about things in general. Neither one of us went so far as to disclose our own deepest feelings but that didn't seem to matter. Just sitting with her, gave me a certain sense of peace. She had that unbelievable quality about her that quieted one down. Nobody in the family ever felt pressured by her. When heated discussions went on, she'd just sit back and listen. I often wondered why she never offered any opinions but let the men take over most dinner conversations. I chalked it up to her New England background. I figured she had been lucky enough not to make serious decisions by herself. She had always had a husband and now her children were helping her out. Sometimes, I wished I had that privilege, but then I don't think I would be where I was now. We all loved her and she became the first matriarch-figure in my life since my grandmother.

My own kids plus my extended family throughout the latter part of the 70s slowly began to engulf my life. Not that I didn't enjoy a lot of it, especially on holidays, but I could feel a slow decline in my own work and interests in New York. I began to rethink my priorities. While I'm on top of my career, why not retire and let the young girls take over? I really gave it a lot of thought. I didn't mention it to anyone except Bill. He didn't sound too happy over my decision but left it in my hands to make up my own mind. And I did—I decided to take early retirement. This would give me a good career to look back on, some perks from the company, like a small pension, life insurance, health care and a chance to work freelance for them. I would not stop writing, that's for sure, but it would be easier for me to pursue my own projects. After many years of always meeting a deadline, I could relax and choose my priorities. I felt financially secure because I had been saving up for sometime and felt I had a big enough "egg nest" to hold us for awhile.

Nobody took me seriously when I said I was going to take early retirement from Hearst, not my top editors, not my kids, not even my women friends. They all said something like, "Come on, Marie, you've got it made, living in a glamorous world, good salary, three week vacation, trips to new places and all those cosmetic goodies and gifts you get. Give it up? Why?"

It seemed my reasons weren't good enough. One Sunday afternoon, Harriett and I were sitting in the greenhouse cleaning some vegetables for that night's dinner. I started to talk about my dilemma with her. "You know, Harriett," I said. "I'm getting that same "burned out" feeling for my job as I did just before I quit 'Teen' magazine back in 1965. I can't quite figure it out but it's as if I had my challenges in my particular job with each of these magazines I gave birth to and "mothered" until they "grew up," and now it is completed. I'd really like to write something on my own, maybe a novel, a book of verses. I've never had the time to release my own creative thoughts."

"But, Marie," she replied in her quiet, calming voice, "you've done a lot of books. I'm sure you used your creativity developing them and your magazines, too."

"Yes, I guess I have but all that was "how-to" stuff that mostly required research and my experiences in the beauty and fitness world. Not the same. But maybe I don't have it to write a novel or whatever, but I feel it's time to have the freedom to devote my total energies toward it and at least try."

"Well, then, Marie if your desire is so strong, I'd say "go for it!"

I laughed and set my pot of green beans on the table. "Thanks, Harriett, you're the only one who hasn't tried to talk me out of it. You know, my Aunt Fanny said that to me one day many years ago when I was uncertain about a serious decision."

I leaned down and gave her a kiss on the cheek. "I'll finish my "How To Be a Beauty Pageant Winner book, and then I'll give six months' notice to Hearst. With royalties still coming in from my other books, the small pension I'll receive, and Bill's work, we should be able to get along okay."

Harriett smiled and gave me a hug. Liza, my wonderful dog, got up where she was laying in the bedroom and began to bark and jump up and down. It was like she knew what was going on and announcing it was going to be okay too.

The next week at work, I wrote my request for early retirement to my top editors. It was now official, not just talk. In the letter, I gave them six months' notice, explained my reasons for quitting Hearst, told them I'd get 'my house' in order before I left and leave the magazines in the capable hands of my associates. I expressed my thanks to them and the Hearst Corp. for their support and belief in me for the past ten years.

When I handed in the letter, it was like a load off my back. I was going to be free to be my own person for the first time. No more commuting, no getting up to the ring of an alarm clock, no more putting on makeup and fussing with my hair every day. I would let it all hang out. There were so many jobs to catch up in and around the house.

Still nobody really believed me. My retirement letter was never acknowledged. It seemed that everyone took it as a whim. Three months later, I wrote another one. Finally, the wheels started to turn and the retirement department called me to fill out all sorts of papers. When I mentioned all this to Bill, he didn't say much but I could see that he was happy that I was happy. I hadn't thought of it before but I wondered if he felt threatened he would have to bring home the "bacon" every week, I put it out of my mind.

Bill's daughter, Tracey, was now working part time for him. She really liked doing the woodworking. I thought this a little unusual for a girl but kept in mind it did keep her closer to her father and might teach her a skill to use for the future. She was able to make extra money during the summer and still have time for her friends.

On October 20 of 1980 I came to work with a couple of shopping bags tucked under my arm in order to pack up all my stuff from my office. I spent the morning piling in personal materials in the bags—photos, things from my desk, etc. My associates stopped in to see how I was doing. "Marie, you will be back after lunch, won't you?" Susan asked? "Yes," I answered. "I'm going to have a facial at Georgette Klinger's at noon, then I'll be back to give you all a kiss goodbye."

I left my office on my lunch hour and grabbed a cab to the prestigious skin salon on Madison Ave. Their skin treatments were always like a therapy session for me. I was pampered, soothed and enjoyed the quiet of a darkened room. Oftentimes, I would fall asleep during the treatment. It was expensive but I would receive a discount because I was a beauty editor and had mentioned the salon in my magazines. I used to try to imitate the treatments as best I could on Harriett when she came to visit. She always enjoyed them.

The moment I was left alone in the little cubicle of the salon with the mask on my face waiting for the cosmetician to return to remove it, I began to feel elevated into another world. This day's "out-of-body" experience was one I'll not forget. Late that night I wrote it down and months later it was published by Country Press, a small avant-garde publisher.

4. JOANNE—MY FRIEND & I IN NEED

AFTER THE FAREWELL party at my office, John Mack Carter, the Editor-in-Chief of Good Housekeeping Magazine, took me to the side and said that Hearst Books (one of the many divisions of the Hearst Corporation) was looking for a writer to do four beauty/fitness books for them and they asked him for a writer. He gave me the name of the Editor, said I should call him. "Marie, this could be a money-maker for you but I can't promise it'll work out. Wait a few weeks, then give them a call." I gulped my champagne and said thanks. It seemed I was back in the "thick of things."

For the next week, I thoroughly indulged myself as a lady of leisure. I slept late, puttered around the house, did some shopping and stayed out of my little office. After awhile, I felt the need to go into the city. I called my dear friend, Joanne, and asked if she could meet me for lunch at Yangsee River restaurant which was near her office in Lincoln Center. I hadn't talked with her since a terrible tragedy occurred in her life. She was pleased to get my call. I was anxious to know how she was getting along.

She looked as elegant as ever as she sat across from me in the booth.

"Joanne, it's so good to see you. How are you doing?" She had phoned me some time back that her younger daughter, Pauline, had been attacked on her bike while she was riding through Central Park, hit on the head with a baseball bat, rushed to the hospital and died several days later. It all occurred shortly after Rick's suicide. Somehow, neither of us could come face to face with each other until now. I felt this luncheon would give us the time to commiserate about our individual tragedies. I could feel her hurt and I am sure she realized mine too. Still, I was fearful it might be too soon for her to talk. As it turned out, it was a good therapy session for both of us.

As we sipped our tea and slowly ate our lunch, Joanne told me the whole story about Pauline's death and how she and her other daughter, Andrea, and her new husband, Dick, were handling it.

"Marie, it hurts so much because I feel I could have avoided it."

Those were the exact words I said back to her when I recounted Rick's suicide. We kept talking for over an hour. When one of us weren't in tears, the other was. We released our guilt feelings, expressed our grief about loosing two wonderful, talented young people and how we realized these terrible happenings would remain with us forever. I repeated the age-old phrase: "It's not right that a parent should outlive his child." After goodbye hugs, we parted. I hoped that our "session" helped us both.

When I arrived home after lunching with Joanne, I jumped into the shower and let the warm water trickle down on my body and stood still as if I were standing under a waterfall on a tropical island. My thoughts flowed toward some of the things that Joanne had said during our meeting. "Marie, I'm glad I have this job at Lincoln Center. It keeps me so busy that I don't have time to dwell about Pauline's death. I think if I sat at home alone with nothing much to do, I'd go crazy."

For the last few weeks, being home alone while Bill and Todd were away for the day, I began to find myself reliving my life when Rick was alive. When I'd see some of his friends at the post office, library or just driving down the road, they'd greet me friendly-like but even their faces brought back memories of my son. The magnolia tree which Rick planted himself and which grew outside our bedroom, brought back memories every time I walked out the door. I realized I was fighting "demons" inside me and that I'd better find work to get my mind on another track.

As I toweled off after my shower one morning, I thought it would be a good idea if I took my former editor's, John Mack Carter's, suggestion and called Ed G., the Editor-in-Chief of Hearst Books about the series of beauty books he was planning to publish.

I reached Ed and we talked for over an hour on the phone. He explained that he wanted four books on beauty, fitness, diet and skin. The job would pay well. He said it would be okay to do my writing at home. Also, when I came into the city to confer with him and the art director, I could use an office on the same floor as his in another Hearst Building on 57th St. I was overjoyed with this generous offer and immediately accepted.

"Ed, I know I can do these books updating all my past writings from Good Housekeeping and Cosmopolitan; we can even use the photos I took. Since we are a part of Hearst we have the rights to do this. With a good art director, it should work out perfectly. I still have my connections with the cosmetic, hair and fitness people so that shouldn't be a problem."

"Okay, Marie," Ed answered, "Let's go for it. Meet me for lunch next week and I'll bring the contract for you to sign and we can talk more. Glad to have you aboard!"

It all sounded too perfect—$100,000.00 for writing about what I've written about for 20—odd years. I realized that it would take up most of my day but then being allowed to work at home most of the time, was very tempting. Just think, I said to myself, all I have to do is slip on my casual outfit, walk ten feet to my office desk and do my work; no commuting, no makeup sessions, no editorial meetings. It was an offer I just couldn't resist. There was only one negative. When do I start my own creative work? What about my novel which I'd already titled, "A Real Woman"? It looked like I'd have to put that on hold for a while.

That weekend all the Griffings came over for dinner. Todd was there too and Heidi came in from the city. I announced my new project. They congratulated me and Bill, especially, was pleased that I accepted the offer. I guess we both figured it was too early for me to walk away so quickly. He and I thought it would be a good idea if I incorporated myself for money matters—$100,000.00 was not to be sneezed at. The IRS would be looking at that. The following week I became "Marie Fenton Griffing Associates, Inc."

For the next year I worked on the first two books for Hearst. My new art director was a talented young woman who worked as a freelancer and often came to my home at night to collaborate with me about the page layouts for each book. And my weekends were free to be with family and friends. I went back to my Saturday night poker sessions with my friends.

When I had my weekly salary to rely on for food and other household expenses, I didn't realize the high cost of living. Now, going into my savings account each week, I found it worrisome. Then there was Todd's college tuition. I was pleased he had found a school he liked (NY Institute of Technology) and especially a career he'd wanted to follow—TV/Communications. With him living at home now, I could observe him more fully. He was serious about all this. I could see it was hard for him to travel by bus and subway early each day into NY, attend classes, and come back home late to study again into the night. I admired his determination and focus. He was making me proud especially when he graduated with honors and found a job as a photographer at a cable TV station in New Jersey.

When my friend, Joanne and I would lunch on my days—in to NYC, we'd discuss how well our kids were doing. Her Andrea would be graduating from college. But almost every time Joanne and I met, I could still see the pain in her eyes and I'm sure she saw mine. We tried to focus our luncheon conversations on our own work and other topics, but occasionally Rick and Pauline's name would enter. We'd look at each other, take a deep sigh, hold hands and try to dismiss our hidden grief. Our children had grown up together and we had been there, recognizing each of their talents. Joanne was like a sister to me.

I told her I was doing the Hearst Books. "Marie, it'll keep your mind distracted for a while and after the books are completed, just think, you'll be rich and be able to write that famous novel of yours!"

Joanne was uplifting for me and I always looked forward to our get—togethers. What I didn't see coming was that our meetings would end because the whole book deal was going down the drain. I had produced two complete manuscripts together with layouts when suddenly my editor, Ed G. was taken off the project and I was advised that the other two books I was supposed to write were cancelled. I was devastated. John Mack Carter called me into his office one day and said my boss, Ed had run so much over budget not only on my books but others he was handling that the whole how—to section of the publishing company was being shut down. I would be paid for one of the two books I'd done but they'd never be published. "Sorry, Marie," John said, "not your fault; you did good work, but you know how it is . . . 'the bottom line' is what counts." I shook his hand. "It's okay, John." I answered.

My stomach felt empty as I walked to the garage to pick up my car. "Now what?" I asked myself as I drove up the Palisades Parkway to Sneden's Landing. "Well, I've got enough money in the bank to last me for a year. I guess I'd better hustle for new work." Then I laughed. "What would Joanne do? I know. I'll think about it tomorrow."

5. THE FIRST GRANDCHILD IS BORN
AND THE WOMEN INVOLVED

I T WAS THE middle of summer, 1981. My Hearst Books deal had been shattered even though I'd made $20,000 out of it. I was sitting in my office trying to figure out what direction I should go. For sure, I didn't want to commute to NY every day and get another job with a magazine. I was enjoying working at home with my writing. I decided that I'd try to work out some sort of public relations freelance part-time job with one of the many connections I had in New York.

I went through my files and found an organization that might be interested in me and my qualifications although I'd never done PR work in my life. It was the Solomon Organization which did promotions for Miss Universe and Miss America. The president of the company, Steve Solomon, was an old buddy of mine. I was about to call him when Tracey, Bill's daughter walked into the house asking for some tool that Bill had in one of our closets.

Since school had let out in June, Tracey was working with Bill at his shop and getting paid for it. Bill and I had agreed since Tracey liked working with wood, it would be a money-making summer vacation for her. I hadn't seen her for months. She was back living with her mother and would stop by occasionally. She always seemed agitated and would drop in for a minute, then leave quickly. That behavior frightened me and I asked Bill to check out her living arrangement at home. But nothing was reported back to me. He said Tracey was doing a good job at the shop and seemed okay to him. I left it at that.

Most of time I saw Tracey, she was always dressed in jeans and a T-shirt. Since the age of 10 when I first met her, she was never thin/thin, but lately she gained weight. I would be the last to mention anything. Being a stepmother to this delicate child wasn't easy. I avoided giving her any personal advice. I felt it wasn't right for me to do so.

Tracey walked into my office and stood in front of me saying she had found the tool. We talked a few minutes about the work she was doing.

My eyes suddenly noticed a huge bulge under her T-shirt. I gulped and thought to myself, "This girl is not only gaining weight but she looks pregnant."

I, being familiar with pregnancy, having had three children of my own, recognized the unique look of this condition. I gave her a kiss goodbye. Then I immediately picked up the phone and called Bill.

"Bill, I just saw Tracey and I swear that she is pregnant. Haven't you noticed? I'm worried. Will you call her mom? Maybe she knows something we don't."

Bill took my call seriously and called his ex-wife but unbelievably, Lois never noticed any signs. Then when he and Tracey went to lunch at a diner near his shop, he casually asked her how come she was gaining so much weight. She only raised her shoulders and said she didn't know. Finally, Bill asked the ultimate question "Are you pregnant?" She nodded and started to cry. "How far along are you," Bill asked. "Seven months," Tracey answered.

When Bill arrived home that night it was like he was in a stupor. I'd just come out of the shower. He looked at me and said, "Marie, you are right. Tracey is going to have a baby." I dried off, put on my robe and laid flat on the bed and whispered to myself, "Oh, my God!"

We announced it to the whole family. Everyone was awe-struck. Who? When? Where?—questions everyone asked. I cautioned Bill to delicately query Tracey about all the facts: who the father is, why she never told us before this, would she finish out her senior year in high school, had she'd seen a doctor?

She told us that she'd gone to Planned Parenthood when she was already four months pregnant. They left it up to her to either keep the baby or put it up for adoption.

When Bill and I talked with her a few days later, she said she'd have the baby but would give it up for adoption because she felt she was too young to care for the child. We agreed and tried to comfort her during this stressful time. She never revealed why or how this all happened. But she did give us the name of the father, Joseph, who lived down the block from her mother's house, a young boy who was a senior in high school with her. Apparently, the sex was consensual but under what circumstances is still unknown.

When Bill heard this news about the boy involved, I felt he wanted to take a shot gun approach. But he didn't. Having the common sense he was born with, he talked with Joseph's father and mother. By this time,

Joseph was already headed for Texas to enter a university there. By doing this, the other family conveniently avoided a confrontation. The untimely incident disturbed us all. Now it was up to the Griffings to stand by Tracey and calmly work it out. To say the least, this event distracted me from my own thoughts of a new job.

Bill and I decided it was necessary that we have a meeting with the family members: Harriett, Bill's mom, his son and daughter-in-law Mark and Debbie, his sister Ruth and her husband, Al, his other son, Billy and partner, Lorraine, who lived in Rhode Island couldn't come down. Everyone met one night at our house in Snedens to discuss the situation and see if we could come up with ways to help Tracey get through this traumatic affair. She was still living with her mom, Bill's ex-wife, Lois, because of her illness (MS) couldn't come. Bill would have to get her input separately. This was all scary for me. I didn't have much weight in any decision. I really wanted her to keep the baby but knew I had little voice in such a decision. I felt everyone's life was about to change depending on the final decision. In such a close family as Bill's was, I believed there was room to raise one little child. I was anxious about Harriett's reaction to all this, knowing her to be a conservative New England raised Protestant.

We all sat around the large oak table in our living room. Bill took over the meeting by describing the circumstances of Tracey's pregnancy and then asked for any ideas on how to handle the situation. Following, as I can recollect, are some of the opinions offered from the women:

DEBBIE: As you all know, Mark and I have been trying to conceive a baby for a few years now; we've undergone all sorts of tests and consultations with doctors but it doesn't look good for us and we really desperately want to have children. Now there is one being born right here in our own family. We know Tracey is too young to care for the baby on her own. We feel it would be wonderful if Mark and I could adopt the child after it's born. We would like to ask Tracey if she'd agree to it.

RUTH: Al (her husband) and I think it's the perfect solution. Mark and Debbie would adopt the baby. If Tracey put it up for adoption, we may never see the child again. I wouldn't like to see a Griffing child taken care of by anyone else but us.

HARRIETT: It's difficult for me to think about all this and that my only granddaughter could have fallen into such a tragic situation. She is so young and vulnerable it hurts me to think what this is going to do to her future. I feel it is best I leave it up to all of you to make the right decisions. I will go along with Tracey's, too. I'm sure the Good Lord will accept what happens from now on because He knows we all care and love Tracey. And we should still keep on loving her no matter what she decides. She stood tall but there were tears in her eyes.

MARIE: Somewhere in all of our lives, at one time or another, we've taken the wrong path—consciously or unconsciously and have had to pay the consequences. This is a major "wrong turn" for Tracey and I think she is the one we should consider first. I'm sure the baby will fare well being raised here within the family. I have qualms about the baby being adopted by another family. But, I feel for now our concern should be focused on Tracey. Bill and I agree she undergo therapy as soon as possible to help guide her through this traumatic period. Of course we'll all be beside her and protect her, but I feel she needs some outside counseling by an expert in this case. Teenage pregnancy out of wedlock is a growing problem in our country. We have to handle it with caution.

This was the first of many meetings that the Griffing family held around our round oak table in Snedens. My son, Todd, and daughter, Heidi, didn't want to be involved in this decision making and I agreed with them. Heidi felt adopting the baby within the family would only be a constant reminder to Tracey about her mistake. Even though I probed Todd for his opinion, he "stood on the fence". "Mom, it's up to you guys but I think Tracey should be the one to make the final decision about the baby."

And so it went for a month until we met with the therapist and Tracey.

"No, I don't want to keep the baby. I don't want to give it to Debbie and Mark. I want to put it up for adoption."

These were definitive words that Tracey kept repeating at the meetings of the therapist from Social Services, Bill and me. At later meetings with the family, Bill announced the matter was closed. He arranged with a lawyer to find a family who'd adopt the baby. The only monies discussed was a small fee to help pay for hospital expenses and getting Tracey back into therapy after the baby was born. The adopting family agreed, the lawyer prepared all the papers and the new parents would pick up the baby at the hospital.

MARIE FENTON GRIFFING

It must have been about 5 a.m. on September 15, 1981 that we received a call from Lois, Tracey's mother that Tracey had gone into labor and was on her way to the hospital in an ambulance. Bill and I both got dressed quickly and sped to New Jersey. When we arrived, Tracey had been admitted. The nurses said she was doing well and would deliver in a few hours. Bill immediately called Mark who came over quickly.

I was a nervous wreck. We were all anxious—pacing around the waiting room. Finally, Bill asked the nurse if he could go in to see Tracey. She said "No, only the father can go in." Then Bill approached the doctor as he was walking by. "This young girl is having a baby and needs someone beside her. I'm her father and I insist you let me into her room. The baby's father is not around." The doctor lowered his head and seemed to think about what Bill said. "Okay, you can go in but no one else."

Bill left to go into Tracey's room. Mark and I sat outside in the waiting room. Debbie arrived later. After 3 cups of coffee, my stomach started to pain—it was like I, too, was in labor. I went to the bathroom and vomited. It was weird, like I was having the baby. Mark suggested I go home and rest until it was all over. When Bill came out of Tracey's room a few minutes later, he announced that Tracey was coming along very well but it would take a few hours before the baby was ready to come out. He could see I was wasted and said he'd drive me home which was only 20 minutes away.

I apologized for my condition. I truly was distraught and he understood. He dropped me off at the house and drove back to the hospital. I told him to call me when the baby was born. He said he would.

At 9:30 a.m., the phone rang. I was resting in bed. "Hey, Marie, Tracey had a beautiful baby girl, healthy and strong. I've seen her and held her. She's gorgeous." I sighed and started to cry. "I'm so happy everything is okay, Bill. Come on home now. You need some rest."

When Bill arrived at the house, he was smiling from ear to ear. Tracey had an easy labor and Bill was allowed to hold the little being in his arms—his first grandchild. I was happy for him but I knew that giving her up to others would break his heart. I never mentioned my feelings to him. Three days later he went to the hospital and together with Tracey who was leaving the hospital, carried the baby over to the adopting family who were in the parking lot. Then he took Tracey back to her mother and came home. I could see the tears in his eyes. He showered and with his chin up said he was going to his shop to do some work. I was fixing a dinner for us in the kitchen. I started to cry but quickly wiped away my tears, He kissed me goodbye and I hugged him tight. "It's going to be okay, Bill. You know the old saying 'It'll all come out in the wash' well, things will be back to normal soon." I knew what I had said was not to come true. All of us were involved and the loss of Bill's first grandchild would effect us in different ways—sooner than I thought.

That afternoon while preparing dinner in the kitchen, the phone rang. "Mrs. Griffing this is the lawyer for the adoptive parents of Tracey's baby."

"Yes", I said with my eyes open wide and my heart starting to palpitate.

"The couple has decided they don't want to keep the baby—not that the baby is sick or anything. She's beautiful and perfect. They've suddenly become frightened about the results of their decision. They want to return the baby. To whom can I deliver her?"

I couldn't believe what I was hearing. "Gosh, I don't know. I guess you'd better come to my house. Bill isn't home but I'll call him."

"Okay. Sorry about this. I'll bring the baby over in a half hour."

My vegetables were over boiling on the stove. I turned them off and the roast I had in the oven. I immediately called Bill at the shop but didn't explain much, just said the baby was coming to our house soon and for him to get back quickly.

It was like a "lost weekend" from then on. I ran around the house like a wild rabbit trying to think how I would handle taking on the baby. I had no crib, no diapers, no special milk. I stood in our bedroom, tried to calm myself down and concentrate on a plan.

First, I pulled out a large, deep drawer from our upright clothes chest and placed it on the camel saddle stool that was at the end of our bed. I tossed all the clothes in it to the floor; I lined it with a soft, light, white throw from the bed; and found another soft throw from the couch to use as a cover-up. I grabbed other light blankets from the linen closet and spread them on the bed. Then I just stood by the front door and waited.

Suddenly, I saw two cars pull into the driveway. One I recognized to be Bill's station wagon; the other I figured was the lawyer's. It was. The lawyer climbed out of the car carrying a small blanket bundle in one arm and a large plastic bag in the other hand. Bill ran from his car toward the man and grabbed the blanketed bundle from his arm and raced to me. I had the door open and was just standing there like a statue. His faced looked strained. I think my mouth was wide open as he placed the bundle in my arms and ran back to the lawyer.

MARIE FENTON GRIFFING

The bundle felt warm and I took it immediately into the living room, peeled back the light-covering. There was Tracey's baby, sleeping peacefully in my arms. I sat down on the couch, cuddled her and kept looking at her face. I must have sat like that for ten minutes until Bill came into the house.

"Okay, Marie, the plan has changed." Bill said. I could see he was shaken. I beckoned him over to the sofa. "Look at her. Isn't she beautiful?" It felt like holding my own babes for the first time so many years before. Bill sat down next to me; took a deep breath and gazed down at the "sleeping beauty." We both sat there for a while before we came to our senses.

Bill carried the baby to our bedroom and laid her on our bed. We removed the blanket around her. She had a pretty baby sleep outfit on and in the large plastic bag we found all sorts of things—baby bottles, milk formula supplied by the hospital, diapers, plus packets of sleepers; wipe tissues; a little hat, a pretty embroidered blanket, and other baby essentials that the adoptive parents had bought and passed on to us.

I was relieved because I wouldn't have known how to cope without these immediate necessities. Bill and I were now the caretakers for his grandchild.

I felt sorry for the couple who had anxiously waited to adopt the baby. I could only surmise they were frightened that Tracey would ask for the baby back. Bill and I knew she wouldn't do that. I guess they felt it better not to go through with the adoption, even if it was a last minute decision. I was sorry for the woman who went out and shopped for the lovely things she bought for the baby. I could imagine how she was hurting having to return this beautiful child. Television recently brought out bad adoption experiences and that could have influenced them.

Bill and I circled the bed peering at this little being sleeping on the bed. I started to put things in their place; prepared a bottle for her, laid out the diapers and other things. Then I gently picked her up and placed her into the blanket-lined drawer. She kept on sleeping; I covered her and breathed a sigh of relief. She was safe.

Bill went to the phone and called the Social Service woman that we'd dealt with throughout this whole saga. She knew that Tracey was giving the baby up to a couple but she said if it didn't work out to call her and she'd put her in a foster home for six months until Tracey decided to give the baby up for legal adoption with her agency. It was Friday afternoon and the woman said it was too late to do this now. We would have to keep the baby until Monday and then bring her into the agency. Bill told her okay—we'd take care of her.

Bill started to call members of the family. They said they'd be over on Saturday and Sunday to see the baby. When he reached Tracey and explained the circumstances, she didn't say much. He told her if she wanted to see "Jessica" (the name that Tracey had given her baby just after it was born), it was her right but only if she really felt the need. She said yes. She would be over the next day.

It astonished me how I quickly got the "hang" of taking care of a newborn. We women do have a strong maternal instinct. Realizing that made me feel good. I diapered, bathed, powdered—all the things a "mommy" does with a baby; it all came back to me. Bill and I finally settled into bed but all night long we were awake from time to time, feeding Jessica and diapering her when she awakened at 2 p.m. Sometimes one of us would quietly get up to check her out and see if she were breathing. We were two nervous people that night. Tanya, our dog, who always slept in our bedroom at night, left the room and went to the living room to get some sleep. She apparently became nervous of all the commotion and this "thing" in the drawer. She had never seen a baby before except her own.

The weekend was unbelievable. The whole family arrived to look and hold the baby. Tracey was the most unbelievable. She arrived with a girlfriend and spent at least two hours lying on our bed with Jessica next to her. I would peak in once in awhile. She only stared at the baby, touched its arms, fingers, toes as if she couldn't believe that this human had been in her stomach for nine months.

Meanwhile, Mark and Debbie (Bill's son and daughter-in-law who were not able to conceive and wanted desperately to adopt Jessica) were troubled we were going to take it to the New York Social Services on Monday to be put into a foster home. Bill and I tried to calm their concerns and advised them to wait and ask Tracey again if she'd like to keep the baby in the family. We sent them home. Harriett was the most amazing woman throughout this "saga." She saw the child, admired her, and held her but never expressed any grief or other feelings. Her last words as she left the house were, "Let Tracey make her own decision."

MARIE FENTON GRIFFING

6. COMPLICATIONS SET IN; WOMEN HELP OUT

F OR THE NEXT six months, Bill and I couldn't help but put our full concentration on Tracey and her newborn, Jessica. The Griffing family was wonderful in that they didn't try to influence Tracey on which direction she should take. Of course, Debbie and Mark were hoping she would change her mind and allow them to adopt the baby. She had six months to decide. Jessica was in safe keeping in a good foster home set up by Social Services.

I'll never forget that Monday morning after 3-day-old Jessica spent the weekend in our house and how we all fell in love with her. Bill was so sad when we wrapped her up in a blanket for the trip to Manhattan. I held her during our drive. We were going to pass her over to a stranger at the Social Service office who in turn would give her to the foster parents.

When we arrived at the dingy building and walked into the waiting room, I handed Jessica to Bill. When the lady arrived to take her, tears rolled down his eyes and it almost seemed as if he didn't want to let go of this babe, his first grandchild. But he did. I personally felt it would be a good waiting period for everyone concerned—Tracey, Debbie & Mark and Bill to consider all options and which would be best for the baby. I knew in time it would be resolved. For the time being, the child would be properly cared for. Tracey was even allowed to visit her baby at the foster home anytime she desired.

Meanwhile, after so much disruption in our lives, Bill and I seemed to be growing apart. We were not communicating much any more; our interests divided.

Now that Tracey had graduated from high school, we suggested she enter a community college in New Jersey to continue her education. She went along with it and took up courses in design, drafting—subjects she was most liked. She also became interested in a religious movement, popular at the time, and kept in close contact with an older woman member of the group. That concerned me and Bill but we thought it was just a phase.

My life became confused. Debbie and Mark were still anxious to know about Tracey's final decision about Jessica. Harriett was coming over every weekend, Deb and Mark were stopping by too, Heidi was flitting from one job to another, Todd was coming and going with his school work, How could I handle all these changes and primarily how could I concentrate on my own endeavors? I decided to take it day by day.

It did make me happy when everyone came for holiday dinners. I always loved to cook up festive dishes so I threw myself into keeping everyone together and happy. Meanwhile, I was trying to get my PR work going plus writing some articles for Cosmopolitan and other magazines.

I lost my most loving dog, Tanya. She died of old age and I missed her so. Heidi and her new friend, Janie, brought me Janie's dog to take care of while the two girls were busy working at a summer camp for children in New Jersey. At first, I refused but gave in because I love dogs. My cats, Poker, Mite and Calico seemed enough for me to take care of, but a dog definitely is a better companion when you're home alone, and that's where I was most of the day. Bill worked diligently again at his shop but would come home tired. I began to feel that we were falling backwards instead of forward because of so much attention to family problems.

For the next several years, my life passed too quickly to recall all the ups and downs; so many things happened so fast, it is difficult to recall all. One of the happiest times I do remember very clearly was when Todd graduated from the New York Institute of Technology with honors (Summa cum laude). Bill and I went to his graduation and I sat next to his favorite teacher at the luncheon. He had only high praises for Todd and said he would be successful in TV. I was so proud of my son. As for the main players on stage at that time of my life, here is what I can remember:

Tracy: She made her own decision in six months following the birth of Jessica. She asked that Debbie and Mark adopt her baby. She also asked to be allowed to see her from time to time. They agreed and were very happy about the decision. Needless to say, Bill was thrilled too.

She stopped her education because she couldn't cope with the studies and went to work with Bill in his cabinetry shop. She moved out of her mother's house and became friendly with a young woman. They lived together. I had suspicions of her being a lesbian, but I did not express them. She was a good worker for Bill and he was happy to have her "under his wing" again. I admired her determination to go forward with her interests. I knew she was a survivor and would find the right road to take for her future. I often wonder if I would have held up as strongly as she did during all this conflict. The ease she showed in the handling of her problem made me look at the way I was now handling my own. I decided to stop feeling sorry for myself and to start being grateful that I have a good life and realize that others have far more worries than I. My step-daughter taught me a good lesson.

Debbie: She was excited about having a baby to care for. For the last several years, she and Mark tried everything but couldn't conceive. She adored Jessica and was a good mother. Then out of the blue, six months later, she became pregnant with her own child. It was like a miracle, but many medical experts say, this often happens. The family was growing bigger and I had to add more chairs at our dining room table. It was fun to have Debbie and Mark's children over to visit. I always looked forward to having my own grandchildren, but knew I would have to wait awhile for that. So now I felt lucky to have these new additions to our family—Jessica and Justin. Then along came Cameron, Debbie's own second baby.

She was ecstatic about her good fortune and I could associate with that. When Todd was born, I remember how happy I was and felt my family was as perfect as I wanted it to be. Debbie was a good mother and I knew she would put all her energies into making every member of her family the best they could ever be. That thought made me somewhat envious because I knew my career won over sometimes when it came to focusing on family or work. I think I will always feel guilty that I was not the best mother I could be. I did my best but Debbie showed me I could have done better.

Heidi: She decided to quit her job at the summer youth camp and enter another type of community living—Kripaula Center in Massachusetts headed by an Indian guru who had successfully established a legitimate site for outsiders to come and reap the intellectual pursuits of gaining a calm existence through meditation, proper foods, exercise without drug use. To me, that sounded wonderful. The only thing—I was skeptical of this plan. It looked to me like he was using young vulnerable people to operate his "camp" and it sounded like a cult to me—there was a lot of this during this era. However, Heidi seemed happy in this new environment and that was most important to me.

I was beginning to better understand Heidi and her multiple work interests. I came to the conclusion she was searching for something that would fulfill her and she had not found it as yet. Also, dealing with the early death of her father and the horrific choice Rick made, I could only imagine she was hurting deep down. The poetry she wrote told me that. At times my heart swelled over with compassion for her and I only wanted to hold her in my arms and rock her back and forth like when she was my little girl who bruised her knee. But she had a lot of changing moods and sometimes it was like walking on egg shells when she would come home for a visit. I could only stand back and let her find her way. I hoped the love I offered her would help guide her forward. I believe she showed me to become more patient and understanding about the different paths she took—and I thank her for that.

Harriett: A lovely lady who was now in need of family support. Bill would pick her up every Saturday morning to spend the weekend with us. She did have a day-care person with her in her house during the week, but little by little her friends who used to stop by to play cards with her, passed away or were in a retirement home. We had no recourse but take her "under our wing." I spent each weekend catering to her needs, bathing her, serving breakfast, lunch and dinner. I really didn't mind because she was a quiet, obliging person. I let this all sink in because I knew some day I would come to the same point that she was in life and I knew it was important that I don't forget Harriett's strength throughout this time and the wonderful accepting way she faced the future. There were lessons to be learned here—knowing one's limitations, "grinning and bearing" and "it is what it is." Harriett taught me all these to store and remember for my old age.

My public relations jobs fell apart mainly because I gave them little concentration. I did try to start a novel, "A Real Woman" of which I wrote 300 pages, but let it drop. All of my savings were gone. Bill and I were having a tough time making ends meet. His shop was not making money either. His own shop expenses and giving Tracey a small salary, he didn't have much left over for us. "You can't get blood from a rock!" he'd answer when I asked him for financial help For the first time, we began to squabble and shout at each other. It was not a good relationship.

One Sunday afternoon, my friends, Margaret, Chappy and Sally asked us to join them for a jazz festival at the 76 House, a nearby gourmet restaurant. Bill and I were not feeling friendly towards each other at the time, so he opted not to go.

The jazz concert was wonderful. We had a front row seat, drank a lot of wine and when it was over we went to the bar to have another drink and talk a little. That was my nemesis. Somehow the conversation drifted to my first husband Bob and I made a toast to him. Sally and Margaret giggled and said "and to all his lovers in Snedens."

I was shocked. I just blanked out for a second. "What are you saying? Bob fucked women in Snedens all the time I worked my ass off in New York. This is something I never knew. I don't believe this; he would never do that to me."

"Marie," said Margaret, "You never knew?"

"I don't believe you," I answered.

"Yes, Marie, Max found him in bed with his wife, Barbara."

"No, No. I do not believe you."

Then I started to cry. It was like my whole world had been blown apart. It was the last thing a woman who adored her husband would like to hear from others. I was absolutely devastated. I ordered another martini and asked again to tell me all the details because I was ignorant of it all.

I guess they saw my anguish and didn't respond.

"Tell me, tell it to me—everything," I screamed.

Nobody answered at first. Then Chappy said that they were making it all up—like a joke. I knew better. I just hung my head and cried. Sally drove me home. I rushed past Bill in the living room and fell into my bed sobbing. It was a night I'd never forget. No real answers even to today. Will I ever know the truth? How can I trust anyone anymore? How about Bill? Can I trust him? I questioned myself for days. Even had the nerve to call up Bob Meisner, Bob's closest friend, and ask him about all this. Of course, he would not say anything. Nor did other friends I asked around Snedens. I finally put it far back in my mind and never brought it up again, although I'll never forget that incident.

1985 was not a good year for Bill and me. We quarreled a lot, mostly about finances. Meanwhile, we were trying to keep up a front for the family. Todd was back living with us. He had started a new job in television and doing well. I was pleased. I asked him for help with the household bills and he responded. That helped but I was terrified of losing my home. I was two months in arrears with the mortgage.

One night the "straw that broke the camel's back" happened and I asked Bill to leave the house and not come back. He had nothing to lose except me. He packed up and went over to his mother's house to live. I had no idea where I'd go from there but I needed space from him to collect myself.

The family was distraught by this situation but I didn't care. I knew it was coming. For the first week or so, I felt a sense of relief—no more arguing over money matters. In a way I felt free now to make new decisions. I would let the dust settle and then take it from there.

I did compulsive things—like, selling beauty pageant crowns at an art festival. I did make $50. I cooked up three soups and with the help of my friend, Greta, tried to sell them to a local gourmet shop. That fell through. I went to the bank and tried to get a loan, but because my credit record was low, they refused me. And to make it worse, the bank charged me $200 just to apply for a loan. I even tried to put my house up for sale but didn't have the guts to sell it. The market was especially low, so I gave up on that. I was at my wit's end. I finally had to borrow money from an old friend to get me through for a while until I could get the courage to look for a job in New York. It was like living the months after Bob had died and I was penniless, but like then, I was determined to work at getting through this difficult time even though I knew I would miss having Bill around. I truly loved him. I felt lost and helpless. I decided to wean myself off my daily booze intake of Scotch and water to Vodka and grapefruit juice—Vitamin C is good for me, I told myself. Oh My!

CHAPTER NINE

MY LIFE COMES
TOGETHER AGAIN . . . .
(1985 to 1987)

1. GETTING BACK MY SELF ESTEEM —WITH HEIDI'S HELP

I WAS A mess by the middle of 1985. A call from my daughter Heidi, saying she had bought a plane ticket for me to meet her and her friend, Janie, in Las Vegas for a week sounded very inviting. I was in the "blues" after Bill walked out of my life.

Even though my finances were not doing well, I figured I'd take a little R & R. I felt I needed to make myself feel alive. So, I accepted Heidi's invite to meet with her in Las Vegas and then take a trip across the desert in her van to visit my brother, Pat, in San Diego, and see a close friend, Boyd, (the best man at my marriage to Bob in Mexico). I prepared myself for the trip. I trusted Todd to take charge of the house and the animals. I thought it was a good idea to advise Bill who was still living with his mother

It's strange, but I couldn't get him out of my mind. I still felt angry but my underlying love for him was still there—and that bothered me. I wondered why I was so weak when it came to my emotions. Maybe a few sessions of therapy like Sally advised would be a good idea. I would confront that when I returned from Vegas.

I felt liberated as I flew on American Airlines from Newark to Las Vegas. I relaxed for the first time in months, listened to the music on the ear phones—one of the songs from Aretha Franklin fortified my feelings—"I don't have room for the pain."

I couldn't wait to see Heidi. I knew in my heart that she had wanted me to take this trip to get me out of the doldrums, and she was right. I appreciated her caring for me. My daughter came through when I needed her. I'll never forget it.

I felt new and almost reborn when I arrived in Vegas. Heidi and Janie reserved a nice room for me and we had lots of fun going to the shows, seeing the sights, eating wonderful foods, playing in the casinos. All the activity took my mind off my troubles and I even didn't think about Bill. Well, truthfully, only once in awhile. After a couple of days, we left to drive across the desert to Los Angeles to see my friend, Boyd, and then spend a couple of days with my brother Pat. Little by little, my head started to clear; I became myself again and knew I could face what would come when I returned to New York.

The overnight with Boyd was great. "Mom," Heidi asked me while we were visiting there, "How come you never married Boyd—he seems perfect for you." What could I say to my daughter—that I loved Boyd but not in a sensual way. He was a loving friend, a great pen pal. I replied, "The timing was never right, Heidi."

At my brother's house, we had a good time. Pat and his wife, Beverly, were very hospitable. My brother was big on vodka martinis. I could see Heidi wasn't happy seeing me back on the booze again, but I went with the flow. I met all my nieces and nephews whom I had not seen for years. We recalled all the good times when they came to our wonderful house in Tarzana to swim and have barbecues. No questions were asked about my separation from Bill. On the last day of our visit, I had the need to call him and let him know what was going on. I felt we should meet when I got back to New York. I hoped we could take time out to communicate, do some therapy and find our way back together again. It was strange—being so far away from him, only made me realize that I shouldn't give up on him so fast.

Heidi and Janie drove me to the San Diego airport where I boarded the plane to Newark Airport. On the plane, I was able to reflect on how Heidi had come so close to me during this trip. When we parted, I thanked her. She suggested I see a family therapist along with Bill and try to work out our differences. She also urged me to stop smoking and curb my alcohol drinking. I embarrassingly nodded yes. I had never gone to a therapist on my own behalf before—now I felt it might help. Since the early 70s, I had sat in on therapy sessions with Rick a dozen times at least and the same with Heidi. I thought it a waste of time and I became belligerent, especially with some of Rick's doctors. Yet, I knew Heidi was trying to throw me the last "straw" to grab so I could hold on to the marriage. It was like a turnabout—a daughter now trying to help her mother find her way. Maybe, that is what having children is all about—we go full circle.

When I arrived back home in New York and lay in my own bed, I knew that it was time I get my scene together. My heart told me I still was in love with Bill but I couldn't accept him back on his terms—it would have to be on mine.

The months to come would prove me right.

2. BILL AND I FOCUS ON OURSELVES; WOMEN FRIENDS OFFER SUPPORT!

THE WEEK AFTER I arrived home from Las Vegas, I was busy with domestic work. I did a lot of food shopping for Todd and me; reshuffled my bills to see which to pay first; had the gardener in to make the grounds presentable in case a buyer for the house came by (Yes, I decided to put it up for sale). And I rejoined my old poker group on Saturday nights.

Everyone knew that Bill and I had split up but not much discussion about it. Only a friendly "dig" from one of them like—"We knew it wouldn't last." That was painful to me but I laughed it through. Meanwhile, I kept thinking of Heidi's advice to see a therapist. After one of the poker games at Sally's house, I cornered her in the kitchen to ask if she knew someone, reason being she underwent some sort of group therapy after splitting with her own husband years before. She suggested her "newest" therapist, a psychologist in New Jersey about 20 minutes from me. "He's not expensive Marie," she told me. "I think he's good. He's young and quite good looking." I laughed, "Sally, I don't need a good looking therapist, I need someone who can help me get through this trauma."

I took her advice and called him for an appointment. The first few sessions with him were difficult—I cried a lot. Thank goodness he had a big box of tissues handy. He was a gentle spoken man in his late thirties and seemed truly concerned about my situation. I came to trust him. Our weekly sessions seemed to strengthen my own convictions.

In October of 1985, a hurricane-like storm struck our area. I remember the day well. Todd and I were up early. He was getting ready to go to work. The winds were blowing 50 miles an hour and the rain was coming down in torrents.

I was fearful of the big oak tree just outside my back door. It was hundreds of feet tall and there was always a thought in my mind that if it were toppled, it would fall on my house. I was thinking of that when the windows started to shutter and I couldn't see beyond the back step because of the torrential rain.

Suddenly, I heard a couple of loud claps of thunder which almost made the house shake. Then a bright light came through the window in my bedroom, a loud cracking sound, a thump right outside. I ran to the family room where Todd was donning his jacket for work. He heard it too and looked stunned.

"Todd, I think we've been hit by lightening, but I don't know where." We hugged each other and Todd told me to stay put and he'd check outside. I looked above me and saw the roof was still intact. Where did the lightening hit? I wondered.

"Mom, it's okay," Todd said as he shook off the rainwater from his jacket. The lightening hit the big ash tree behind the garden. We're okay but the huge trunk is split in half—you should see it, unbelievable!"

After the storm calmed down, so did Todd and I. We walked out and far back in the garden, I saw the damage. I couldn't believe it. This tremendous trunk of a tree was split in two. Was this a symbol of Bill and me? I just gazed at it for minutes. It was like a sign for me. The lightening strike came so close but thankfully caused no damage to the house or Todd and me. How come? Todd finally left for work when he saw that I was calmed down. I went to my typewriter and off the top of head wrote a verse about the happening—something I usually do when a crisis arises. For some reason, I felt the lightening strike had a part of what I was going through at the time. Recording my feelings has always helped me through difficult times.

I had another therapy session that afternoon and I brought the writing with me to read to the doctor—for whatever it was worth. Maybe it would help him better understand me or maybe he'd think I was a just another "crazy lady." I had to take the chance. Here's what I wrote:

MARIE'S TREE

"My tree came falling down today. This beautiful, majestic ash, hundreds of feet tall that I could see from my bedroom window had been hit by lightening. It was scorned by Hurricane Gloria, split in half from the torrential winds and lightening strike. I gasped when I heard the terrifying noise and felt a wrench in my gut. When I saw the damage, I was spent. I sadly shook my head and thought, "It's symbolic of what's going on with my life now."

There it sits, tipped on angle—this strong beautiful tree. Half is standing tall and straight with its flowing leaved branches waving back and forth in the breeze. The other half is split from the base, wedged between other trees, still aloft but in a dangerous, precarious position—to fall or not to fall. Why do I feel such a personal attachment to this wondrous tree? How can I help it? It's in such a painful position. Like me, it's one half is leaning, supported by other trees (my friends, my kids?) I know it will have to come down to solid ground (like me?) and find a restful position.

Somehow, I feel the split tree correlates with my own life situation. Bill and I had "split." We're both adrift. Is it a new turning point in my life? Am I "on tilt?" Or should I compare myself to the other half of the tree standing upright? I need answers. I need help on where I'm headed.

I walk around the tree, touch it, smell the fresh leaves on the fallen half, then I look upward to the other half still standing strong. I still cannot make out which half am I."

Martin, my therapist, seemed very interested in my piece "Marie's Tree." He interpreted my writing differently than I. My viewpoint was mixed, he said. "Marie, you are questioning the symbolism of this fallen tree. You are trying to figure out which part of the split trunk is you—the tall half or the fallen half. I believe that you, Marie, are the whole tree. Part of you has fallen down. The other part of you is standing tall. I do not see your husband Bill in this. This tree is you, Marie, and in it you see your pain."

I thought about what he was saying and it made sense. "I think I know what you're saying, Doctor," I replied. "But speaking symbolically, what happens to my broken side?"

"Well, let's start by symbolically suggesting that you cut the fallen part of trunk into pieces, burn them slowly; then concentrate on nourishing the other half of the trunk that is still standing strong so it will continue to grow. Discarding the fallen pieces will be difficult but I've always discovered with my patients that whatever pain they go through in their own particular life crisis, they grow stronger because of it—and I think you will, too. Look at yourself. You got through your first husband's death and the unfortunate death of your son, and all the worries about your daughter, but consider how you have changed a lot of your thinking, how you've found the strength to go forward. Don't let this new trauma bring you down. You can and you must overcome. May I suggest that you ask your husband, Bill, to join us for a few sessions—if he is willing to do so.

I think that by both of you talking with me about your differences and anger could be helpful. If not, I feel that just you and I will make some sense of all this."

I left Martin's office feeling stronger and more in touch with myself than I had in a long time. I decided to call Bill and ask him if he'd go to my next meeting with me.

When I arrived home from my session, I saw Bill and Todd hacking away with axes on the fallen tree. I walked out to the garden. They were both sweating but pointed to all the blocks of wood we'd have for a fire that winter. They were both smiling and I started to laugh. "Good work," I said. Then I asked Bill when he was finished if he would come inside so we could talk. "Okay," he replied.

My stomach went queasy when I sat down with Bill in the living room. His hair was ruffled, his shirt sweaty—still the handsome man I'd married. I so much wanted to hug him even though I was angry for being in this terrible predicament.

I first asked how he came to know about my tree. He answered, "Through the grapevine." Who could have told him about my dilemma? I thanked him for his help. Todd, meanwhile, was in his room taking a shower. I felt uncomfortable but I forced myself to ask him about the therapy session.

"Bill, if there's any chance of us getting together to talk about our breakup. I think it would be a good idea if you and I met together with my therapist. Maybe he can help us settle this separation in a friendly way."

Within a few seconds of my remarks, Bill nodded. "Okay, no problem. Tell me where and when and I'll meet you there."

I was astonished at his answer. When he left, I breathed a sigh of relief. Hopefully, the session for the following week would help us both.

I immediately called my friend, Sally, and my other friend, Greta, who had been supporting me all the way. We planned to meet for lunch soon. I knew both of them would give me feedback on this situation. I figured I was very lucky to have women friends in whom I could confide. For me they were almost as good as going to my therapist. I thought about Bill and how he was probably holding in his anguish and mixed feeling within himself. Men don't confide in each other as easily as women.

MARIE FENTON GRIFFING

3. LUNCHING WITH THE "GIRLS"

I FELT THE need to talk with women friends about my separation from Bill and ask them for feedback on how I was handling this situation. I knew that a few of them had been "f . . . ." by their men and ended with divorce. I was hoping against hope that it would not happen to me. Greta, Sally, Lucie, Helen and Susan were all intelligent, educated women—all some years younger, but I felt they were wiser than I in many ways and could offer me advice on how I should settle my problem.

I phoned them during the next couple of weeks to get together, one on one. We all opted for lunch. Three met me in Tappan and Nyack, near my house. The other two, Susan and Helen, met me in New York City.

The experiences were wonderful and most uplifting. The three who had had troubled marriages and two of them divorced, gave me a lot of support in the direction I was going—therapy for Bill and me. The two divorcees (one of them did remarry), agreed that finding the problem early and settling it was the best recourse. "Divorce, is terrible," said Greta. "It wrenches you completely, takes away all your self-esteem plus leaves the wife trying to build a whole new life for herself while her husband, in her case, had his lover to support him." She continued, "It has taken me many years to build myself up, find that new life. I discovered in therapy groups that I was not alone. Other women in their 50s who raised a family for 30 years were dumped because the husband had the "gray itch" but I overcame.

"I echo that," said Sally. "Here we spend many years supporting our husbands, raising kids, cooking, cleaning, moving from place to place and it seems when they feel we're used up, they go for a younger woman and leave us in the "dump.""

Then I got opposite views from Susan and Helen, my co-workers from Good Housekeeping who were in their 30s and experiencing the good side of marriage.

"Marie, you and Bill were meant for each other. He has in many ways taken care of you, your house and has been caring to your own children.

Give him another chance to show you his true love for you. Don't act too quickly."

"Marie, take a few breaths before you decide on a divorce. It can be a terrible ordeal on everyone concerned. You have a large extended family and this will definitely affect everyone. I agree on a 'meeting of the minds' with the aid of a therapist. If that doesn't work out, then do your best to continue your own goal in life—concentrate on your writings. I know you will find the answer."

All of this advice came flooding in within the week that Bill and I were scheduled to meet with my therapist. It was mind blowing.

I called Harriett one day before the meeting with the therapist. She and I hadn't really talked since Bill and I split up. I missed her presence and considered her a friend not only because she seemed like a "rock" throughout Tracey's dilemma but was to me the best mother-in-law any woman would want. I needed to talk with her. I realized she was a good friend, too.

"I hope you and Bill get together, Marie," Harriett responded to my phone call. "You have been good for our family and I hope we have been good for you. I know that Bill loves you very much. I don't know the exact reasons you've split up, as I try not to interfere with my children's doings. They are now adults and have to handle their own problems. I'm too old to carry their burdens but if they ask of me, I give my honest and best advice. Marie, I love you and I hope you and Bill can work this out so we can become a family again."

My last meeting was with Lucie. The old restaurant close to the Journal News where we both worked together was gone. So we met in another spot in Nyack.

It was so good to see this lovely woman again. At first we talked about our children and how they were doing. We had our favorite drink, a Scotch Sour. It was like old times again. We did some small talk about little things and then during our salad, I told her about my dilemma and asked for advice. She was blunt and I took her opinion to heart.

"Marie, you're not getting any younger, neither am I. Men our age can go out and easily find a new mate. I know from what you tell me it has been monetarily difficult for you, but Bill hasn't messed up your life, otherwise, as far as I can see. He has cared for you, your kids and you've done the same for him. That's what a good marriage is all about, caring and loving. However, I understand that protecting you should be part of the bargain and if you are going to lose your house and not be able to

MARIE FENTON GRIFFING

provide for your kids, then he is not doing his part. And somehow, he has to find a way to turn that around."

"I agree with what you're saying, Lucie, and I've considered all those points and it's the money part that's tearing us apart." I answered.

"I don't know but maybe he'll find someway to meet your needs. Give him time. When you've found a really good man who loves you, think carefully before making final decisions. I say go with him to the therapist. It can't hurt." she replied.

We tipped our glasses together before we left the restaurant. "Okay, upward and forward!" we toasted.

And so it went. One after another, my women friends gave me their support, their opinions and most importantly, being there for me. I took all their feedback to heart and slept on it the night before meeting Bill the next day at the therapist's office. I knew what I had to do. I only wondered if my husband would open up to me and if he could "fix" it for us. It was finally up to him.

Bill's and my first therapy session was a fiasco. He "flew off the handle" a couple of times about things I said. Ten minutes before our hour-long therapy session was over, he got so upset that he stomped out of the room and left. I tried to keep my calm during all this. The experiences I had joining Rick and Heidi in therapy, helped me understand Bill's reactions. After all it was his first time.

The next couple of sessions were better. It was strange driving up to the doctor's office in my car and seeing him pull up right behind me and then the two of us silently going into the office. I could feel his strong vibrations as we sat on the long couch. There was one session I even walked out on. But after a few more, we settled down.

After the last session, Bill followed me home on the Palisades Parkway and waved me over to stop at one of the lookout points. My attitude was still belligerent. I kept my calm as we sat on a stone bench overlooking the Hudson River. It was a beautiful late fall day.

"Marie, I truly love you and will try to help you financially from now on. I'll really try my best but I can't promise I can do it all."

I guess that's all I really wanted to hear, that for the first time he was committing himself to paying the bills. I asked him to come home and we'd work it out one more time. There definitely was a strong chemistry between us as well as an emotional attachment, and it won out ahead of my rational thinking.

Bill moved back into the house and it was funny to see the reaction of our extended family when we announced it. All of them gave a sigh of relief.

From then on Bill gave me $400 in bills to help pay expenses. Where he got it, I didn't ask. I started to feel secure again. Our attitude toward each other had changed and our love and sex life seemed to grow stronger.

The Christmas holidays came and went. It was a joyous time. The whole family gathered together at our house and everything seemed back to where it used to be. Whatever—the therapist's input, the support from the family, help from my women friends, the strong love between us, I don't know which one it was or was it all that gave us a second chance. Anyway, we were living as husband and wife and I felt like my old self again.

I searched around and got a job as a public relations spokesperson for North American Pageants. It was on a retainer basis but it helped me get back into writing again. I took my house off the "selling list." Bill helped a lot more around the house on weekends to get the place back to normal. I wasn't looking forward to a freezing February and March. I talked with Bill, occasionally, about us moving to California. I craved warm weather and hot sun. Twenty-five years in New York was wearing on me. It was not only the snow shoveling and icy roads but how much New York City had changed as well as parts of our own suburban community. A big IBM establishment was being built a few miles from Snedens; condos were being built in Nyack, on the Hudson. Fancy huge homes were being built in Snedens; local schools were being closed. It was like progress was taking over this wonderful quiet community. I felt, somehow, it was time for us to move on, but I didn't quite know how.

One morning in early spring of 1986, Bill's younger son, Mark came over to the house. I wondered why he'd stop by so early.

"Marie, my company has opened a branch sales office in Florida," he said sipping on a cup of coffee. "We need a good salesperson—I know my Dad is good at sales. What would you think if we asked him to be our representative down there? He'd get a weekly salary of close to $500 a week."

I was blown over by this news. "Thanks, Mark. Let us think about it." I replied.

Quickly, I ran to the phone to call Bill.

4. OFF TO FLORIDA . . . GOODBYE'S ALL AROUND

IN LATE 1986 Bill flew to Florida to begin his new job with son, Mark. I had second thoughts about it. I didn't much like being separated again from Bill, but after discussing all the pros and cons, we decided it might be a good way to start over. I was looking to California but Florida has warm weather too—and lots of oranges. Our only hesitation was leaving family and old friends. For me, it was nothing new. Todd was my main concern. Heidi was now on her own. Bill, however, had lived his whole life in the area, except for a few years in the Navy. He was the one who would feel the separation the most.

I held up the fort in Snedens while he went to Florida. He called me every night. I did miss him. Within a month he told me that this would work for us and that I should fly down and plan to stay awhile.

I did and the moment I arrived in Ft. Lauderdale in November, leaving the cold temps in NY, finding balmy breezes as I got off the plane, I knew this would be a good change for me. I had wanted to go back to CA, but at this point, I opted to settle in FL.

And so we did. We rented an apartment in a condo called the Parker Dorado in Hallandale—a small town between Miami and Ft. Lauderdale.

My son, Todd, said he would continue to live in and take care of my house in Snedens and the cats, too. That was a relief for me. However, I had to call Heidi and Janie about the dog, Brandy, whom I had adopted for a year. I loved Brandy, but I knew that Todd couldn't handle all of the animals. Janie came by and picked up Brandy. Now I was free to relocate to FL. and find a whole new lifestyle.

I packed a few bags, said goodbye to friends and off I went into a new adventure in my life. After my first visit to Florida and its wonderful climate, I knew I was making the right decision.

The penthouse we rented in the Parker Dorado Condominium, a 327 apartment complex on Ocean Drive in Hallandale, FL. was furnished right down to sheets, dishes—everything we needed. We were on the 17th floor overlooking the Intra-coastal. It was many years since I lived in an apartment. I was ecstatic!

I discovered the amenities of the condo: a library, an exercise room, a sauna, large rooms in which people could play cards plus a beautiful lobby and three elevators. And just a step outside was a huge pool with lounge chairs all around, and down the stairs from the pool deck was the wondrous ocean.

I felt like I was back in California. Flora and fauna were exactly the same as I remembered. It seemed too perfect. But there was something missing. It was my friends. I called back to my "buddies" in New York to hear their voices, talk about my new home, to just connect. This continued for several weeks until I realized that I was running up a big phone bill and opted for writing letters.

One day as I was looking at a boat going down the Intra-Coastal Waterways, I saw the people on deck, smiling and waving to others in small boats going in the opposite direction and I thought how much this scene related to me. Hello—Goodbye. That was what I was doing again. I didn't feel sad. I felt a little scared. A new dawn awaited me.

5. YOUNG GIRLS BOOST MY SPIRITS

B ILL AND I were adjusting to this new life in Florida. Even after having to sell my house in Snedens in order to get an income for us to live on, going back there, packing up my stuff, helping Todd find a new place to live in, saying another goodbye to my women friends, I was in pretty good shape. However, Bill wasn't. He was out looking for a job. I was very worried about his mental being then. But in 1987, he got lucky and found a job as manger of cabinetry at Denison Marine, a big boat company in Davie, FL only 20 minutes from us. He would be bringing in a weekly check, We both breathed a sigh of relief plus this was a job we knew he would like because he loved boats and this company built big yachts, each worth a million dollars or more. So every morning he went to work. I packed him a "brown-bag lunch". He was happy as a lark.

One day in August, 1987 I met two young girls, ages 11 and 12 while swimming in the ocean. They were from Montreal, Canada, visiting their grandma in the condo. We became friends. They were here for only two weeks but the three of us "played" together. We laughed a lot; enjoyed making muffins, romping with a dog on the beach, preparing a "dinner fest" for their parents, and the most fun, my teaching them how to play poker.

Those two weeks sparked up my life. With Bill and me alone here without any family or friends, meeting these girls was just the medicine I needed to make me feel young and vibrant again. When they left we all promised to write back and forth until their next visit around Xmas. Their names are Alanna and Jaclyn and they are still my friends today.

Bill and I became accepted as members of the Parker Dorado Condo community, so much so that he was voted in as President of the condo Board of Directors. That made me the "first lady." I joined the shuffleboard club, and became director of the library which I really enjoyed. I met a lot of residents this way. I also helped with the social activities programs in the building; even worked with the ladies serving coffee at the monthly condo meetings. All this was a little out of character for me. I never liked joining clubs, but it seemed to lift my spirits so I accepted the socializing. All the women were friendly but no way would I get too close to them. My previous experience with Sadye kept me at bay. I didn't want to be upset again. I felt more comfortable talking, joking and playing shuffleboard more with the men in the condo than with the women. Since I was about 10 years younger than most of the women here, they slyly watched my association with their husbands. I found it rather intriguing but kept my distance from too much familiarity.

My New York women friends started to come down to Florida to visit me. It was great to see and talk with Sally, Margaret, Tilly, and Paula. My sister-in-laws, Ruthie and Bernice Fenton came too. We had a busy year in 1988.

The finale of all these new pleasant happenings occurred at Xmas time when I met another young girl, Samantha, also from Montreal who was visiting her grandma in the condo. She was playing shuffleboard with her grandpa and asking around for two other players to join them. Bill and I accepted. She was about 10, the same age as my other Canadian young friends, and like Jaclyn and Alanna, Sam was very bright and had an outgoing, jovial personality. I've always liked that in children . . . somehow I can communicate better with kids like that instead of shy, inhibited ones. I played my best at the shuffleboard game and beat her. I think she expected me to let her win. From time to time as we played, I gave her some tips on how to hit the opponents disk or how to shove her disk into the right number. We laughed a lot. I liked her immediately and asked her if she knew my other two young friends, Jaclyn and Alanna who had also come down for the holidays. When she said no, I asked if she would like to meet them.

"Sure, Marie," Sam said. "It gets boring here with all the old people and not knowing anybody."

I decided to set up a meeting in my apartment for Sam to meet Jaclyn and Alanna. "How would you like to bake corn muffins with my other two young friends this afternoon? Check with your grandma and see if it's okay."

When I got phone calls from each of the grandmas that they were delighted to have me "babysit" for their kids, I set up the kitchen so each would have her own job making the muffins. I hadn't done anything like this since my daughter, Heidi, was a little girl.

We had a great time; made loads of muffins, some of which I let them take home to their grandparents. They really perked up my spirits, especially their laughter as we goofed sometimes baking the muffins.

They felt free and creative—I enjoyed this new companionship. Bill even said he'd never seen me so joyful since I came to Florida.

There was one thing that bothered me. The newspapers and TV always had stories about "pedophiles"—men or women who befriended young children to sexually abuse them. I certainly did not want the girls' relationship with me to be thought of as something like this. What I was trying to do was be a mentor to the girls, guide them in a way that I felt was helpful, only in a surrogate grandmother manner. I was aware my life had not come full circle, not having grandchildren. With almost every elderly lady in the building boasting at least one grandchild and I without any, I wanted to fill this void—and I guess that's what I unconsciously was doing.

Out of the blue, I decided to initiate a Youth Art Program in the condo library. The girls thought it was a great idea. I outlined the program and all three got involved making posters to advertise it to the other visiting children in the condo. We hung up Hanukkah and Merry Xmas banners in the library; I bought lots of art materials and favors for the kids. We decided on a theme for the program—"My Florida Feelings." Most of the kids were from up North—Canada, New York, Boston, Chicago, etc. This activity was new to them and they came in droves. Some even brought friends from other condos.

I solicited some of the condo unit owners who had businesses in hair accessories, children games and straw cowboy hats to donate their wares as rewards for the kids' art work. I asked others for shells they collected from the beach so the young artists could glue them on their drawings and collages. Then we planned to have the drawings exhibited in the condo lobby the day after the art program. It all worked out beautifully. We had over 30 children participating. When the parents and grandparents saw the results in the lobby the day after the program, they were thrilled. Without the help of my three young friends, I couldn't have carried it off. They, too, were pleased with the project. I told them that this would be an annual event and hoped they would like to help the following year. They agreed.

After the program, which took up a lot of my time and energy, I realized it was almost Xmas Eve and Bill and I hadn't put up a tree as yet. We bought our first fake tree and some decorations. When I saw the girls at the pool, I told them about my having to "dress" the tree. They eagerly asked if they could help. I knew they were Jewish and celebrated Hanukah so I checked first with their parents to see if it would be okay.

We had a blast trimming the tree and even had time to bake cookies for the neighbors; the girls loved to deliver them.

I missed the companionship of the girls when they left for home but they promised to write and would be back in August for summer vacation. I did have my two parakeets to amuse me. Bill built a little house and attached it to the cage so that Mr. Green and Ms. Blue could mate if they had the yearning. And for sure, they did. Now I would be a "grandma!"

6. GETTING TO KNOW YOU

IT WAS EARLY summer in 1988 when Bill's mom moved down to her new "home" here in Florida. Bill and I worked furiously to get the apartment set up for her. She had sold her home in New Jersey, her precious paintings, little pieces of furniture and other stuff were shipped to Florida. Before she arrived, Bill and I tried to make the place a friendly setting for her. We worked day and night.

Harriett accepted it graciously, which is a wonderful part of her personality. We knew it was a difficult transition for her just like it was for us. We talked up all the wonderful ammenties she would have here compared to living on her own in New Jersey. She agreed but I could tell it was hard to leave her old friends, her weekly card games, her house that she was so accustomed to. I related to all her feelings—I had been there.

She brought down a remarkable caretaker, Irene, an immigrant from British Guiana, who was very attentive to Harriett's needs. She lived in and took care of my mother-in-law's needs which were many—Harriet now had Parkinson's disease.

To me it was a revelation how women take care of women. Irene was very uplifting to Harriett. She, too, inspired me. So much in fact that I started to be a second caretaker for Harriett—then I progressed to giving help to old people on my floor of the condo—Max, my 80-year-old neighbor next door, Rose, my 86-year-old neighbor across the floor and another, man, Max, only 60'ish, down the floor who was suffering from Lou Gehrig's disease. Everytime I make my famous chicken soup, an applesauce, banana cake, corn muffins, whatever, I made for them all to share. I slowly became the Parker Dorado "Meals on Wheels" for all these old people. I received a lot of gratification for doing this work. I knew they appreciated my efforts and their responses to my giving made me feel good. Bill thought I was overdoing, but I convinced him to let me do my thing.

While doing all these activities, I was keeping up my writing pursuits and met Dolly, a formidable woman who had lived off and on here in the condo for many years. She was on the Board of Directors for the condo.

Dolly was articulate, knew volunteer work as she had worked for years for The Hadassah and she was always in control whenever a crisis arose in the condo. I admired her drive and direction she took in containing problems in the building. She had an inner strength that I tried to learn from. She asked me to continue as a volunteer and handle the library, do the condo bulletin, help with general meetings. The way she put it, it was an offer I couldn't refuse. I had never met a woman like her who had it all together. Dolly became my mentor even though she was almost the same age as I. She had a good sense of humor, an intelligent, caring way of handling people in the condo who didn't abide with the rules and regulations of the building. When it came to delivering a speech at the condo meetings, Dolly was very articulate; the best. I always had stage fright when I had to make a speech. Dolly showed how to make it easy; be yourself; know your subject.

I pursued and succeeded to get new PR jobs with various companies but they didn't last but six months—either the businesses went under or they couldn't afford me anymore. I was devastated but realized Florida was unpredictable for people starting new companies. Even some old established companies went bankrupt. It was 1989 and the country was still trying to catch up after the recession a couple of years before. Florida was lagging far behind.

I kept striving, then let it go and prayed to God to provide for us while we survived after Bill's layoff from his job at Dennison Marine.

It was Harriett who helped me "keep the faith." I began to realize my own mortality after caring for her. She was in her middle 80s and I was in my 60s, yet I began to fear the thought of getting old and incapable of caring for myself when I grew older.

Bill started up his cabinetry work again and rented a small shop about 20 minutes from the condo. We "begged, borrowed and stole" to keep our bills paid up. We "damaged" our credit cards a lot in those days.

But within a few months things started to turn around. Bill got orders to do three kitchens in the condo and little by little, I was able to pay off some of the card charges and even put some of the money he got from his jobs into an envelope in a drawer . . . I called it "our stash."

By now, Harriett had adjusted to her new lifestyle and enjoyed the warm climate. With Bill holding her, she even went into the pool. In her middle 80s, she showed no embarrassment wearing a bathing suit. When I'd see her terribly wrinkled skin on her arms and legs, I gulped . . ." would my body look that way in 20 years. It scared me.

"I guess it gradually creeps on you," I told Dolly one day, "and suddenly you just don't pay attention or maybe don't look into a full-length mirror anymore."

"Marie, seeing our parents grow old-old, is trying thing for people like us in our 50s and 60s, but we must realize that the life-span has been extended because of the miracles of medicine. I think the most important thing to guard against as we age, is keeping our brain in good shape and that means keep it active—read a lot, seek creative outlets, solve problems whether they be cross-word puzzles or balancing your checkbook."

"Yeah," I laughed, "I guess I'm the best problem solver in our family. I've had a lot of practice."

Once in awhile when Dolly and I would be pasting up the monthly condo bulletin, she'd talk about her parents and how she cared for her father who was stricken by Alzheimer's disease. Both were dead now. She said Bill was lucky that Harriet still had "her marbles together." I knew what she meant because my mother got it when she was in her early eighties and ended up in a nursing home where she died. I always felt guilty that I couldn't be there for her—my brother, Pat, handled that burden. She was in California and I was working at Good Housekeeping then and wasn't able to move back to California. I'd always given it thought and wondered if I had inherited the gene and would I also get the disease.

Being able to talk about all these things with Dolly helped to release some of my fears of aging. I became more laid back and decided to enjoy each day. After all my life was full—all our kids came to visit us more times which I really enjoyed.

Bill, and Mark, his son had finally resolved their anger about Mark firing Bill from his first job here in Florida (I helped to resolve that issue) my young friends always boosted my spirits when they came down from Canada; Bill's and my health were good even though he had to have a hernia operation and I had a partial hysterectomy; Bill's three grandkids were growing nicely; we were socializing with nice people; my becoming a blonde did make life more fun again; I was into the serious creative writing I'd been wanting to do for years—my collection of verses and autobiography were coming along just fine; and best of all was the wonderful sunshine almost everyday and the therapy of going swimming in the ocean and pool as well as when the "snowbirds" came down for the winter and I had fun playing shuffleboard every afternoon. Yes, life was good to me.—I was happy . . .

CHAPTER TEN

ADAPTING TO MY NEW LIFE
(1990-1997)

1. MEETING NEW AND DIFFERENT WOMEN FRIENDS

S UDDENLY ONE DAY, someone rang my door. It was Sadye, a neighboring woman in her early 70s who offered me a cake and said "Welcome to the Parker Dorado." I thought it to be a nice gesture and invited her in. We talked and I told her about Bill and me then she forewarned us about some of the Jews living here. I didn't understand her attitude since she was Jewish herself. She said "You and Bill are the first "goyim" in this mostly Jewish condo." I was shocked by her words, but decided to let them slide by. I just nodded. I certainly was not prejudice to Jewish people, nor was Bill. I had many Jewish friends, plus relatives. I thought, "Wait until they hear I once had a Jewish husband."

Sadye became our friend. She guided us through all the politics of the Board of Directors; the condo meetings we should attend; the rules and regulations . . . like wearing a cover-up, sandals when walking in the public areas . . . and buying a special yellow towel with our name on it to use on a chaise lounge, putting on the timer when we did wash in the laundry rooms, and so much more. I was glad to have found a new friend.

Little by little I met people around the pool. Sadye introduced us to a few; almost all had thick Jewish accents and I could feel them scrutinizing us as we lounged on the deck.

Sadye popped into my apartment almost everyday with all sorts of goodies she'd cooked; we played games with her; we invited her over for dinners. She was a very outspoken person but I trusted her. She had a lot of strength, caring for a sick husband. She had a strange sense of humor, most of it mocked her Jewish friends. That side of her I didn't like, but all in all she was friendly toward us. Bill and I decided that we would continue to live here while he was working for his son. The nearness of the ocean won us over. I loved my daily walks on the sand and swimming in the pool. And I was working on a beautiful tan.

Since our rental lease would be over in May 1987, we decided to start looking for an apartment to buy in the condo that would be larger than our one bedroom. Sadye found us one on the 11th floor. Another apartment was also available on the 7th floor, so Bill decided that he'd talk his mother in New Jersey to buy that one for herself. He had wanted for months to bring her down here so she could be close to us. I didn't object. In fact I thought it would relieve him of a lot of stress because he was worried about her being alone except for occasional visits from the kids. She was in her mid 80s and most of her friends were either in nursing homes or had passed away. It would mean selling her house, but in the end she said okay and we closed the deals on both apartments.

After the contracts were signed, Sadye suddenly stopped seeing or talking with us. Someone in the condo told me that she expected a commission for finding us the apartments. I was totally surprised. Bill and I planned to thank her by taking her and her husband out for dinner. Giving her money never crossed our minds nor did she ask or mention a "finder's fee" when she told us about the apartment. I guess she just expected it naturally. Here I thought I'd found my first friend in Florida. Instead, I discovered there are people in the world who have different ways to count friendship. My eyes were opened. This experience devastated me. I guess our backgrounds and values were just too different.

Anyway, I was joyous about our buying a new home. We immediately started to make plans to refurbish it to our liking. I felt we needed advice and contacted a woman that my friend Jerry Silverman in New York had said I should look up. She was a decorator and said she would be happy to help us.

We invited Muriel and her husband, David, over for dinner one night and was taken by their friendly manner and eagerness to advise us. Before they arrived I told Bill I didn't want another episode like we had with Sadye, so we made sure they knew we wanted to compensate them financially for Muriel's services. But they firmly rejected any payment. The following weekend they invited us to their apartment in Fort Lauderdale. It was a beautiful showcase for her creative talent. I couldn't wait to see what she would do for our place. While she scouted out furnishings for us, Bill, being the wonderful handyman that he is, helped repair certain bathroom and kitchen cabinetry in their apartment. This, in a way, was following the "barter system", a pay-back practice that appealed to all of us. We continued to see each other on weekends.

Bill noticed how close Muriel and I were getting to be and warned me about being too trusting, but I was "hungry" to have a woman friend to confide in, I again lost my "footing" and a few years later, Muriel severed our relationship over some insignificant mishap but for her it was a major crisis. As it turned out, Bill was overdue with a job that was to be delivered on a moment's notice when Muriel called him and asked that he rush over and fix a broken faucet in her bathroom. He told her it would have to wait until later. She broke off our relationship. Again, I was devastated. Would I ever learn that new friends have to be approached slowly and carefully until a solid footing occurs, and that takes a long time, even years before you really get to know all about the person.

It's strange that throughout my 60 years, all my women friends and I got along even when we had misunderstandings. No matter what we may have said or done, our friendships were too strong and close to keep us apart for a long period of time. We always managed to "make up" and remain friends for years on end. Maybe I had to learn new tactics when taking on a new friend at this age. I don't know. I can't figure it out. Maybe in time, I will.

Anyway after we got our new "home" together, a terrible thing happened with Bill's job at his son's company. Bill knew that his work was progressing slowly but blamed it on the Florida attitude of doing business down here—they call it "manana." Anyway, I thought it would work itself out, but his son, Mark, fired him one night before he took off to New Jersey. Bill was devastated, swore he'd never talk to his son again. I felt this attitude was self-destructive for Bill as well as Mark and his family. After all, Bill's grandkids were Mark's kids and I knew it was important for Bill to stay connected with them. It took time and a lot of convincing but I eventually got the two to make up.

So here we were again without any cash flow or what Bill calls it, "between a rock and a hard place."

2. LORRAINE & HARRIETT—LEAVE ME WITH LASTING IMPRESSIONS (UNWRITTEN AT THE TIME OF THE AUTHOR'S DEATH)

3. HEIDI COMES INTO HER OWN
(UNWRITTEN AT THE TIME OF
THE AUTHOR'S DEATH)

CHAPTER ELEVEN

MY SECOND REBIRTH
(1997 - 2004)

1. DOLLY AND ME—BUSY BEES (UNWRITTEN AT THE TIME OF THE AUTHOR'S DEATH)

2. MY GUARDIAN ANGELS
SHOW UP UNEXPECTEDLY
MY GUARDIAN ANGELS SHOW UP UNEXPECTEDLY

3. THE SAGA OF MY CANCER—I FIND STRENGTH! MY GUARDIAN ANGELS SHOW UP UNEXPECTEDLY

4. IT'S ALL UP HILL FROM A LITTLE HELP FROM 'FAMILY' MY GUARDIAN ANGELS SHOW UP UNEXPECTEDLY

5. LILA—MY REMARKABLE NEW FRIEND & GURU
MY GUARDIAN ANGELS SHOW UP UNEXPECTEDLY

CHAPTER TWELVE

MY HAPPY ENDING
(2004 - ON & ON)

(unwritten at the time of the author's death)

AN UNWRITTEN CHAPTER

It was Marie's wish that the birthday letters that she wrote to her firstborn child Rick after his death be an Addenda to her book. She stated that she would never consider him dead until she herself died. Then she wanted a plaque added to his father's grave, naming her unbearable loss.

RICK'S BIRTHDAYS

RICK'S BIRTHDAY GREETINGS FROM HIS MOM

Following are 30 years of birthday greetings written by Marie Fenton Griffing to her son, Rick David Fenton, after his suicide on July 4th, 1975. He left a note declaring his self-afflicted act not realizing the consequences that it would bring to those he left behind. Because his body was never found, there was sadly no closure for Marie. She continued to hope for some miracle right up until her own end.

Nobody who knew Rick well can easily accept his action but always recognized the terrible mental pain he was undergoing. Everyone who loved him is still trying to cope with his drastic decision and regrets that he/she could somehow have helped prevent it. Each person close to Rick has been living with the scars of this horrible tragedy and trying to come to grips with . . . . why he was so desperate and why he didn't realize that help was all around to guide him through his difficult times.

With all that "water under the bridge," his mother who loved her first-born so much has kept his spirit alive through her poetry, her writings. She will not acclaim his death until the day she passes on . . . then it can be so noted.

By the Editor: Lila Lizabeth Weisberger

IMAGES

I experienced a weird sensation yesterday.
I never cease to be amazed at the queer
workings of the mind. They sometimes can
be so scary. I find that no matter how
hard I work to keep my thoughts off Rick's
action, all sorts of images of him appear and
reappear in my head, and at the strangest
times—when I'm in the middle of a conversation
with someone, brushing my teeth, in the coffee
line at Chock Full of Nuts. Like yesterday, for example,
I was having a facial. The setting was quiet.
I was relaxed. My mood lately improved;
I'm still uptight but I think I'm in control.
The cosmetician had applied a mask, dimmed
the lights, put some cotton on my eyes
and left the room to leave me rest awhile.
I was in complete darkness, slowly getting drowsy
when suddenly Rick came to mind. I felt frightened,
almost panicky, as if he were in the room; the thought
of seeing him—like a ghost—was the reason.
I took off the cotton from my eyes; no more darkness,
just a dim-lit room. I looked around, felt reality back
with me again. I relaxed and replaced the pads.
Darkness again, but this time my paranoia was gone.
I reflected on the sensation I had just had and wondered
about it. People have written about such things
happening, so why couldn't it happen to me?
Then I wondered how—a light, a glow, what?
In my head I pictured Rick as I had seen him last,
then in a split second I saw him when he was about 12,
then as a little boy, a baby and then an incredible feeling
occurred. I felt a stirring in my stomach, my womb,
and I had this warm rush of love, the protective kind
I had experienced when I carried each of my children.
The door opened, the cosmetician came in to wash off
my mask, the lights went on bright.
—1975

Verses by Marie Rick's birthdays (from 1976 to 1996)

IT'S BIRTHDAY TIME AGAIN!

Rick, you are 25 years old today and even though you are far away
I have to say while I sit alone at this typewriter that I miss you much,
and would love to touch you, ruffle your dark brown hair,
hear your laughter, make you spareribs,
see you blow out the candles on your cake and watch you get excited
opening presents . . . but this is a dream from which I have to awake.

I can't seem to awake. I've shed many tears and feel the sorrow
of your woes. Somehow I've survived the year since you left us.
I can't blow up any balloons for you today.
I can only talk to you on this typewriter tape.
Oh, how my tears now flow.

I slept in late this morning. It wasn't until I looked at the clock and
saw it was 10:30 . . . the hour you were born in Paris.
I was so happy then to see my little boy.
For so many years you've given me much joy.
I don't understand why you left us stranded without you.

I'll not forget your special day as long as I'm alive.
when I die, then I'll admit you've died . . . and we will meet in another life.

June 8, 1976

HAPPY BIRTHDAY, RICK

It's your special day again . . . June 8.
I remembered it the moment I awoke.
I wanted to run to your room and dry out "Happy Birthday, Rick!"
but I didn't . . . cause you weren't around.

Throughout the day I kept thinking of you throughout the years
when the breezes were fresh and cool
and I said quietly to myself
"Happy Birthday, Rick" just to calm down my fears.

I want the night to come and morning even faster
so I can stop the thoughts and tears, get on with living again.
I'll try to forget how much I miss you, love you
but I know in the a.m., my heart will not mend.

June 8, 1977

HAPPY BIRTHDAY, RICK

Again your day comes up, the date of your birth.
I almost forgot until last night I started to feel cramps
in the pit of my stomach and I wondered why.
They were like I was giving birth again.
Then I recalled that 27 years ago I delivered a son.

You were a beautiful baby, kicking and fussing
with thick brown hair and big blue eyes
that later turned to brown and a smile that melted my heart.
Little perfect fingers clutched onto mine and never let go.
But in time they slipped out of my grasp . . . you were on your own.

I'm so sorry I couldn't hold on tighter,
and that you tumbled into a darkness where I couldn't find you.
If you walked into my life today, I'd hug you, kiss you lightly
and wish you the best of birthdays, ask you to cut your cake.
Maybe if it really happened, neither of us would make mistakes.

June 8, 1978

HAPPY BIRTHDAY, RICK

Going back and forth each day over the George Washington Bridge,
I always think of you and it was here where you said you fled.
My heart twitches, I breathe deeply
and hope when I get home I'll get some news about you.

I check in with our local police to find out if they've found you,
either alive and living someplace with a friend.
I think they get tired of me calling all the time.
They just say that so far they're at a dead end.

I don't give up easy because in my heart I feel you near.
Where? Maybe many miles away, I don't know.
I worry about you and think of December when it starts to snow.
Keep warm then . . . best wishes for now.

June 8, 1979

MARIE FENTON GRIFFING

HAPPY BIRTHDAY, RICK

Five years now, come the 4th of July that you wrote your suicide note. I read it from time to time, over and over again and still can't believe it's true. I'd like to bake you a cake today . . . it's your birthday. But I don't dare because everyone will think I'm going crazy.

Sometimes, in a way, I feel like I'm going mad . . . maybe it's that I'm angry that you left Heidi, Todd and me in the lurch . . . didn't give us a chance to change your mind. Oh, Rick, what a legacy you left behind.

Because it's your birthday, I can only hope you are happy wherever you are and ask that you don't forget us all . . . we love you so.

June 8, 1980

HAPPY BIRTHDAY, RICK

It's a sunny day in Snedens today. The magnolia tree that you planted five years ago outside the front door has a few flowers still wafting in the soft breezes.

Do you remember? It was only three feet tall when you shoveled it in there. I helped dig out the soil . . . it was like you were planting a part of your soul. Now it has grown to 10 feet tall.

I always think of you when I pass by and wish you were here to see its glory when it bloomed in the spring. I would pluck some of the pink flowers and bring them into the house for all to admire.

Keep safe, Rick. I'm here waiting.

June 8, 1981

HAPPY BIRTHDAY, RICK

I can't believe another year has passed without seeing you.
Do you realize that you're thirty-one . . . and I'm fifty-seven.
I can't fathom it.
Too many candles to put on your cake.
I miss you so much.
Please come back!
I'm so sad. You should be here to enjoy all the things I have
that I would share with you now and ever after.

June 8, 1982

HAPPY BIRTHDAY, RICK

It has been eight years since I've seen you. I do see you in my dreams and oftentimes a resemblance in young men's faces I pass on the street . . . but they don't have your smile, your laughter, your expressive eyes.

Sometimes, I kind of wish I could go to your grave and visit, say hello and know you were there, safe and sound . . . but I can't lay you to rest right now. I have this gut feeling that you are alive and well somewhere.

As you know I've always and will be an optimist. I know I'll see you again and we can talk about all the things both of us have done. I hope it's next year . . . if not then, maybe in never-never land. I realize I keep repeating myself; can't help it. By the way, can you believe you are 32 years old today?

June 8, 1983

HAPPY BIRTHDAY, RICK

I wish you were close to experience the changes going on in my life.
I could really use your support to go forward and continue.
That would lessen my strife.

But today is your special day and should be joyous.
I look out at my beautiful yard and think of you.
I gaze at the dogwood tree under which our favorite dog, Tanya, is buried.

Like you, she was a blessing to us all.

June 8, 1984

HAPPY BIRTHDAY, RICK

It's your 34th year . . . it's a good year. I remember my 34th year . . . your brother, Todd was born, just four days before your 13th birthday, which we celebrated in Tarzana. He was 4 days old so we had a party for you to announce your special day. Dozens of people came to your party and see little Todd, too. It was a wonderful day . . . everyone was happy, delighted and made such a fuss about the two of you.

Today, on June 8, 1985, I was puttering in the kitchen and heard the song, "Jean . . . Jean" and recalled your girlfriend from high school. You two were so close for many years. In 1970 you both left each other to seek other goals . . . Jean went down South and got involved in a religious cult . . . you went to Northwestern University to find an acting career. Stupid drugs you both were taking crazied your minds and souls. I'm so sorry for that but I had no control over that horrible period . . . I just feel sad it all had to end this way with my trying to communicate with you on my computer . . . in 1985.

Wherever you are today, I send you a kiss, a hug and all the pleasurable times you've always given me. God Bless.

June 8, 1985

HAPPY BIRTHDAY, RICK

I can't believe the age you are . . . 35!
And how much I've missed
seeing you all these past 11 years.
Now again today come all the tears.

I see you taller than at 25; maybe your waist a little more wide,
your shoulders more broad,
but know your smile is the same as before.

I'd love to sit down with you; tell you about my move to Florida,
and talk to you about my transition,
listen to your thought and what you think of my new position.

I understand there'll be no meeting until I die.
Until then I'll keep in contact with your spirit, not close the door.
It won't be too long 'til we meet and hug once more.

June 8, 1986

HAPPY BIRTHDAY, RICK

You were born on June 8, 1951 and you left us on July 4, 1975 . . . what a short time to have had you around. At first I was angry at you when you cut out but today I can only feel sad that my firstborn left me behind to survive.

I'm sure you are pleased how Todd and Heidi have progressed. It has been hard for them to come to grips with your actions. They are suffering like me and your leaving has left deep scars that none of us will be able to heal.

When I swim in the warm ocean waters by myself, I look up to the cluster of clouds and sometimes see your face in them. I throw you a kiss and meditate . . . my tears are swept away in the waves. I hope you are happy wherever you are and hear my good wishes to you your special day.

June 8, 1987

HAPPY BIRTHDAY, RICK

My Rick . . . another year has passed since your last birthday and your memory hasn't missed a beat . . . it never will.

Every time I see a little boy child running around on the beach . . . a teenager shopping in the mall . . . a young man standing tall and handsome on a movie line . . . there isn't a time that I don't see you.

Yes, after 13 years now since you physically left my life, I still see your likeness around wherever I look. I imagine your funny laugh, your smiling eyes and whenever I see an old Charlie Chaplin film on TV, I remember when you were just 7 and dressed up like him for Halloween.

When I went in for my surgery some weeks back, I thought maybe I'd die on the table, but I didn't. I wasn't scared because if I did die, it would be the time that we'd meet again . . . but God apparently didn't call "time."

June 8, 1988

HAPPY BIRTHDAY, RICK

It has been 14 years since you walked out of my life.
Too young for you to leave us.
How I wish I could have had a hug or kiss goodbye.
Instead you vanished . . . I still can't understand why.

They say you never get over the loss of a child.
I know that's true and realize I'm not alone.
You left a diary and poems I have tucked away in a drawer.
I have read them over and over again . . . and moan.

You'd be 38 today and with all your talents, I'm sure you'd be a star.
But now you're a star in the heavens and shining bright.
You'll always be alive to me like you were in '75.
Be happy today. I'll love you forever.

June 8, 1989

MARIE FENTON GRIFFING

HAPPY BIRTHDAY, RICK

I awakened early this morning. My stomach felt queasy.
My nerves were jumpy; overall I felt uneasy.

Then I saw the date on the Today Show and I realized why
I was feeling out of sorts . . . "It's Rick's birthday," I sighed.

Thirty-nine is almost middle age and I try to imagine what it would be
like for you to open the door and walk in.

I can't believe you've been out of my life for 15 long years.
I think I must have shed 100 buckets of tears.

I'm getting older too, but know there will come a day
when we will meet again . . . I wonder what we will say.

June 8, 1990

HAPPY BIRTHDAY. RICK

OH, RICK, I CAN'T BELIEVE YOU'D BE 40 TODAY!
Could it be that now your hair would be turning gray
and you'd be wearing bifocals,
going to bed at ten,
having oatmeal for breakfast?
Oh no, not you Rick.

I imagine you as a loving father
with a pretty wife and two cute kids,
coming over for dinner,
helping set the table like you always did.
Oh yes, how I wish, Rick.

It's hard to think what you would have become
and what your interests would be.
I bet they would be fun,
like some job acting in a movie or TV.
Oh boy, that'd be great, Rick.

I do know I wish you were here now
so we could swim together in the ocean,
and I'd bake you a cake,
give you a hug and that all was OK.
Oh heck, it's not to be, Rick.

So, I speak to your spirit
and hope you hear my words
because somehow I need to reach you,
relieve my pain and calm my nerves.
Oh maybe, you'll answer, Rick.

MARIE FENTON GRIFFING

I'll always remember the good times,
cause there's no reason to recall bad days.
I'd rather cherish the wonder of you
and each year 'til I die, wish your Happy Birthday!
Oh Rick, I love you.

June 8, 1991

HAPPY BIRTHDAY, RICK

Another year has passed; you'd be 41 today
and in the prime of your life.
I try to imagine what it would be like
but a vision doesn't come in sight.

On the plane yesterday coming back to FL from LA
I carried thoughts of you.
I'd visited our Tarzana house and cried walking through it.
Memories of happy times flashed before my eyes; I sighed.

Other people live there now and it's not the same.
It looked smaller than I'd remembered.
The whole place has changed.
I could only wipe away tears; close the gate behind me.

How I still grieve for you, Rick
You'll always be with me and in my heart until I die.
When that time comes, I'll see you.
For now, I'll do what I have to do.

June 8, 1992

MARIE FENTON GRIFFING

HAPPY BIRTHDAY, RICK

I can see your smile and your laughing eyes,
the cleft in your chin, the joy on your face,
opening your birthday surprise.

I can see your thick, wavy dark hair, your long sinewy finger
that give expression to every word you speak
or heighten the meaning of your silly giggles.

Yes, despite all the years that have passed
since I last saw you--I remember this day when you were quiet and meek.
I see you clearly, tall and straight, and feel the kiss you planted on my cheek.

June 8, 1993

HAPPY BIRTHDAY, RICK

It's so nice that I can just pick up the phone and call Todd on his birthday
or Heidi on her birthday.
I can speak to them, give them my good wishes and love.
I so long to be able to do that on your birthday . . .
but I can't. So, I write these messages to you on your special day
and hope they reach you wherever you are.

I look at photos on my bedroom wall
and reflect on our many years in Snedens. You grew into such
a fine young man . . . anxious to go to college, then everything
seemed to go downhill. You got lost in drugs.
I tried to reach out to you but you were already gone.

I keep telling myself that's all water under the bridge
but question the decision I made to allow you to go so far away
when you were young and vulnerable yet so determined
to prove yourself as a man and make me proud.
Maybe I should have kept you close to home and be your guardian angel.

June 8, 1994

HAPPY BIRTHDAY, RICK

I almost forgot it was your special day until I heard the date on TV.
I felt bad that it had slipped my mind because I never, ever wanted to forget.
June 8 . . . is an important date no matter where I am.

The sun is shining bright here in Florida and I'm on my computer
writing you this birthday wish . . . to think you'd be 44 blows my mind.
Somehow, it makes me feel old, but I guess I am. I'm lost in time.

I think of you when you were a beautiful babe in France,
a toddler in Germany, a little boy in Tarzana, a young man in Snedens.
Was I the mother who nursed you, diapered you, calmed your cold sneezes?

Am I beginning to forget all the wonderful things in our lives?
No, I'll not let it happen because you'll always be in my heart.
I will keep your memory alive until the day I die . . . we'll never part.

And as I whisper my last breath
I'll say your name . . . Rick.
As of now, I can only remember . . . even if it's a little bit

June 8, 1995

HAPPY BIRTHDAY, RICK!

I bet that if you were around today,
you'd be healthy, wealthy and wise,
and have the four kids you always said you'd have
which would make me a proud grandma, but alas, no way.

I'm slowly running out of what kind of greetings to send you,
and what news to send you 'cause you're getting further away from me.
I don't want to repeat myself except to say, "Best wishes, Rick, I love you,
and wish you were near like so many years ago, the way you used to be."

June 8, 1996

HAPPY BIRTHDAY RICK

I wish you were here to see my new cat, Minou.
She doesn't look much like my first Minou but has the same demeanor.
Remember when my Siamese, Minou, gave birth to two black kittens?
It was 1973. You called me at work to tell me they were born on your bed.
I rushed home to see this wondrous event.

You loved caring for them until they were ready to be adopted.
One we gave to Robbie, but kept the second for ourselves.
Now we had four cats. We knew Mite was the father of Minou's black male.
Since he was conceived during a poker game . . . "Poker" became his name.

But do you remember the tragedy six months later?
Poor Minou was killed by a car . . . you & I buried her under the grapevines.
So then I only had three . . . Mite, Calico and Poker . . . a lot of mouths to feed.
I cried when I lost Minou but now she's reborn again after 20 years.

After 10 years of not having a soft-furred pet around,
my new Minou has sparked up my life here in Florida.
I play with her, pet her, feed her but unlike my former cats,
I have to clean up her crap in the litter box . . . really not too bad,
since she offers me much joy in this loveless life I've had.

June 8, 1997

HAPPY BIRTHDAY, RICK!

Another year of my not having you near me in person.
This birthday of yours almost passed me by,
but last night I had a dream about you.
It was a good one and you looked like you were twenty-five.

Then I awoke this morning and realized that you would be forty-seven.
How the years do fly!
I imagine you being a star on Broadway or a computer genius.
You always had a great memory, at least ten times better than I.

I miss you posing in photos I take of Todd and Heidi.
You would have so enjoyed knowing them today.
They have changed, grown and matured to become
my strength to help me continue my life until into the sunset I sail.

Love, Mom
June 8, 1998

MARIE FENTON GRIFFING

HAPPY BIRTHDAY RICK!

The sun is bright and warm at 10 a.m.
It's June 8th, your 51st birthday.
Seems so long ago since you were with us
I almost forget what you looked like
but I'll never forget the day you went away.
I have a wedding to go to at seven,
but I'm not happy about that.
Don't know why I am feeling this way,
must be cause it your 51st birthday.
At the wedding I imagine it's yours
and I'm the proud Mom standing near you,
then I scatter the thought, it never came true
I pushed back the tears feeling so sad
that none of my kids found a right mate,
which leaves me wondering where I went wrong
or somehow missed out doing right for all three of you.
I'll never really know because that's the way it is.
I'll "go to my grave" with all this guilt, feeling doomed.

June 8, 2002

HAPPY BIRTHDAY RICK

Fifty-three is a good age to be.
You're right in the middle of your life,
You can look back with pride,
or on so much time lost
and what could have been.
But never with regrets
because that solves nothing,
just leaves you feeling sorry for yourself.

This is my advice to you, Rick
whom I love unconditionally,
my first born, the sunshine of my life.
You left me too soon without a clue
and I've searched for answers,
what could have changed your mind,
what would your life . . . and mine . . . become?
I'm afraid to know the outcome.

You are my second "sunflower" to bow its head.
I thought I gave you so much TLC
it would last you all your life,
but it wasn't enough,
because you needed more than love.
You needed a miracle to set you straight.
You needed an angel to guide you home,
and she did that long ago night in 1975.

June 8, 2004

MARIE FENTON GRIFFING

HAPPY BIRTHDAY, RICK

Hardly a day goes by
that you don't come to mind,
either because of a voice I hear,
or something on TV,
a face I see in a crowd,
my heart jumps a beat,
and I feel a shiver of fear.

I just can't seem to forget,
the last days I saw you,
and never had a clue
that you would destroy yourself,
leave me wondering why,
looking for answers in the sky,
clouds floating by, reminding me of you.

It's your birthday today,
and fifty-five is a good age
to take stock of your life,
but I will never know
what sort of life you would have lived,
but hope it would have been free of strife,
sadness and pain—unlike your early years.

Love, Mom
June 8, 2006

HAPPY BIRTHDAY, RICK

I don't know what to say
now that it's again your special day.
My pen makes a deep black spot on the paper,
poised to record my thoughts,
but not moving ahead,
no words come to mind,
maybe I should wait 'til later,
'cause now my heart aches so,
I know I haven't said all
that should be said,
except you shouldn't be dead
before me . . . not fair
that I'm left behind to never get over
your tragic exit, leaving me
with unanswered questions
that leave me wanting,
more and more with each passing year,
not knowing the whole story,
I so desperately need some sort of closure
from a son I hold so dear.

Love, Mom
June 8, 2007

HAPPY BIRTHDAY, RICK

En fin! I feel the call
the call to tell you
I am ready
to greet you anew.

I don't know why
I waited so long
to send you my love,
but I'm here now, that's what counts.

I've thought of you often.
Wondered why I hesitated
to sit down and write my annual poem,
Just an odd time, I was frustrated.

Now I'm here
talking to you loud and clear,
wishing you were here,
to see how good I feel
now that the end of the year is near.

Marie Fenton Griffing
Sept. 29th, 2009

HAPPY BIRTHDAY, RICK

I'm searching but can't seem to find
a cheery greeting for you.
I'm searching for closure
(whatever that really means)
but there are so many
things I can't seem to put out of my mind.

For example, the other day
when I watched the news.
The story was about bodies
of those who died unidentified,
and I thought of you still waiting
to be found in some spot where you lay.

I count the years—35 in all.
That means 35 birthday greetings
I've written, showing my love
for you is still strong.
So here I go again and I'll never waver
to always wish you, Happy Birthday, son.

Marie Fenton Griffing
June 8, 2010

IN THE PRESENCE OF MY SOUL
BY HEIDI FENTON
1978

Three years ago, my brother left a suicide note,

and then disappeared, never to be heard from again

These thoughts are for people, like me, who have

lost someone, and have to live with the reality

of never having that person around again,

in their life.

He terminated his sufferings with

a discordant note that blamed no one. But,

through his disappearance, the lives of

many have yet to regain their ability to

live.

A death-people seem to be able to

handle. It's tragic and heartbreaking, but

the reminder is there, you can touch the

absence. But an unresolved ending is

incapable of supplying a finality. Not

to know, creates an unstable feeling to try

and live with. Part of you says he's alive,

but the other knows he doesn't eat at your

table anymore; he doesn't play his favorite

records at ear-splitting levels; he doesn't

sit at the piano and play those old songs;

he doesn't touch your life directly with

his own; he doesn't call your name.

We are all susceptible to the dark

entanglements our minds hold for us, and

for some, this gnarl turbulence invades the

only clear path open, and closes it down

for good. All the help, and the guidance

cannot save those who find it intolerable to live

I think I understand some of the

conflicts he had. When one feels out of place

in their own world; when they walk through

a crowd, and really feel as if no one is

there. When the heartbreaks and sorrow of

each minute topples your soul, when you

honestly feel as if you are so totally

different from anyone else, as you try so

hard to blend in, then it is almost impossible

to redirect the negative flow that is

flooding your body.

But how do you convince someone of their

unique individuality. How do you assure

someone that all of these seemingly unimaginable

horrors compose their singularity that makes

them so special. How do you prove to them that

understanding your individuality sometimes causes

great pain.

It seems to me, that most of us learn

things too late, and unfortunately, that only

helps build up the guilt we get, when we realize

later, of all the little things we could have

done to help. So we confuse our minds with

reprehensible thoughts that help us believe

that it was us, who caused his downfall, instead

of his own lack of strength.

I sit here, after saying all I have said,

and believe honestly, that I could have

helped him more, I could have helped "cure"

him. We, who cared, say this often, but

there was no "cure." There was no magical

potion that we could have given him, no hellfire

speech we could have served him, nothing

we could do could ever, totally convince him

of his worth.

But we blame ourselves nevertheless.

I blame myself. I still feel that I could

have done something extra, tried harder,

cared more. And people will say, "it's not

your fault", and I'll agree with them. But

there is something that feels uneasy within

me, and no matter how I, and other people

try and convince themselves that there was

nothing they could have done, there will always

MARIE FENTON GRIFFING

be that undercurrent of guilt for those

of us that were close.

So, no matter what I say, you will

always question your direct or indirect

participation with his life. And especially

on holidays, when family and friends should

be together, your association with his spirit

will be great, and your sorroww immense.

Try and reflect on his individual essence,

his style, his squawking laughter, his calming

voice . . . . his hysteria and hysterics, his kindness,

his smile and his heartaches. And bask in the

richness, that his life has touched yours, and he

shall always remain within you.

AFTERWORDS

MARIE AND BILL had many full years in their condo depite difficult and challenging illnesses. Marie died September 20th. 2012 at the age of 87. Their home was up for sale and they found the Independent Living facility they would move into. Marie died before moving there and Bill, now 86 is living there alone. His adjustment is difficult and although he misses the love of his life he has the support of closeknit family and friends.

Marie had asked me, one of the newest women in her life, to review each chapter of this book after she wrote it. During the last ten years of her life we discussed her book chapter by chapter. In 2010, we determined she would need to end the book with a chapter about her early years in Florida. She no longer had the energy to do additional writing. She had more to add to her book as you will note from her Table of Contents. Her life ended before her book was ended.

This book is as I found it on her computer and with the addenda on loose pages.

As she was driving back with Bill from her last doctor's appointment, she wrote notes on a yellow pad about her feelings. These are the final written words we have found. She was to see her doctor again in three weeks, and was being helped by hospice, Bill and her family and friends in her own home on a hospital bed in the living room.

Yes, Marie, even sunflowers die.

From Lila Lizabeth Weisberger

MARIE'S LAST WRITTEN WORDS:

Marie's unfinished notes written in the car, driving home from her final appointment with her oncologist:

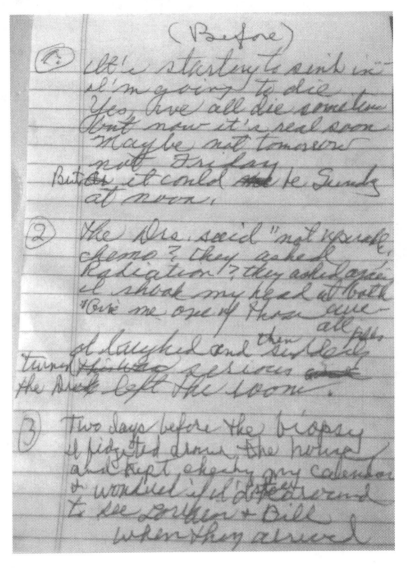

or would they come
just in time
to toss my ashes into
the ocean under the full moon.

numbness, I guess, is the
word ~~other~~ for what I'm
feeling.

(4) I'm not nervous or
scared;
It just feels odd to
suddenly get a ~~short~~ sharp pain
~~around my chest~~ of breath
when I utter the word
"die" under my breath

(5) Before they set up my ~~picture~~
I ~~inevitably~~ would begin to
pack my belongings.
Our home was up for sale
and people were coming & going.
So each I didn't get a price,
there was one bid but
it was too low

It was then I sensed
an eerie karma around me.
Should I keep packing stuff
or only the precious dishes
and jewelry.

The pain pills have taken
over my mood swings.
I feel comforted just
sitting in my chair, leaning
back and wonder how
much longer I will
turn to it and use it
to make plans for
the year ahead

When I hear
we say, "hang in
there!", that's a lot
of meanings —
be patient, stay put,
don't change a thing!
Yet, how I felt was
for the doctor to call.

and my eyes slowly closed
it fell deep asleep.
A few bumps later, I
woke to my own breathing,
and your hand touched mine,
"We're home, honey," ya
said

(b) They say most cancer
patients go into denial at first,
and I must agree to that.
I found myself writing down
things to do by months from
now, then suddenly stop
and think ~~so, I won't~~ probably
not be around
~~but pick up clothes~~
"I'd make a note to
call Randy to clean our carpets,
then put down the phone — how
many days do I have left? A
more important question to ~~asked~~
to ~~myself~~ cling to — I almost
am my ~~truthfulest~~."

3.

I expected the answer
but not quite on target.
No pedantle, no day, no hour,
just one appointment for
another scan, to see an oncologist
and maybe radiation too
or a pill to "make it go away"?
No, not the one my mother
gave me when I had an earache.

Driving home had a calming
effect on me
not that it helps anyone
but a strange numbing feeling
overcame me.

the white puffy clouds
moved just above the sky
cars sped by us slow
and drivers slower than usual?

My hands clutched my
My arms gently spread
of course on my chest
I felt a half-smile form
in my life

letty me know what
my biapsey revealed
But my cell came
and that drove me mad
How long can you "hold
on" without going mad?
that depends on how
long is
an hour or a mile,

I came, I saw, I asked
the docter "Why didn't you
call me?" He said
He looked at me
"You're free now"
Like the good
patient I should have bowed
but I didn't. I said
"When is my death
warrant?" to which he
laughed, tilted his head back "Oh, Wow"

6) ~~strikethrough~~ I'm sleeping better than ever.
must be the pain killers I'm taking
My pain is different from any
other kind I had before
and I began to wonder
what death would feel like
which made me laugh
at something I was not
~~supposed~~ supposed to feel
anything at all — that's right,
feel nothing at all. Or
why not consider that bright
white light some people said
~~they~~ saw — when they had been
~~told~~ they had died. So complicated
what I say there's a door
you open to get to the other side?

Now
But it's hardest to
deal with when it comes to
family + friends.

(Before)

1. It's starting to sink in—I'm going to die. Yes, we all die sometime but now it's real soon. Maybe not tomorrow not Friday but it could be Sunday at noon.
2. The doctor said "not usually chemo? They asked radiation? They asked again. I shook my head at both. "Give me one of those cure-all pills." I laughed and then suddenly turned serious. The doc left the room.
3. Two days before the biopsy I fidgeted around the house and kept checking my calendar and wondered if I'd still be around to see Lorraine and Bill when they arrived or would they come just in time to toss my ashes into the ocean under the full moon.
   Numbness, I guess is the word for what I'm feeling.
4. I'm not nervous or scared; it just feels odd to suddenly get a sudden pain in my chest when I utter the word "die" under my breath.
5. Before they set up my—I originally was beginning to pack my belongings. Our home was up for sale and people were coming and going. So even though we didn't get a good bite there was one bid but it was too low. It was then I sensed an eerie karma around me. Should I keep packing junk or stuff or only the precious dishes and jewelry?
6. The pain pills have taken over my mood swings. I feel comforted just sitting in my chair, leaning back and wonder how much longer I will sit in it and use it while I make plans for the years ahead.
   When after we say, "hang in there!" has a lot of meaning—be patient, stay put, or don't change a thing. That's how I felt waiting for the doctor to call, letting me know what my biopsy revealed. But no call came. How long can you "hold on" without going mad? That depends on how long is an hour or a mile.
   I came, I saw, I asked the doctor "Why didn't you call me?" He said "you're here now." And like the good patient, I should have bowed, but I didn't. I said "When is my death warrant?" to which he laughed, tilted his head back "Oh, wow."

3. I expected the answer but not quite on target. No month, no day, no hour, just more appointments for another scan to see an oncologist and maybe radiation or a pill to "make it go away." No, not the one my mother gave me when I had an earache.

4. Driving home had a calming effect on me. The white puffy clouds moved faster across the sky. Cars sped by us (was Bill driving slower than usual?). My arms gently lay spread crosswise on my chest. I felt a half-smile on my lips and my eyes slowly closed. I fell deep asleep. A few bumps later I woke to my own breathing, and your hand touched mine, "We're home honey," you said.

5. They say most cancer patients go into denial at first, and I must agree to that. I found myself writing down things to do a few months from now, then suddenly stop and think no, by that time I'll probably not be around. Or I'd make a note to call Randy to clean our carpets, then put down the phone—how many days do I really have left? An important question to add to a dozen or so I already have on my "doctor's list."

6. I'm sleeping better this week, must be the painkillers I'm taking. My pain is different from any other kind I had before and I began to wonder what death would feel like, which made me laugh at something. I was not supposed to feel anything at all—that's right, feel nothing at all. Or why not consider that bright white light some people said they saw—when they had been told they had died. So complicated. Who's to say there's a door you open to get to the other side?

Now

But it's hardest to deal with when it comes to family and friends.

MARIE FENTON GRIFFING

POSTSCRIPT
MORE ABOUT MARIE'S LIFE: POEMS

SENDING MY BABY?   ROLLING THE ...

PLEASE GET ME OFF THE TRACKS IF   IN MY ACCOUNT

DO YOU THINK HE MEAN WANTS   TELL ME HOW IS THAT

Spoken!

WHAT DID HE MEAN BY THAT

Music by: Manny Vardi; Lyrics by: Si ...

PEACE

Take away my window where I meditate,

Take away the pool I swim in,

Take away my book nearby,

Take away my cat on my lap,

Take away my flower garden,

Take away my husband cuddled next to me,

Take away my shower water gushing over my head,

Take away my keyboard that makes words,

Take away my spice rack and stove,

And if you do, you take away all the peace in my world,

because these things make me whole if only for a while,

I walk away with good feelings and a smile.

4/7/05

I FOUND ME

I found me
when I found you
in a smoked-filled bar
with people chatting loud
and a cold wind blowing outside
as I walked to the door,
looked back at you,
waved a soft goodbye,
fighting the urge to go back,
afraid of the ties
that commitment brings,
not ready to say 'I do"
needed time to think it through,
then, feeling the icy blast on my cheek,
I sensed that one day soon
I'd walk in the sunshine with you,
and we'd call ourselves 'we',
discovering in my heart
that when I found you,
I would find me.

Marie Fenton Griffing, April 20, 2008

I am blessed to have lived this life so long,
crazy as it was at times. I had fun-filled days
and fantastically love-filled nights.
So let the wrinkles come with every laugh,
frown lines not allowed on my brow.
May Bill, my family and new friends stick around
to celebrate my hundredth birthday pow-wow!

....Marie Fenton Griffing
  4/11/08

HE HURTS, I HURT

His eyes are set deep into his face,
they've lost their luster, with no gleam,
not even a hint of color.

They mirror the pain he is feeling,
he clutches his side with one hand,
smoothes his tousled silvery locks
with the other....

He hurts and I hurt to see him this way
like he's a little boy, holding my hand,
with nothing to say.

When he hurts, I hurt. I feel a sob,
a growing sob down deep in my groin,
or is it my spine.

I do not cry out, just my insides sobbing,
until I feel his hurt fading.
He smiles down at me; my hurt is fading

Marie Fenton Griffing   11/09

STEP BY STEP

With my head held up straight,
my shoulders back,
I plunge ahead,
not knowing if or when I'll break.

But break I do not.
I bend my knees,
my elbows and my neck,
stretch my arms—then stop.

It hurts and it pains,
but as they say,
"no pain, no gain,"
and above all, I want the gain.

I'm moving forward each day,
It may take weeks,
or even months,
but I keep repeating, "Marie, be brave!"

One day I will walk in the light,
with my head up straight,
knowing I have overcome.
I gave it my best fight.

Marie Fenton Griffing
2/10/09

MY SAY ON GROWING OLD

At the age I am...83 today,
I'm happy with who I am.
Oh, not my wrinkly face,
and saggy butt; I've stopped
agonizing over them.
It's a fact—I like who I am.

I would not exchange my life,
or Bill, my friends and family
for all the money in the world.
Living on my lowly social security,
is okay, as long as my good luck
gets me a jackpot at you know where—Hard Rock!

I feel I'm at that stage of life
when I can treat myself to things
I never dared to years ago—
like a giant soft ice cream cone
at 3 in the afternoon, or
buying six books at one of
my favorite stores, Barnes & Noble.

There's great freedom for me
in growing old—like taking a nap
no matter the time of day,
whispering "I love you" in Bill's ear
for no reason at all,
or saying 'no thanks' to the police
asking for money on the telephone.

The sad thing about growing old
is losing old friends who listened
to my joys and woes—they listen no more.
And crying when my cat died too early.
With her purring on my lap when I was sick
helped me fight the cancer that invaded me.

VALENTINE LETTERS—FEBRUARY 14, 2012

Feb. 11, 2012

Dear Marie...

Today a day, one of many, many days, I am thankful for your love and caring. I am aware of people thinking it wouldn't last. I have been blessed with two loves in my life. Ours has been the longest and I hope will have many more good years ahead.

I was lucky to have your love and the love and understanding of our combined families—they are all very special to me.

I know it has been hard on you with my back problems along with your own difficulties. I have met with Dr. Cohen and when he said I would be able to walk straight again, it was like a dream come true. I look forward to not having to have help carrying my coffee, let alone help getting up a curb or being afraid of slipping on the floor—I have a hatred of all of that.

I love you very much and I always will.   Bill

THE DAY I FELL
IN LOVE WITH YOU

I wasn't paying attention to the weather outside. It was warm and cozy in Polly's Cage. With Lucy and Sue flanking me at the table, my friend, John could only flirt with me as best as he was able. We all knew about his Mafia ties but we liked him for his jokes and deep blue yes.

As we sipped over Scotch and beers, the front door swung open and with the gusy wind you blew in. The light was behind you and your tall frame and broad shoulders made a silhouette to set off fears. And that it did with John as you headed our way.

I smiled and waved but my heart throbbed so loud I could barely say "Hi, honey, what a surprise. You know Lucy and Sue, but you haven't met John."

The wave in your blonde hair dipped over one eye and you barely gave him a half smile. Then you gently took hold of my arm, handed me my purse from the table and said "We're going home now; you'll see your friends later."

I didn't know whether to be angry or not, or what, but suddenly I felt a warm surge of warm in my gut...that special feeling when you know you're in love.Oh My God, I said to myself as walked out of the bar and it didn't take long to realize then were the one for me. To end on an amusing note, I never asked you...did my running back from the car to the bar upset you? I just couldn't leave that bouquet of flowers that John bought for me, and I did come back; no way would I leave you waiting—after all, you did rescue me. Truly, you are my hero...my Sir Lancelot! Love, Marie

(END PAGES)
GAMBLING

Marie believed in her luck, and one of her pleasures was playing the slot machine.

1. THOSE COSMIC RAYS written by Marie Fenton Griffing

When you are 81 years old and have been lucky in love but never lucky in money-matters, a sudden windfall makes you wonder if those cosmic rays really do work. I have always loved the excitement of gambling. It all started back in the 1930s when I was a little girl and I learned how to play poker with other kids on my block in southwest Los Angeles. We had no money to play with so we used matchsticks or tooth picks. Then came the game Monopoly and even winning the fake money was fun. In high school, I loved going to the horse races at Santa Anita with my parents. During my college days at USC, poker was a big sport, and you had to be a good one when you sat down at a game that suddenly turned out to be "strip poker!" In Europe as a reporter for The Los Angeles Times, I discovered the thrill of playing roulette in Monte Carlo.

When I got overstressed as an editor at "Teen" and Good Housekeeping magazines in Manhattan in the 1960s and 70s, it was a relief to come home to quiet Sneden's Landing outside of the city where I returned to my first love, poker—a Saturday night game with my neighbors became a tradition. You would think that retiring to Florida in the 1980s and being invited to Tuesday afternoon Bridge in the condo card room would fill my gambling urges. Oh no! The cruise ships awaited me at the docks with their slot machines and black jack tables. At ten a.m., once or twice a month, I, along with hundreds of elderly people (mostly women), sailed off for the day from the Fort Lauderdale coastline on the Sun Cruz or Sea Escape ships, enjoy a lovely lunch, a Las Vegas style show plus try our luck at the gaming tables or slot machines. I never bet a lot of money, I never lost a lot of money nor did I ever win a lot of money, but I felt one day I would hit it big.

Last October, during a visit to Rhode Island to visit family, my daughter-in-law, Lorraine, who likes to do a little gambling too, and I drove to the nearby Foxwood Casino to play the slots. Lorraine is lucky. She has won a number of big jackpots that she used to help pay off a house mortgage. I followed her around trying to discover her secret method of playing. She laughed and said that I would start winning when the cosmic rays found me. That night they did. I won a $700 jackpot and the following night, $1,200.

When I came back to Florida, I told my gambling buddies, Sally and Margo, about my good luck. When they asked me to go to the Seminole Hard Rock Casino nearby, I was a little hesitant. I had been there once and did not like the type of slot machines—they weren't like the Las Vegas ones that worked with coins. They are computerized and pay out winnings on paper. I like to hear the jingle of coins come tumbling out when I win.

But I said okay and on December 13, 2005 (a date I thought would be unlucky for me), I walked into this huge casino, holding arms with my two thrill-seeking friends. I was amazed at how many seniors were there, even a couple in wheel chairs.

In a couple of hours, I had but $20 left to play. Feeling dejected, I sat down to one of my favorite machines, slipped the bill into the opening and saw it disappear. I shook my head and said to myself "Come on baby, pay off for mama." After hitting the button a couple of times. the lights on the machine went off. I pressed all the buttons even the "cash out" button-nothing. I was upset and called out to a casino service person who came over and called someone on his walkie-talkie. I swiveled around and around in my chair then heard the man's voice, "Mam, you have just won a jackpot." I couldn't believe my ears. I turned to look at the screen on the machine and there was a blue sign that read, "Congratulations you have just won $8,550!" I didn't know what to do. There were no bells ringing or music playing. Then people started to gather around me and congratulate me. I laughed and told them it was the cosmic rays. When I showed Sally and Margo the $5,000 check and $3,550 in cash they just nodded their heads and said, "Blow some of those cosmic rays toward us!"

"Wow, Bill (my husband) will be surprised." said Margo. "How will you tell him?"

I thought about it and told them my plan. "He will be in his chair, watching TV and I'll walk quickly to the bathroom, waving hi and saying I have to go right away. Then I'll Scotch tape all the $100 bills around the front of my naked body. Won`t that be a surprise?" We couldn't stop laughing. Of course I didn't do that, but when he saw all the money, it was a pleasant surprise.

When Lorraine and Billy (my step-son) came to visit over New Year's, there was no doubt that she and I would spend a few hours at the casino. I was astonished one of the Triple Diamond machines paid me a jackpot of $1,600. This time bells and music went off and Lorraine who was nearby heard it and came running over. We jumped up and down saying "Those cosmic rays are working good!" A few weeks later, Margo wanted to try her luck at the casino and asked me to go with her. I said okay but was a little anxious. Now that I had been winning, I felt there was no chance that I would be lucky—my breaking even was dubious. I had been playing cautiously at the 25 cents machine when I decided to move to the $1 machine. Within a few tries, I saw these three diamonds appear in a row on the screen in front of me. The music went on and the light atop of machine began to flash. Another jackpot!

Needless to say, I was flabbergasted and so were the casino people. Only time will tell if this mysterious stream of winnings will continue. As of now, to quote the 'high roller' "I am holding my own". The cosmic rays seem to be waning, but like the other little old ladies who go to the casino for excitement, I continue to look forward to the thrill of yet another win.

2. Marie GAMBLING: It's All In The Attitude by Gene Weisberger

Over the years Marie and Lila became fast friends. When I was writing short stories for an upcoming book of travel tales, I asked Marie, whether she would do some editing for my new book. I became very comfortable working with Marie. During the next decade, Marie and I became good friends. I have summed up Marie's work ethic as always creative, never critical.

A few years ago I got the idea to invite a score of my friends to submit stories for a book that I called "Somewhere A Story." I was certain that any story Marie wrote would be an asset to the book so I made hers the first story in my book.

In addition to our writing connection, Marie and I became good friends. She often told me about her love of the excitement of gambling. I remember her excitement the day when she won the jackpot.

She often invited me to join her and her lady friends when they planned to go to the Indian Reservation for a night of gambling. But I never did find the time when we were in south Florida as "snow birds."

But then there was this morning—

The telephone rang at a little before nine. It was Marie.

"Hi Gene, how are you? say my friends and I are going out on the casino boat to do some gambling. How would you like to go?" For a moment I was silent. Then, I thought. "Nothing to do, why not? Sure" I said. Soon we were walking up the gang plank.

The four of us had seated ourselves on the deck as the boat sailed into the ocean from the Intracoastal. The crew served a small breakfast and we found comfortable lounges until the ship reached the three mile country limit. The United States regulations does not permit gambling inside its borders, so we could only begin gambling the moment the ship reached international water. They very carefully follow this rule but the very instant the ship is outside United States the gambling activity begins. In minutes the gambling machines were stripped of their covers, theswitches were throw, the gambling lights went on all over the ship and people lined up to get betting tokens.

Marie knew the type of machine she wanted to play and was ready for action. As soon as they were open I saw her buy her tokens and I watched Marie as she dove in.

I use the expression "dove in" because that is the way Marie took to her gambling. She did it with great enthusiasm as if one was diving into a pool.

I watched Marie for a while as she played her machine incessantly and then I thought I would try my luck. But I was not exactly an overenthusiastic gambler. I would gamble for a while and then watch the others continue their play. But of all the gamblers I watched that day, it was Marie who was the most enthusiastic. I would say Marie just loved her gambling. I gambled on and off for the four hours that we stayed out past the three mile limit, but Marie stayed at the machines for the entire time.

We had lunch at the cafeteria which was very delicious, but I could tell Marie's heart was with the slot machines and she headed back to her slots as soon as she could. She sat at a variety of machines for the entire time and stopped gambling only when the ship came back into the United States waters.

I do believe Marie won a few dollars that day, but I think I remember her losing just about the same amount. But we did have a good time. The ladies laughed and joked around a lot. You could that they really enjoyed the activity. Marie asked me if I had a good time. I said that it was great. The way she threw herself into her gambling was such fun to watch. She really had the idea that she was going to win and with that thought of winning the gambling must be so very exciting.

I think she really had the right idea about gambling. Go to win. And that's how Marie lived . . . .

3. ONE MORE TIME: Those cosmic rays are working good! by Lorraine Kaul

Marie's Last Hurrah!

There was always that special something about Marie, her passion, her humor, even her head strong stubbornness but most of all her unwavering attitude in completing her goals that is what most impressed me. It did not matter if the goal was one of her lifetime achievements, a work project, or finding the perfect gift for someone; once Marie decided she was going to do something, most could agree that it would happen, and it would happen "Marie's way." When faced with objections and obstacles she would always utter the words, "Give Me Strength" and do what was needed to push forward. That "special something" that I could never quite grasp or describe, I later called it her impish and captivating character.

So here I am, friend, follower and Daughter in Law, down in Florida for what was to be our last visit/journey together in this life. I had made the journey from RI to her home in Florida every year. Among the many things we loved to do was gamble: horse racing or slots, it did not matter. We both loved the thrill, the risk, the adventure of our favorite "sport". When she came to visit me, we looked forward to our visits, but most of all we looked forward to, our PLAY TIME. We felt like kids in a sandbox when engaged in our "sport."

This time it was a somber occasion, Marie was diagnosed with stage four lung cancer. Although she had survived cancer of the jaw, breast cancer, COPD, and insurmountable life stressors, this hydra headed monster was too much for even the strongest of warriors.

It was her last couple of weeks of life. I came to help care for her and get support services into her home as she finished the last leg of her life's journey. The fire breathing monster brought with it anxiety attacks, severe nausea, vomiting, emotional pain, hallucinations and unforgiving physical pain. Despite all my attempts to care for her, I remember how truly helpless I felt.

In between the attacks however, Marie would bear her own armor against the monster. She would laugh often, even make jokes of her situation, then she would busy herself organizing the household bills, deciding who gets paid, and who must wait. She called friends to thank them for sharing her life and exchanged whatever closure conversation that she felt was needed. She knew and discussed openly that she had only days left to live and asked me to keep refilling her root beer glass. She had pretty much stopped eating but she said, the root beer made her feel nostalgic. I was awe struck at her unshaken courage. She told me that she had been excited for me to come down, so we could go gambling and then stopped in the middle of the conversation and apologized that she was dying and I might have to meet her at the slots "on the other side." She laughed and said, the big "Jackpot" would be awaiting us. I laughed and told her that she better remember to save me some of the gold coins. I filled her root beer glass. She promised me gold from the other side.

The week, was long, the Hospice Aides, Nurses, Spiritual Advisors other Social Workers came in and out. Marie was sick and tired from the sickness, sick and tired from the care, and sick and tired of what she called the "slow process of death." She said, "I want to get on with it. I have always sort of wondered what it's like on the other side." Despite it all, she was cordial and tolerant of all her well-meaning guests. Well, until Friday. I was due to go home to RI the next day. Marie's son and daughter would come in soon, the support services were in place. Marie had just woke up from a very frightful horrid night in the hands of the monster's fury. It was the anxiety and respiratory attacks, the nightmares, followed by medicine induced hallucinations that beat her into a deep exhausted sleep.

I stayed by her side, with wet cloths, holding her hands, trying to comfort her talking her through the experience. We both woke up exhausted, from the ordeal, but it was now Friday and Marie knew that I was going home the next day. The morning began with administering all her medications, but Marie was unusually alert. It seemed, out of nowhere, she got up went briskly to her dresser drawer and got her purse. She began counting money and announced that we were going to go gambling today. She said, you are going home tomorrow. I might even be dead tomorrow, but we are going gambling today. Wherever the monster was lurking, for this minute, Marie had apparently, won a battle.

I was surprised and stunned at the abrupt turnaround. Here was this eighty seven year old maybe, ninety pounds soaking wet, little spitfire, who has just gone through hells battlefield, the night before, prancing around the room announcing the plan for the day. She added, "It's my last hurrah and I'm going gambling." I was magically re-energized and ready to go!

She however, had an appointment with the Hospice nurse. We, my husband, her husband and I would feel better if we had medical approval before we accommodated this last "aspiration." It was not delivered as a demand, but it was definitely not a request. Life even in its final stages has a way of tampering with a good plan. Later that morning, we received word that the Hospice nurse was coming later than originally expected. Knowing that she had a short reserve of energy to get through the day, this news put a damper in Marie's plan. It was at this time, Marie became intolerant of her well-meaning guest, the Hospice nurse, and then insisted that we get her here immediately so she could go gambling. With that positioning we did as she wished and the nurse changed her schedule and approved our plan for "recreational therapy." My husband and I hooked up the portable oxygen tank and we all headed off to the casino. Marie's husband, Bill wished us well and stayed home for some well-deserved rest. When we arrived at the casino, Marie and I found our slot machines, and my husband Bill followed us rolling the oxygen tank as we played. I won $400.00 in the first few minutes. I knew that would hold us in the game for the duration. Who cared if we lost all of the money, this was Marie's last hurrah. I asked Bill to go get me some pizza. He left us there, just the two of us in the large dark room with the bright lights from the machines. It was our heaven and for now, a safe haven from the monster. We laughed and agreed that if there was glory in a kingdom, we were there.

We continued shared some laughter as we played together but then Marie, knowing the casino like it were her living room, became intolerant of her machine. It was not being cooperative. She cursed it, called it "stupid" jumped up and began whipping around from machine to machine like a frenzied fire fly. She forgot that she was quite frail, hooked to an oxygen machine, which I am holding, let alone knocking on death's door. She was high spirited and not self conscious. So, now I am also whipping behind her, one arm extended to balance her, the other arm extended in the opposite direction guiding the oxygen tank, my neck is twisting forward to see where she is going and backward to steer the oxygen tank, trying to cut the tight corners around the rows of machines, and yelling at Marie, "Hey slow, down I can't keep up with you!" She turned around, laughing and howling, "Well, speed up!" The sight of me flailing behind Marie, pleading for patience, turned many patrons from their machines to focus on our escapade and she brought down the house with laughter. Finally she landed, uttering her famous statement, "Give Me Strength" releasing a long sigh of relief. She finally found a machine that cooperated. Her wish for strength was granted and she gambled for four hours straight. Marie decided it was time to go home, she said, good bye to the casino, blew kisses and thanked the slot machines for all her joyous adventures. She went home a winner in more ways than one. She was determined to have her last hurrah, Marie's way.

Marie died the following week, leaving family and friends with many memories and an indelible story of courage and will etched in our thoughts and hearts forever.

HOW TO STAY YOUNG

Throw out nonessential numbers. This includes: age, weight and height. Let the doctors worry about them.
That is why you pay "them."

Keep only cheerful friends. The grouches pull you down.
Keep learning. Learn more about the computer, crafts, gardening, whatever. Never let the brain idle. "An idle mind is the devil's workshop." And the devil's name is Alzheimer's.

Enjoy the simple things.
Laugh often, long and loud. Laugh until you gasp for breath.
The tears happen. Endure, grieve, and move on.
The only person, who is with us our entire life, is ourselves.
Be ALIVE while you are alive.
Surround yourself with what you love, whether it's family, pets, keepsakes, music, plants, hobbies, whatever.
Your home is your refuge.
Cherish your health: If it is good, preserve it. If it is unstable, improve it. If it is beyond what you can improve, get help.

Don't take guilt trips. Take a trip to the mall, even to the next county; to a foreign country but NOT to where the guilt is.

Tell the people you love that you love them, at every opportunity.

AND ALWAYS REMEMBER:
Life is not measured by the number of breaths we take, but by the moments that take our breath away.

Script by George Carlin

MARIE FENTON GRIFFING

EULOGY

For Marie from Martha Albrecht

We should define a woman by what inspires her
What raises her
Marie was a woman with many elements
Her honesty and integrity an inspiration
Her love of family: flawless

She was gifted with words, writing was
a perpetual thirst that brought
great pleasure
An expert on what is beautiful
An impassioned woman, settled
Earthbound
A lover of nature
Contained
A sensitive women masked
with profound strengths

Let us honor Marie's Lessons
Be in the world that you shared with her

When a great woman dies
We remember the nuances
Of movement
Of Time

MARIE FENTON GRIFFING